Fall of the Big Top

Fall of the Big Top

The Vanishing American Circus

David Lewis Hammarstrom

McFarland & Company, Inc., Publishers

Jefferson, North Carolina, and London

LIBRARY OF CONGRESS CATALOGUING-IN-PUBLICATION DATA

Hammarstrom, David Lewis.
Fall of the big top : the vanishing American circus /
David Lewis Hammarstrom.
p.   cm.
Includes bibliographical references and index.

ISBN-13: 978-0-7864-3169-4
illustrated case binding : 50# alkaline paper ∞

1. Circus — United States — History.   I. Title.
GV1803.H35 2008   791.30973 — dc22   2007035672

British Library cataloguing data are available

On the cover: "The Bird Cage Girls" conceived and directed by Barette
for Polack Bros., 1956 (Circus World Museum, Baraboo, Wisconsin)

Manufactured in the United States of America

*McFarland & Company, Inc., Publishers
Box 611, Jefferson, North Carolina 28640
www.mcfarlandpub.com*

Fondly remembering
White Tops editor Walter H. Hohenadel,
who bylined a 14 year old

Contents

Preface

Writing this book has reminded me of how much circus history I have lived through.

I was about ten when King Brothers Circus came to Santa Rosa, California, where I grew up. Perhaps no one event had ever thrilled me so much — and, consequently, no one event disheartened me more than what happened in Pittsburgh, Pennsylvania, a few years later on July 16, 1956. That evening, across our television screen flashed the sobering news that Ringling Bros. and Barnum & Bailey was giving its last performance under canvas.

Fifty years later, I am still poring through old scrapbooks stuffed with newspaper clippings from Pittsburgh and Sarasota that I collected of that gloomy day — the first drafts of history, luckily saved by a distraught young circus fan who had seen the Big Show under canvas just once. Like a lot of teary-eyed adults, I had dreamed it would one day return. It never did.

Raised in the 1950s, I grew up spoiled on two types of circus riches: the gigantic three-ring spectaculars of John Ringling North's "Greatest Show on Earth" (which Cecil B. DeMille turned into the 1952 film), and the single-ring supremacy of Louis Stern's Polack Brothers. Both presented some of the finest performers one could ever hope to see: the Wallendas, La Norma, Francis Brunn, Lou Jacobs, the Zoppes, Rose Gold, Sonny Moore's Roustabout Dogs, and on and on. At the Santa Rosa fairgrounds pavilion where the Polack show played each early spring, one evening before the performance I got up the nerve to approach the great Barbette, who directed the spectacles and production flourishes. While he fussed over some lighting equipment, Barbette chatted with me in a rather friendly and flip manner, not at all condescending. And I beheld close up the bohemian face of the circus.

Perhaps it was he who inspired me to write my very first circus review in 1955 — of one of the shows which he himself directed. I sent it off to *White Tops* editor Walter H. Hohenadel, who, amazingly, published it!

Some years later on my twenty-first birthday, while I was "performing" as a first-of-May clown for Wallace Brothers, they stopped the show during a comedy gag. My fellow joeys pranced around me in the center ring and sang "Happy Birthday!" Ringmaster Robert Mitchell, a circus fan with whom I had been corresponding, had suggested I join the company when I looked him up on the Cleveland lot. It sounded exciting and glamorous, so he ran me past "Papa" Cristiani for family approval and they made me an usher. Within another couple of weeks, I advanced to clown alley. Every Friday, I stepped up to the office wagon to receive a paycheck from horse rider Norma Cristiani, whose smile and friendly charm made all of the unexpected hardships and emotional shocks easier to absorb. How could I have ever guessed way back then that one day I would be interviewing both Robert and Norma for a book about an institution sadly on the wane?

In 1967, I witnessed the mesmerizing artistry of the Moscow Circus at the Oakland Coliseum. Twelve years later, I was in Russia with tape recorder in hand, talking to Soviet bear trainers and acrobats, directors, administrators and tanbark intellectuals. Ten more years and that state-supported empire of *sixty* permanent circus arenas spread through the fifteen Soviet republics would begin to crumble along with the Soviet Union. In another ten years, many of those gifted artists who had seemed so mystical behind a secretive "iron curtain" were now free spirits, freelancing on American sawdust and, between shows, networking on cell phones and watching favorite tv shows in their Airstream trailers. Few of them were seeing anything about themselves in circus program magazines, not even a listing of their names — for on some of the shows in which they now performed, there were no program magazines.

Polack is gone. King and Wallace are distant memories. Ringling struggles to redefine its identity in the modern age. So do New Cole and others. But this fascinating delight full of spectacle and surprise has a way of reinventing itself. New acts and new modes of showcasing them come along to fill voids left by fleeting impresarios with names like Vargas and Pisoni.

Now and then, too, the art form invented over 200 years ago by English equestrian Philip Astley advances by breathtaking leaps and spins. On my birthday in 1981 (August 19), something monumental took place in the circus stratosphere: In Long Beach, California, on that very day at around fifteen minutes before midnight, trapeze wizard Miguel Vazquez flew the *first* quad. The following summer on September 4 at the Cow Palace in San Francisco, the city of my birth, I watched Vazquez achieve another first: After catching the quad, on his majestic return to the fly bar he turned a perfect pair of mid-air pirouettes!

Nothing I have lived through, though, can compare to the shrinking present tense, for these are traumatic times that threaten to render a great American holiday a relic of the past. And to think that I witnessed the birth of the single most powerful challenge yet to the very foundations of what circus entertainment has meant to most of us. Advance to Los Angeles, 1987, where I have just beheld a quiet revolution-in-the-making under a yellow and blue tent in Little Tokyo. Here are the exact words from a freelance review I sent off to *Variety* in New York:

> One of the hottest tickets of the Los Angeles Arts Festival, Cirque du Soleil, is a wow of a show and the talk of the town. The youthful company, based — along with a burgeoning circus school — in Montreal, and sponsored here by Canadian Airlines International, offers a revelation of the infinite viability of circus art. They take it to new heights with deft creative direction incorporating a bold original score played on synthesizers, a sax and drum.... The results are fairly miraculous.... Cirque du Soleil, which has only been in operation for four mere seasons, is already a company of world class stature that bears watching closely. It's likely to have an impact on the way other circuses are produced and directed, and on the way they're perceived by the public.

Variety refused to print. So, after seeing the same show out in Santa Monica a month or so later, I sent off a second notice, purposefully toned down a little. Maybe, I feared, they thought that my rave was too good to be true. Again, "the Bible of Showbiz" refused to publish.

I knew I had seen something that could profoundly change the sounds and sights of big tops. When friends asked me for a recommendation on Cirque, I told them that if there was only one circus they could see in the next ten years, this was the one to see. At the same time, I did not know, nor could I have guessed, what the future might hold for this ground-breaking troupe. It seemed likely to me, having watched so many upstarts come and go, that Cirque would soon become a caricature of itself, wear out its welcome, and fade into oblivion after six or seven seasons.

In the early 1990s when I turned my pen from the big tops to Broadway, I imagined that, were I to one day write another circus tome, surely it would be about the remarkable rise and the creative glories of Cirque du Soleil. However, as the years passed and more Cirques were born, a more dramatically engaging story emerged: How the American circus itself is struggling to survive in the face of not just the Cirque du Soleil phenomenon, but of the animal rights movements. Thus, the book through which you are about to travel.

So much we took for granted not that long ago is now gone or seriously in jeopardy. Can circuses survive without animals? Without genuine daredevils? And if they do survive, will they be circuses? Or are we transforming our expectations and preferences from authentic big top realities to something that might be called circus ballet?

Here is a more wide-reaching view of the story. The arc of change began long ago, as far back as the early twentieth century, when show owners began to retire the grand free street parade. The Great Depression took a terrible toll on the business, but hard times can inspire new showmanship. Nothing springs overnight from out of nowhere. Just as John Ringling North's bold creative inclinations drew from ideas already evidenced, so did those of Cirque's reigning impresario, Guy Laliberte. So here is an exploration of how we have arrived at where we are today. It's been a rewarding adventure in discovery to research and write about.

A number of people agreed to talk to me while a tape recorder was running, and for that, this book is infinitely better informed and more relevant to the pressing issues at hand. And for that, my lasting gratitude to Michel Barette, Bunni Bartok, Paul Binder, Barbara Byrd, Alex Chimal, Michael Christensen, Norma Cristiani, Raffaele De Ritis, Calvin DuPre, Tito Gaona, Tommy Hanneford, Geoff Hoyle, James Judkins, Andre Kovgar, Chris Lashua, Dale Longmire, Robert Mitchell, Bob Moore, Picasso Jr., Larry Pisoni, John Pugh, Paul Pugh, David Rawls, Svetlana Shamsheeva, Bill Taggart, Vallery, and Sylvia Zerbini.

Others, along the way, answered questions and supplied additional information: Ken Dodd, Fred Dahlinger, Kevin Woodson, Jim Royal, Slava Troyan, Jim Culver, Garry Darrell, Sherwood Kaiser, and Patty Campbell.

The Circus Historical Society's Web site, Circus Message Board, took a trio of my big-picture questions and helped direct me to critical source materials. Likewise, back issues of their *Bandwagon* magazine supply rich historical detail.

The wonderful photographs spread through these pages come to you through courtesy of two major sources: At the Ringling Circus Museum in Sarasota, its curator and archivist Deborah Walk granted me access to their ever-bourgeoning collection of digital images. Assistant curator Jennifer Lemmer Posey, aided by Melissa Porrfeca and Liz Gray, helped coordinate my search. In Baraboo, Wisconsin, at the Circus World Museum's Robert L. Parkinson Research Center, I can't say enough for archivist Erin Foley, who went out of her way to track down so many of the photographs I hoped to locate. My thanks also to Phillip Thurston at the Big Apple Circus, to Ron Mandelbaum at Photofest, to Chris Lashua, Larry Pisoni,

Veronna Boyd, and to the late Ted Sato. The availability of relevant images and the prices in play meant that not all areas of my narrative could be as ideally illustrated as others. Visually, any perceived slights — trust me — were unintended.

My greatest regret? That I was never able to talk to, let alone find, the legendary Miguel Vazquez. He, too, is now history.

Never count tomorrow out. New visions can spring from out of nowhere. Could be from Silicon Valley. Could be from Sarasota or Harlem — or Ireland: In the year 2007, after a forty-year hiatus, a member of the Ringling family was once again directing the destiny of an American circus. He is none other than Ireland-based John Ringling North II, who purchased the Kelly-Miller show and operates it with Jim Royal. Will North be inspired by the inventive flair of his legendary uncle to forge a fresh vision over sawdust? To find a way out of the current malaise? (As of mid-season, Royal reported North to be "thoroughly enjoying his new role as circus owner" and making plans for the 2008 tour.)

Will others, too, find the creative inspiration to keep a foundering American institution viable and attractive to future generations? The answers to come are sure to add chapters to the ongoing saga. And let's hope it's ongoing. I still wish to believe in the grounded optimism of Earl Chapin May, who described this thing we call circus as being "ever changing, never changing."

I have lived through epochs that still influence today's younger stars. While I was talking to multi-faceted performer Alex Chimal, it turned out that we were both similarly moved by one of the big top's golden-age icons — except that, while Alex only saw him on grainy video footage, I actually saw him perform in the flesh. And, who was that figure? Well, you'll find him on the inside ... waiting to thrill you ... so come on in, folks! Continuous shows, all alive, all real, happening right now!

1

The Big One Falls

Gather round, folks! Step right down to our vanishing midway of the great American circus! Behold the tattered bannerlines before you of a once-great holiday! There's room for everyone, and it's all free!

Yes, I can hear you asking — where's the mammoth big top waving majestically in the breeze that you fondly recall from childhood? Why no smells of sawdust and cotton candy? Where are the elephants? And why are there no barkers shouting, "Doggie, doggie, hot doggie man! ... See the side show first! ... Continuous shows! ... Stranger than fiction! They're here! They've real! And they're on the inside!"

We know; they're not here anymore. In fact, a lot of things you may be looking for are not here anymore. So, gaze upon the canvas pictorials of the strange and wonderful things that once thrilled your mom and pop. And let me tell you the story of why *that* circus will not be coming to town today or any day soon.

You might say it began to unravel back on a drab asphalt parking lot next to the Heidelberg Raceway set in the mountains outside Pittsburgh, Pennsylvania, fifty years ago. It was a muggy July morning in 1956. Onto the lot that day rumbled the late-arriving wagons of the Ringling Bros. and Barnum & Bailey Combined Shows. They came loaded with the props, the seats, the canvas and the costumes for a gigantic three-ring spectacle. Our first great tradition to leave the midway — ample cheap manpower to move it all — had already begun to disappear. Slowly, a meager army of roustabouts and performers struggled that morning to set up the show in a space not large enough for everything. So, they had to "sidewall" the menagerie into an area designated by a circular wall of canvas rather than the regular tent.

One after another, wagon and truck and float rumbled onto the small parking lot, each late by many hours. The three sections of the circus train had been arriving in towns behind schedule for days, standing up crowds one after another. Some matinee shows had been skipped. Many night shows started late. Everywhere, there were striking pickets from the Teamsters' union, bent on either organizing the men who moved the show or shutting it down. With the working ranks desperately understaffed, morale had sunk to an all-time low. Still, the performers did their routines, the crowds cheered them on, and the circus limped on to the next stand.

The last unloading at dawn: Ringling Bros. and Barnum & Bailey arrives in Pittsburgh on July 16, 1956 (Circus World Museum, Baraboo, Wisconsin).

Following its annual spring indoor engagements in New York and Boston, Ringling had raised its tents over Maryland on May 24th to commence the canvas tour. Pushing into the future, they raised a brand new "poleless" gorilla tent in which the late Gargantua's "bride," M. Toto, was exhibited. This revolutionary prototype for a much larger big top to follow proved too difficult to erect given the crippling lack of seasoned hands. So it was soon sent back to winter quarters. The circus was having a hard enough time keeping its conventional tents in the air against the threatening resistance of Jimmy Hoffa's striking teamsters, who circled the show at every stop.

Two months later, the beleaguered enterprise was faltering through New York state, where in Geneva, a windstorm ripped through the big top, blowing it down. They hauled out the canvas from the previous tour, which they carried on the show for such emergencies. Into Pennsylvania they moved — to Warren and Erie, and then to Meadville, where, for the first time in its history, the show appeared without seats.

Then into Ohio, where at Canton, one section of the train was bumped by an errant yard engine; the incident was believed to be the work of a bribed engineer in collusion with Jimmy Hoffa's men. Dozens of circus personnel were thrown to the floors. The next day, in Alliance, circus owner and producer John Ringling North came onto the show to implement cuts in the rolling stock and reduce payroll, measures that had been addressed two weeks earlier in a special board of directors' meeting in New York. The goal was to trim the daily nut by $3,000.[1]

During setup, however, North's belt-tightening resolve was chilled when he took an eye-opening walk through the main tent with his good friend Rudy Bundy, who managed the front door. Everything looked run down and dangerously ill-maintained. North was so put off by the unkempt condition of the seats alone, that right there he made a fateful decision which would change circus history forever.

As the trains were being loaded up late that night for the 75-mile run to Pittsburgh, North was mulling over how to word the greatest turning point in his career. A little later, in his private car, the Jomar, while the train rocked from side to side down the tracks and Bundy looked on, North took out a pen and paper and began to write out a note of grave consequence.

Many thousands of Americans at that moment in dozens of cities up ahead were waiting to thrill to the day-long spectacle of the world's largest and grandest circus clanging into town at dawn, throwing up its wonders and escaping the next night to another destination. Waiting in towns named Moundsville and Zanesville, Dayton and Middletown and Milwaukee. Newspapers ahead were heralding circus day in splashy ads. Onto bare walls and in storefront windows, posters and lithographs were appearing.

"It's coming! Ringling brothers and Barnum & Bailey Circus — four long railroad trains loaded to the gunnels with tons of enchanting cargo!" rang the voice in a radio commercial. "See the world's largest traveling zoo! The Giraffe family! Herds of elephants! Giant and baby gorillas and hundreds of other rare and costly wild animals from the four corners of the world to many new wonders never before seen in America! Magnificent new spectacles and a host of terrific acts and features! It's alluring! It's thrilling! It's exciting! It's the greatest show on earth, now truly greater than ever before!"[2]

After North finished writing out his pronouncement, he handed it to Rudy Bundy and asked him to type it up and issue it to the press the next day. Bundy now had in hand a bold anti-sentimental message that would stun the nation. It was his task to deliver it to the media upon arrival in Pittsburgh on Monday, July 16. North hunkered down in his private car, ready to suffer in seclusion the likely fallout.

Onto the Pittsburgh lot at the Heidelberg Raceway, late the following morning, walked young 24-year-old ticket seller Bill Taggart. He had toured with Ringling in the summer of 1953, working in the horse department and riding in the circus spectacles. He was now a full-fledged season-long employee, and he enjoyed every minute of it. Taggart had been warmly embraced by the Ringling personnel, and he imagined a long career with the Greatest Show on Earth. He had his own private sleeping compartment on car 369, which stood next to the Jomar. Under his bed sat the safe. "That was cool." His neighbors included photographer Ted Sato, who had a little dark room, circus veterinarian Doc Henderson, and Taggart's co-worker in the ticket department, Edna Antes. They socialized in a common living room on car 369.

Bill's closest and best friend on the show was hand balancer Alfred Burton, Jr., "a vibrant, handsome smiling man and a real center ring star." The night before the blowdown in Geneva, the two had stayed over at Taggart's home in Clyde, New York. On other occasions, they went out to restaurants and enjoyed swimming with Antes and Jerry Usicki, North's secretary.

Bill and Edna, that morning in Pittsburgh, had just come from a little diner near the rail yards, where they had treated themselves to breakfast.

Ticket seller Bill Taggart in the "yellow wagon" on the midway (courtesy of the John and Mable Ringling Museum of Art, Tibbals Digital Collection).

Bill typed out a letter to the show's general agent, Paul Eagles, complaining of how slowly the operation had been moving each day. He also wrote how different things were without bandmaster Evans and his wife, Nina, and without treasurer Theo Forrestol and his assistant, Bobby Lochte. Then he helped Edna Antes get the tickets ready for the two performances.

"A short time later," he recalls, "Rudy Bundy arrived impeccably dressed as always and as white as a ghost. You could tell something was wrong. He then showed Edna and I the statement that JRN had ready for the press."

It began, "The tented circus as it now exists is, in my opinion, a thing of the past."

The circus was about to give its final two performances under the big top in Pittsburgh.

"We were shocked as any one would be on a show that was closing," says Bill, "but Rudy made us promise not to tell anyone until he talked with Pat Valdo and Bob Dover and later released the comment to the press."

"I heard it on the radio that morning," remembered the show's feisty legal adjuster, Noyelles Burkhart. "It surprised everybody. Nobody had an inkling whatsoever, but they couldn't go ahead like they were doing. It was the most mismanaged thing I ever saw in my life. ... I'd already been downtown, paid the license, and on the radio came the news."

By afternoon, word had trickled down through the company. A notice was posted on the back of the silver ticket wagon.

Between shows, Bob Dover assembled the cast in front of the wardrobe tent and made the news official. This would the last performance of the season. The train would be leaving for Sarasota. And anybody who did not wish to return could stay in Pittsburgh.

That evening, black and white television screens across America flashed the heart-stopping news: Ringling Bros. and Barnum & Bailey was folding up its huge tented city for good. North elaborated in the press release, "We are considering plans for the future which involve an almost completely mechanically controlled exhibition." He said that the show would go on, as usual, the next season beginning at Madison Square Garden, and thereafter "in other air-conditioned arenas all over the United States."[3]

Cheap manpower was no longer quite as cheap: North had spent many of his years at the helm of the Big One fighting off the growing demands of organized labor, and he had finally lost to James R. Hoffa. The depression years had incited roustabouts to rally for better wages and working conditions. They had staged a walkout opening night, 1938, at Madison Square Garden, and without their returning days later, the circus could not have played out the season. It took hundreds of men to guide the wagons down flat cars and off the "runs" to the street, then to the lot. Hundreds of men to toss huge bales of canvas to the ground, lace them together, hammer the stakes and tie off the ropes, and hoist it all into the air. Hundreds of men to hustle the "city that moved by night" from one town to the next in the miraculous space of mere hours.

The three-ring behemoth required hundreds of performers, too, to fill up its rings and glorify its hippodrome track with color and animation. North had traveled abroad nearly every summer to scout the world's best circus stars. He had spent millions on elaborate wardrobe and floats, on exotic animals and strange novelties from far and wide. In 1955, he had paraded fifty-five elephants into the tent, cast in a fanciful production called "Mama's in the Park." Broadway designer Miles White dressed up every act in dazzling color, making the circus a feast for the eye. Dick Barstow paced it with parades and dancers, with clowns and aerial ensembles. *Life* magazine came out to photograph the highlights. Cecil

Striking teamsters bring the Greatest Show on Earth to a halt (Circus World Museum, Baraboo, Wisconsin).

B. DeMille directed an award-winning movie, *The Greatest Show on Earth*, about it. For a few promising seasons, it looked as if John Ringling North and his circus were invincible.

The anger of labor spoiled it all. So did the competing lure of TV. So did the vanishing number of circus lots close to urban population centers. So did the longer hauls from rail yards to show grounds. So did the skyrocketing cost of rail transport.

When Bob Dover announced to the performers outside the dressing top that Pittsburgh was the end of the line, tears streaked down the faces of many. Some were appearing with the show for the first time. Others were old timers who had been with "Big Bertha" (another one of her nicknames) for many seasons. They were all crestfallen. They all faced a dreary future: where next would they go for work in the middle of a season?

The "afternoon" show, late as usual, got underway at 6:30. The tent was only half full. But as word of the closing spread through Pittsburgh and flashed across tv screens, thousands more were converging onto the grounds, eager for seats to the last under-canvas performance of a show that had been on the road since 1871; for a rare chance to witness circus history. The ticket wagon windows were jammed. Reporters and photographers were everywhere.

Bill Taggart: "I also remember that it was very sad at the cookhouse when Edna and I went for dinner and later for supper. The cookhouse crew were also preparing duckie food boxes for us to eat on the long train ride back home."

This last tented version of the Ringling show was quite different from previous ones. One big reason was that famed bandmaster Merle Evans was not on the show that year. He,

Crowds form to take in the late afternoon show (Circus World Museum, Baraboo, Wisconsin).

along with others like ringmaster Harold Ronk, had quit at the end of the previous tour, too unsettled by the shaky and ill-managed operation to continue. This season's skimpy, scaled-down production frills and floats, designed by the French impressionist painter Vertes, were a sad shadow of lustier, more lavish editions. In the "band," for the first time, were stringed instruments.

The surging mass of curiosity seekers, of devastated circus fans and news-gathering journalists, stood patiently in long lines, hoping for a seat to history.

Bill Taggart was rarely so busy: "I will always remember that last night selling tickets for the show. The long slow line, people full of questioning, the sadness that descended on the show grounds. And, as I was closing the window for the last time, an elderly man handed me a ten dollar bill for the last ticket sold for RBBB under canvas."

The final performance began at about 10 p.m. All 9,856 seats were full. Another thousand or so adults and kids were allowed in, to sit on straw or stand along the edges as a great American holiday played out its final ritual and bid farewell to the world.

As the acts took their turns in and over the rings, others back of the big top sat dejectedly on trunks, holding back tears and commiserating with fellow performers. Some stood in disbelief, frozen in sorrow. Some silently pondered their uncertain futures. Where next? Midget clown Paul Horompo, with the show since 1903, was one of the many suddenly out of work. Tomorrow, there would be no reason to apply greasepaint. Prop man Don Staff consoled a weeping showgirl, Ingebord Hoppe.[4]

First-of-May dancers who graced the parades consoled each other. Some of them, in the short space of half a season, had already grown attached to the nomadic life in spangles and spotlights. It had a way, with its dawn-to-dusk rituals from town to town, of getting into one's blood. It had a way of making one overlook all the hardships — the muddy lots and wet rings, the ominous winds circling a tent — the hard rides in the bunks on the

The big top in all its glory, at D.C., 1954 (photograph by Ted Sato/author collection).

crowded old sleepers. It had a way, with the cheering crowds under hot canvas, with the daily comradery, the laughs and the tears. It had a way.

Inside, acrobats whirled across the sawdust. Unus stood on his index finger. Horses pranced in color-book formations. Bill Taggart's friend, Alfred Burton, Jr., did his alternating handstands at the top of an upright ladder while he caught blocks tossed to him by his father and stacked them one atop the other to build up his elevation. The flying Palacios sailed through the air with breathless ease. And, finally, down the hippodrome track came the last parade, the Barbette-directed "Hoop De Do!"

Close to the end. Close to what nobody wanted to end. In minutes, and then in seconds. Final crescendo. Final bow!

At two minutes past midnight, July 17, 1956, in Pittsburgh, the greatest show on earth under the big top bid farewell to its fans for the last time. The band played "Auld Lang Syne," and the crowd made its way out of the tent. It was "all out and ovah!" as ringmasters once cried. This time, it was forever.

Some gazed back for one last look. Some scooped up sawdust — this, after all, was sacred ground — to save or to sell. Cameras went off. Tears streamed down faces. Crews hurried in as they always did to dismantle the props and lower the riggings, to collapse the seats against the seat wagons. Tractors pulled the wagons out from under the slackening tent and

Early Tuesday morning in Pittsburgh, July 17, 1956, the big top falls forever — 85 years after Barnum, Coup and Costello took out their first tent show (Circus World Museum, Baraboo, Wisconsin).

off to the rail yards. They had things still to do. Poles to let fall. Canvas to drop and unlace and roll up. Ring curbs to dissemble and load.

Down at the "runs," where Ringling flatcars stood silently by, slowly the red wagons of history were being pulled up onto the flatcars, and guided from one to the next to their spotted positions. The three sections of the 79-car circus trains would not be moving out for Moundsville, the next scheduled stop on the route card — nor for Dayton or Middletown, nor for any of the places that had been booked. Already, the first section, called the "flying squadron," loaded with the sideshow and the cookhouse, had rolled out of town for the long journey down to Sarasota.

Earlier that day, the nation had woken up to a bad dream. "An American institution — the circus under the canvas tent — passed away early today into history and folklore," wrote Alvin Rosensweet in the *Pittsburgh Post Gazette*. "It came to a sad and a shabby end hardly deserved by an institution of tinseled glory and laughs that had brightened drab lives of millions of Americans for four generations. But it went out of existence smiling through bitter tears as any one of the cheering 10,000 adults and youths who saw the last performance of 'the greatest show on earth' at the Heidelberg Raceway parking lot can attest."

About the show's devastated workforce, Rosensweet observed, "They stood in groups as though for mutual protection, against the personal catastrophe that befell them without warning, trying to believe that, perhaps, it just didn't happen."

"At least we got rid of the pickets," quipped one of the performers.

"It looks like kids in the future won't know the circus — the thrill of greeting it at dawn in a small town, of carrying water for the elephants in exchange for an Annie Oakley," reflected Rosensweet.[5]

In the words of Bill Taggart looking back fifty years after it happened, "I will always hear the sounds of the teardown that final night, the rattle of the chains, the ringing of the

First section of the "funeral train" arrives in Sarasota, July 19, 1956, amidst an outpouring of public sympathy (Circus World Museum, Baraboo, Wisconsin).

quarter poles hitting the ground, the men shouting, the clank of the caterpillar tractors, the long haul to the train."

Now the doomed Ringling caravan was heading not to towns where circus fans waited to relive a childhood thrill once more, but south to Sarasota. Each section of the train, separated by hundreds of miles, moved slowly down the tracks. Well, folks, they had no pressing engagements to meet. Most of the performers remained aboard. Some remained half in denial, wanting to believe that the show would retool back in Sarasota and return to the road, maybe as it had done in the wake of the horrific 1944 Hartford fire, when it spent the remainder of the tour playing ballparks, stadiums and arenas.

They clung to their withering hopes as the silver, red-lettered cars clanged and rattled past D.C., past Savanna and Charleston, then onto Seaboard coastline rails past Wildwood, Florida. All along the way during watering stops, the let-go employees shared frustrations and grief and dried more tears. For the moment, they had no future. Along the way, too, some of them vented their discontent with the boss, Mr. John Ringling North, whose flamboyant and very costly showmanship many blamed for the early closing. He had spent too much money. He had turned the program into a nightclub revue. He was never around. He should have been solving problems a lot sooner. He had let too many key managers go. He had brought in too many odd ducks from outside to promote the show in questionable ways. He had ill-served a great institution.[6]

But a dreadful circus season provided other reasons as well: The Clyde Beatty Circus had folded in Burbank, California, two months earlier, on May 9, after calling off both performances when the American Guild of Variety Artists (AGVA) struck the show. Its members, claimed the union, were owed back wages totaling $15,000. Clyde Beatty's National Circus Corporation filed for bankruptcy. And another circus, King Brothers, ended up in similar straits, its trucks stranded along a Pennsylvania road. Next to them somebody erected a sign that read, "Donations accepted."[7] Professional circus watchers wondered if the tented industry was on the verge of extinction.

The secluded John Ringling North stepped briefly out onto the Jomar platform near Wildwood. George Bayless, a reporter from the *Sarasota Journal* riding the train, managed to take a picture — only to realize that he had neglected to pull the slide of a speed graphic. Thus, he failed to capture "North's only performance" during the historic rail journey.[8]

What was Johnny North thinking about? Tomorrow or yesterday? Not today, any day but. He shared little with Rudy Bundy as the two sipped drinks and chatted about non-circus topics while the train rattled and clanged down the tracks to Sarasota, now and then being shunted onto sidings as faster, more purposeful freight trains whizzed urgently by. North had competed as best he knew how against rapidly changing cultural forces to preserve the magnitude and magnificence of the circus in which he had grown up. Maybe he was recalling his own enchanted youth in and around the white tops — the days when he marched in the grand free street parade. When he scampered up and down through the seats selling popcorn and soda pop to patrons packed together around the three rings and the four stages of the old 15,000-seat tent.

Maybe he was dreaming of heydays gone by, when the great Alfredo Codona turned somersaults through the air one way, floated back the other. When Lillian Leitzel, high in the big top, spun dozens of circles like a giddy butterfly lost in a rainbow. When fans by the thousands took special excursion trains from small towns to see the greatest circus of all on circus day. Those were the days.

"It just can't be true," said Edna Antes to *Sarasota Herald-Tribune* reporter Stan Windhorn, riding the train to Sarasota. "It's impossible to think of a world without the circus, so it just can't be true."

"We had wonderful crowds in most places," stressed one of the performers, "and everybody thought we were in for a good season."

Circus veterinarian "Doc" Henderson termed the closing "a terrible shock," because attendance had picked up greatly after some bad weather. "No one anticipated the sudden announcement."[9]

Bill Taggart told Windhorn that after the blowdown in Geneva, "nothing seemed to run on time." Still, he predicted to another journalist, "the tented circus will go on again."[10]

At 10:50 a.m., three days following Pittsburgh, the 18 flats and three sleepers of the first section of the train pulled into Sarasota on Main Street and Lemon Avenue at the Seaboard station for a two-minute stop before continuing out to the winter quarters on the edge of the city. A band of former circus musicians led by Merle Evans played "Washington's Post March." A crowd of sympathetic souls were there to greet the show. Signs held high read "Welcome Home, Circus" and "Still the Greatest Show on Earth!"

By now, the national press had issued a grim requiem for the sudden demise of Ringling-Barnum. Melodramatic reports and yellow journalists lent the erroneous impression that it was over and done with, and that it would never go on the road again. Hundreds of newspapers passed editorial comment, offering profound regret and sorrow. In the words of a *Billboard* reporter, the outpouring of sympathy was "fit for the king of the big tops."

Predicted *Billboard*, itself a critic of Mr. North's erratic management style and his controversial emphasis on a "sexed up" show, "Researchers in the future will come across a sorrowful story. And if they begin at the beginning, they will be able to foretell the end."[11]

Yet to arrive in town was the last section of the train, upon which the now-maligned boss himself rode. Along the way, North had declined all interview requests. He kept everyone in the dark on his next moves. Even best friend Rudy Bundy was given few details. Just how might North proceed with his plans to present a full season of shows in arenas, as he claimed he would, when there really weren't enough of them around the country to make a full season possible?

While the emerging class of anti-North critics were speaking to reporters about the disastrously mismanaged tour just ended, hyperbole ruled. A man identified as a "straw boss" called Mr. North "the executioner" and claimed, "He's killed the business."[12]

Other circuses still on the road supplied ample evidence that you could survive on a smaller scale. The Cristianis were now playing to sold-out crowds under their own moderate-sized canvas tent, thank you. Hunt Brothers still pitched its tents in a new town every morning. So did Al G. Kelly and Miller Brothers, and so did Mills Brothers. Jack Mills, when asked if he agreed with North's statement about the end of the tented circus, replied, "Never! John North can speak for himself but not for us — or plenty of others."[13]

The Clyde Beatty show emerged from bankruptcy, reorganized under new ownership — ex-Ringling movers and shakers whom North had fired a year earlier — and it reopened the 1956 tour on August 30 at Deming, New Mexico. Back on the tracks and back under canvas, the circus featured a number of acts off the shuttered Ringling show. By the end of the tour, however, Clyde Beatty would give up rail transport as much too expensive, and transfer to trucks. Another great tradition gone: for the first time in 84 years, not a single American circus would roll into your or anybody's fair city at the break of dawn preceded by the thrilling blast of an engine's whistle.

When the last section of the Ringling funeral train approached Sarasota on a balmy summer night, Mr. North had to be wondering how much longer he could remain in isolation. The 29 cars, containing 250 performers and dozens of workmen, rolled down the Seaboards tracks on Pineapple Avenue at 2:35 a.m., Friday, July 20. They turned east to a siding along Washington Boulevard. After a four-day journey, the train came to the final stop.

Everybody waited for North's next move. Might he have miraculously changed his mind?

They waited and waited, and when at last he emerged in a pair of bright blue pajamas from the Jomar, breaking a four-day silence, North gave vague assurances that the performers would be taken care. As for the future of the show, he stood firm on his Pittsburgh statement. During the next few months, rumors of a possible sale of the circus to this person or that (from Mike Todd to Liberace) swirled back and forth. All the speculation ended when North announced in October that he had hired back his ace manager, ex–trapeze flyer–turned–circus executive Arthur M. Concello. The transition from big tops to hard tops would be engineered under the exclusive control of Concello, regarded as one of the finest big top managers who ever lived. The circus would open in 1957, per tradition, at the Garden in New York, then play Boston and other indoor and outdoor facilities from east to west.

North and Concello did just what they said they would do. Within five or six years, they turned a sad-sack operation (try to imagine watching a circus from a fairgrounds grandstand in the rain) into a thriving all-indoor show that played to millions and once again turned hefty profits.

Ten years later, when North sold the circus to showmen outside the family, Americans that same season were dazzled by another very different kind of circus from Russia which performed in just a single ring.

Now consider this: Fifty years after the hated John North declared the tents to be a thing of the past, the family to whom he sold the show is in essence declaring three rings to be a thing of the past.

And fifty years later, too, Ringling Bros. and Barnum & Bailey is once again surrounded at almost every stand by pickets trying to shut it down: pickets not protesting working conditions or wages; no, pickets protesting the use of animals. Pickets declaring them to be the objects of abuse and exploitation. Angry do-gooders bent on liberating every last performing dog, dancing bear, and cake-walking elephant from the lineup. What's left to declare a thing of the past?

So there you have it. Our first chapter. There's much yet to take in on our midway of fallen memories. We're going back in time to a beginning that is looking, in some ways, more like the present each day. See all the canvas paintings before you — the bearded lady and the fire eater ... Jumbo and Gargantua ... the grand free street parade down Main Street ... acres of white canvas going up ... barkers shouting "This way to the big show!" ... blaring trumpets and thundering drum rolls ... three rings of flyers swooping high over the crowds ... Take a good long last look, and enjoy.

Right this way, folks, to the tale of how it is all disappearing before your very own eyes.

2

Back Before Barnum

In the beginning, circus-going was nothing like the mammoth Ringling-Barnum caravan that folded in Pittsburgh. Nothing so vast or grand as to require hundreds of humans and animals speeding through the night down American rails from one town to the next.

Long before a man named Phineas T. Barnum inspired his business partners with visions of grandeur and American gigantism, what we call "circus" was a smaller, far simpler diversion. We are now going back in time, ladies and gentlemen, back over one hundred and fifty years before Pittsburgh—to a small wood amphitheater on 12th and Market streets in Philadelphia. Back to a place where a crowd of a couple of thousand or so folks sat fairly transfixed over the sight of the thrusting hoofs of a horse circling a tan-bark ring, a rider standing remarkably erect atop it, rhythmically moving his body from one foot to another, then leaping upward and jumping through a hoop ten feet high, landing on the same cantering steed with perfect posture. Spectators whistled and cheered their admiration.

Welcome to the first American circus!

Among its patrons at one performance was none other than our nation's very own first president, George Washington. The general was a riding friend of Bill Ricketts, the man whose circus it was and whose impressive feats of equestrianship provided the program's star attraction.

The date was April 22, 1793, only ten years after we gained our independence from English rule and nineteen days after Philadelphians first laid eyes on horse riders and rope walkers appearing together on the same bill. The nation's abhorrence of British domination did not yet extend to theatre or horse and acrobatic shows. President Washington spent many pleasant hours in the saddle with Mr. Ricketts. The two riders roamed through fields on their respective horses while conversing over political events of the day. One issue they likely discussed was the mounting crisis with France and Great Britain, each country competing to craft an exclusive alliance with the new American government.

On a lighter note one afternoon, the circus man casually mentioned to the chief executive that he had just engaged a rider from abroad who could stand with one foot in the saddle and the other in his mouth as his horse galloped around the ring at a speed of 12 miles per hour.

"Come to my show when you feel like resting," said Bill to George.[1]

18

An artist's rendering of Rickets' Circus in Philadelphia, 1793 (Circus World Museum, Baraboo, Wisconsin).

The invitation, met with noncommittal silence, proved irresistible in time, for after Mr. Washington penned an official proclamation, on April 22, declaring neutrality on the English-France issue, he indulged himself in a leisurely respite away from nation-shaping matters. He decided to take up his friend's invitation to see what all the excitement was about on 12th and Market streets.

At Ricketts' Circus, Washington viewed a display of horse riding maneuvers by his friend that had roused a local resident to write, "Without exaggeration it may be said that he is perhaps the most graceful, neat and expert public performer on horseback that ever appeared in any part of the world; at least the amateurs, who have seen the best equestrians in Europe, are of this opinion."[2]

Here is just one of the many crowd-getting attractions, as touted in a program flier put out by Ricketts to advertise his show and, of course, himself:

> He will ride two horses standing erect, at the same time throwing up two oranges and a fork, playing with them in the air, and receives the orange on the point of the fork; he will put a glass of wine in a hoop, turning it around rapidly, the glass remaining at the same time in its place, takes the same and drinks to the company, the horse being in full gallop, and all without the assistance of the reins.[3]

What a clatter old George's wood dentures must have made when he watched his celebrated friend jump gracefully over ten horses at once, or carry a wee lad on his shoulders while he traversed the ring on horseback "in the attitude of Mercury." Or while he danced a hornpipe atop his fast-moving steed, full speed over the sawdust.

Besides delivering many of the thrills himself, Bill Rickets also engaged other acts, some having nothing to do with horses. This he did to keep his customers engaged and off guard. Mr. McDonald executed comical feats on a horse. Spinactuca amazed with rope walking exploits. On cloudy days and at night, they did their routines under the musty glow of flickering candles. The resounding success of our first American circus gave Rickets the fame, the resources and the resolve to take his show on the road. Up to Albany, to New York, and to Boston he went. Tougher, more sophisticated crowds cheered the novel exhibitions. Rickets returned to Philadelphia once more, and as he toured, the program became more entertainingly varied: Polander Dwarf (yes, a real name) leapt through hoops of fire. Cornplanter (a horse) jumped over another horse, 56 inches high. Mr. Sully the Clown threw a string of "flip-flaps" across the ring. One program finished up with a number entitled "Taylor Riding to Brentwood, on Hunter and Road Horse." Dramatic license was creeping into the programs.

In New York, Ricketts hired Signior Reano to perform a slack-wire routine. He signed William Sully, of Sadlers Wells, to sing a wry ditty, "Four and Twenty Periwigs," which brought down the house. By 1797 —five years later and still solvent— the ever-expanding Rickets' bill included dancers, singers, and comedians. It also featured a pantomime based on the whisky rebellion in western Pennsylvania of 1794. George Washington took in a performance on January 24; President Adams, on October 21 at New York.

Call it an intimate variety and horse show in the round for the common man.

Only four years after taking Philly for a ride, Mr. Ricketts tried his hand up in Canada. Our neighbors to the north responded with their pocket-books wide open. And when the nation's first leader retired, not to a theatre or a ballpark did the merchants of Philadelphia adjourn to host a farewell dinner in George's honor; no, to Rickets' Amphitheater they went. There, the gathering witnessed a pièce de résistance in the form of an illuminated panorama depicting Washington departing the nation's capital, his hand extended to his home in Mount Vernon. The final farewell brought the well-wishers to tears.

Bill Ricketts had followed an evolutionary path very similar to the one forged some twenty years earlier by an English rider, Sergeant-Major Philip Astley. In essence, Mr. Astley single-handedly invented this thing we call "circus." This took place in 1770, a couple of years after he opened a riding school in London and started giving afternoon exhibitions of his own. Born in Newcastle-under-Lyme, the innovator-to-be began riding at the age of 9 while employed as a cabinet maker's apprentice in his father's shop. Eight restless years later, Astley deserted the family business to join the 15th King's Royal Regiment of Light Dragoons, and he never looked back.

Astley rode in combat in the French and Indian war. While in combat, he also mastered a number of impressive turns in the saddle. Upon release from the service in 1768, he began offering horse riding exhibitions south of Westminster Bridge in an open field known as Lambeth Marsh at Halfpenny Hatch. Like so many youngsters at the outset of a theatrical career, Astley passed a hat for donations. His first band consisted of two fifers and a bass drummer, his wife. The performance area was established by ropes and stakes. Two years later, up went a small round roof over the circular ring, originally 62 feet in diameter, soon reduced to the still widely used 42 feet.

Now, Astley was charging the public a one-shilling admission fee, and the public was paying. Now he was calling his exhibitions a "circus."

A natural born showman, Astley's initial one-man exhibitions suffered declining patronage within a couple of years. To revive flagging ticket sales, he added non-equestrian acts to the bill: rope walkers and jugglers, clowns and dancing dogs. He even jazzed up the program with pantomimes. One dramatized Elliot's advance against French fighters in Germany in 1761. Another had a horse appearing to be dead, suddenly summoned back to life to serve his country.

The seats began filling up to capacity once again. The customers returned more regularly, expecting to be surprised by altered programs. Our first true circus impresario had quickly absorbed a box office maxim: Novelty is the surest way to draw a crowd, and the surest road through another solvent season.

The father of the one-ring delight hit the road to international fame and fortune, opening the first circus in Paris in 1782. It was an instant hit with the fussy French. Actually, all who attended Astley's were merely embracing many long-familiar acts in a very new format. For centuries at country fairs, wandering acrobats and minstrels, performing bears, clowns and funambulists had captivated crowds in open fields. Some were revered as artists. Many were dismissed as vagabonds. When Philip Astley brought them all together into one ring, added a band of sorts and dared to charge admission, the concentrated impression created a sensation. But to some, the effects were radically immoral. "What a wicked age this is," wrote a critic of the new circus in 1785, "and likely to continue so! For no less than two thousand persons nightly walk and ride to the Devil — at Astley."[4]

Astley set up circuses in other European cities. The roaring reception that greeted him and his co-entertainers wherever they went only intensified the envy of his principal rival, one Charles Hughes. In prior years, Hughes had worked with Astley before breaking away to form his own show in another London amphitheater, which he called the Royal Circus and Equestrian Philharmonic Academy. And therein lie our roots: Under the tutelage of Hughes, John William Ricketts, a Scottish visitor on English soil, learned to ride. From London to Philadelphia, yes, indeed — our first American circus was thoroughly British.

And it was soon Spanish and French, too — when circuses from those countries sailed across the Atlantic to try their luck from French-speaking settlements in Canada to the lower Mississippi. They usually appeared in wooden structures erected for the occasion. In 1810, the Italian troupe of Cayetano and Company arrived in Newburyport, Massachusetts. It came with half a dozen musicians playing bugle, clarinet, bass-viola and violin. It came bearing military riders, a clown, trampolinists and still more military riders. It came with Master Duffee, "a Negro lad who drew down the house by feats of agility, leaping over a whip and hoop." Duffee also hurried around the ring standing on the tips of his toes. The program finished with a silly farce as Mr. Menial, the clown, assumed the saddle-bound role of "Taylor riding to Waterford" on a zebra. The amused audience issued "cheer after cheer."[5]

Not for long would Americans settle for what Europe had to offer. And not until 1824 did an American troupe incorporate the word "circus" into its title. That was Bancker's New York Circus. Propelled by the Yankee spirit of free enterprise, showmen gradually reinvented the form that Astley had given us into something much larger, more elaborately produced, and more bombastically ballyhooed, thanks to the invention of the portable circus tent. It was designed in 1825 by J. Purdy Brown, a Delaware entrepreneur who was the first to hit the road under canvas. The next year, up in Sommers, New York, Nathan Howes and James

Aaron opened their first circus under a tent. Inside it, they exhibited the second elephant to reach these shores, Old Bet.

Thanks to Mr. Brown's deft invention, showmen could now reach any number of towns that lacked indoor facilities. They could play in smaller hamlets, too, by making brief one-day appearances. Tents up in the morning. Tents down at night and onto the next stand ten or fifteen miles up the road. The circus-going market exploded. Enter the era of the "mud show," the all-night caravan of red wagons rumbling slowly over dirt roads to reach the next crowd in Anywhere, U.S.A.

The nomadic nature of trouping, Yankee style, soon acquired the romantic aura of a day-long ritual. "In wagons, on horseback and afoot, white, black and yellow, men, women and children and old bachelors, everybody and his girl, all came to see the great show with the unpronounceable name," reported the Atchison *Daily Champion* in 1866 about the showing of the Champs-Elysises Circus.[6]

Along with serious-minded consumers of the new art form came the unpredictable moods of local hotheads. They toted guns and they were not afraid to lift and shoot them off over a bumbling ring display that left them unimpressed, or at the sight of a spectator they personally despised. In a Texas town, the Orton Brothers performance was interrupted by 14 mounted gorillas on horseback, who stormed into the ring firing off revolvers, set on a robbing spree. Luckily, a group of soldiers in the audience bolted to the defense with firepower of their own. Nine of the thieves were wounded or killed.

On with the show...

"The circus grounds appeared to be the favorite area for the settlement of the neighborhood feuds that were the characteristics of backwoods communities," wrote showman William Cameron Coup. "Weapons of every sort, from fists to pistols, were employed and bloodshed was the rule rather than the exception."[7]

Local toughs reveled in raising havoc just to show off. "Going to the circus is very much like taking one's first trip at sea on a rough day," observed one Kansas newspaper writer. "When we get out of the scrape we inwardly determine never to go again, and we don't — until next time."[8]

Show owners did not help matters any by forming shady alliances with pickpockets, short change artists and card sharks. Why? A nice percentage of the sanctioned thievery went back to the red wagon and helped offset profitless days and weeks. This riff-raff element gave many shows an odious reputation. At least today's concessionaires who sell their products at highly inflated prices sell them, we trust, on the up and up.

In numerous communities, the public was ill-protected by law enforcement officials, themselves on the take from circus agents who bribed them not to intervene while the light-fingered fraternity worked the crowds. Just getting onto and off the circus lot with your wallet or purse intact was something to feel good about. The show? In rural America, what else came around?

"Ladies and gentlemen, I appear to you on behalf of the circus management. The gentlemanly proprietors request me to advise you that among this large gathering are a number of thieves and pickpockets, and I am requested by the management to advise you to keep your hands upon your pocketbooks!" During the bogus warning, patrons pressed their hands against purses or wallets, thus allowing a band of swindlers to note precise locations. The mass stake-out completed, the cons then went to work, and a number of unlucky customers would walk off the grounds minus their personal assets. Shyster showmen? Yes, often in collusion with city hall shysters.

Still, the public could not resist. Wagon shows offered the average customer a wonderful holiday away from the drudgery of picking apples and milking cows. Even the tawdriest show could bring a degree of glamour and excitement, of laughter and magic to an otherwise humdrum life.

"Ever see a circus that differed materially from its predecessor?" asked the editor of the Levenworth *Kansas Daily Conservative.* "Dan Costello's is a 'circus.' We have no higher commendation for it.... The same horses easily jog around the ring, the same men ride them, and make leaps through impossible hoops, and do much more on the bills than the greatest enthusiast would look for on sawdust. But what of that? You will go. The fat man in the white waistcoat will go, and cool his corpulency with lemonade, and leer and smile at fair forms opposite, whose liveliness should shame him into virtuous conduct, even if his gray hairs do not. You will go! We shall all go, and we will see nothing but what we have seen every year, perhaps, since we wore bids and tucks, and thought the girl in spangles was an angel whom we should like to go to heaven with."[9]

Many a young lad longed to chase after red wagons, to join a way of life excitingly removed from work in a farm or factory. Some did. They would soon enough learn that along with the glamour came the mud and the grueling all-night trips through back-breaking obstacles. "The lot was on a knoll on the river bank. In the morning every wagon was standing in water. We had to have rubber boots to get out. We finally got started; had to go through a swamp road one mile long. Soft mud. We put guy ropes on the side of the wagons, with a man holding on to keep the wagon from going over, but we came through all right."[10] That, from an Imlay City kid — William A. Fairweather, just out of high school and on the road with a family show during 1882.

Always at the center of circus day were the wizards in tights who did wondrous things under the big top. Who gave a public starved for such fare uplifting visions of the human spirit pushing heroically against gravity — maybe against the humdrum regularities of life itself. No circus artist was more rousing to watch then a crack tumbler scampering down a fifty-foot runway at a forty-five-degree angle to a springboard at the end, off which he vaulted himself over six to ten horses, topping off the trick with a forward somersault to the sawdust below. Fast, clean, upright — cheers!

These tent-raising moments bridged all cultures. Circus action was a universal language understood with equal force anywhere around the world. Audiences shared virtually the same emotions of awe and delight, fear and suspense, relief and exhilaration.

Ever up against a public easily bored by the repetition of familiar fare or a stale format, showmen stayed actively open to new ideas. Believe it or not, the first elephant to arrive down a gangplank onto New York soil never made it into a circus show. In 1815, the second bull to reach America made it into the public's fancy on a tour of eastern barns. Old Bet was his name. He had been purchased by a sea-going captain for $20.00 at an auction in London and shipped across the sea. Hackaliah Bailey took Old Bet off the captain's hands for a thousand dollars, and our first touring pachyderm was moved under the cover of darkness to prevent prospective patrons from getting a free look. Along the way, though, curiosity seekers built bonfires and hung out deep into the night, waiting for the rare chance to glimpse the giant creature as it lumbered through the shadows on its way to the next stand.

In 1830, Bailey added the first giraffe to his bourgeoning menagerie, then monkeys and bears. A traveling zoo then might feature a few circus acts; a circus, a few animals. Not until 1851 could the spectator see both for a single price of admission. Another circus man named Bailey, George F., ordered specially built cages for lions and tigers, added an elephant and found it easier to attract respectable customers. A family would go out to the grounds to take in the traveling zoo for educational purposes. And since they were already there, they had a hard time saying no to the entertainment in the bigger tent because their children desired to "see the circus." Minor consent was needed.

And still, the horse was king. And after the horse, probably the clown.

> And then faster and faster they went, all of them dancing, first one foot stuck out in the air and then the other, the horses leaning more and more, and the ring-master going round and round the center pole, cracking his whip and shouting "hi!-hi!" and the clown cracking jokes behind him, and by and by all hands dropping the reins, and every lady put her knuckles on her hips and every gentlemen folded his arms, and then how the horses did lean over and hump them-selves! And so, one after another they all skipped off into the ring, and made the sweetest bow I ever see, and then scampered out, and everybody clapped their hands and just went wild.

The words are from none other than Huck Finn, given to him by novelist Mark Twain describing the heart-pounding spectacle of a mud show during civil war times.

More of the master's prose: "All through the circus they done the most astonishing things; and all the time the clown carried on so it most killed the people. The ring-master couldn't even say a word to him but he was back at him quick as a wink with the funniest things a body ever said."[11]

Enter, according to author extraordinaire Earl Chapin May, who lived into the 1930s, the greatest single draw under a top, big or small: Dan Rice, king of American clowns. He was a jockey at age 7, just for starters, and we could fill up all of our bannerlines with the numerous things this multi-talented character did throughout a checkered and stormy career. Yes, I know, you think of him as a jester. You picture him in your mind as the proudly patri-otic Uncle Sam character, the dude with a long neat goatee and a boxy-rimmed high hat, tight-fitting leotards of red, white and blue. That's only one Dan Rice. There were numer-ous others, from jockey to horse rider, pig presenter to comic vocalist.

Actually, the amazing Mr. Rice drew early fame as a weight lifter, that is, after spend-ing some time as a boxer. His race-track workouts gave him the opportunity to learn how to train horses, too. A young P.T. Barnum, who pioneered, some would say perversely, the sideshow, booked Rice into one of his early-day museums at $50.00 a week, billing him "the young Hercules." Promised P.T., Rice would carry on like a mature Samson. To prove this, the strongman supported a pipe containing 126 gallons of "water" which took ten men to lift into position. At the same time, Rice supported two men standing on his breast. But the pipe contained mostly air — another Barnum hoax. And when the public got wise to it, "Samson" felt relieved, so it is written. Dan Rice did not enjoy practicing humbug, although he was unable to refuse a subsequent offer of Mr. Barnum's to appear as "Hercules" in England when P.T. took his assorted curiosities across the Atlantic. The Brits fell for the herculean hoodwink.

In 1844, Rice went to work for Dr. Gilber R. Spaulding (formerly an Albany pharma-cist), where he delivered a one-man variety show, dancing (yes, a dancer too), singing, cavorting in the ring with a trained pig, Lord Byron, and a wonder horse, and also prov-ing his strong-man credentials. As other circuses in succession lured the highly popular Dan Rice away from each other, our late-blooming jester-to-be was about now drifting into the character role that would set him apart through controversy and fame: the talking clown. And once Mr. Rice opened his mouth, seems he could rarely keep it closed very long. Seems that the rapt attention of an audience on the edge of its seats was more important to Mr. Rice than staying safely above the fray during tense Civil War days.

He was anything but subtle, more often than not propelled by a crude flair for ungrammatical prose and bizarre lapses in logic, all of which, complained a Baltimore drama critic in 1856, "sometimes create a great laugh, of which he is not aware.... The idea of considering Nature as having succeeded in producing a horse of equal beauty of form to those of art, was new, I think."[12]

Or was Mr. Rice just aesthetically ahead of his time?

He ridiculed the ringmaster, whom he was paid to ridicule. He also could annoy members of the audience, whom he was not paid to annoy. Nonetheless, because of this, perhaps, they came out in droves. What would that opinionated character, they wondered, do next when he walks into the ring? And what might he say, and whom among us might be incensed by his fiery tongue to rise up with a cocked pistol and pick a fight?

Rice, considered by some to be the Will Rogers of his era, was a gifted orator, with a voice that carried well. He developed strong bonds with the common ticket holder, if not the comped-in critic. He was a looming

Controversial circus legend before one ring turned to three: Dan Rice, king of the talking clowns (courtesy of the John and Mable Ringling Museum of Art, Tibbals Digital Collection).

figure — 5'11." His popularity went to his head, though, causing him to run for state senator (no luck). Also causing him, another luckless adventure, to run for president. He invited Zachary Taylor to join him on the political bandwagon. Thus was born the phrase "jump on the bandwagon."

Rice played both sides of the Civil War with reckless regard for his life. Trouping through friendly Northern territory, he presented himself as an abolitionist; in the deep South, largely in order to avoid an assassin's bullet, he reversed sides. Even then, Rice took incredible risks to his life and limb on Confederate soil when he could not keep quiet on the subject of slavery. "He would face a mob at any time, under any circumstances," recalled William Coup.[13] When Rice railed against the unjust plight of black people, the circus with whom he appeared suffered dangerous backlashes from the public. At one performance in Memphis, an old Southern hot spot, a man in the seats loudly berated the opinionated jester for his pro-abolitionist views. In brazen reply at the end of his act, Rice sang a song about the outspoken spectator playing cards with a male slave on a log. The audience fell for the ruse, believing it to be true.

The enraged spectator shot to his feet, drew a pistol and demanded respect. Rice stood his ground, unfazed for a moment, then continued to belittle the armed antagonist! Under the glare of a crowd clearly on the clown's side, the spectator fled the tent and the town.

"Dan Rice's circus flotilla was menaced by the mob last midnight," reported the *New York Clipper* in 1861 on an ugly incident in Cincinnati. "They demanded that Rice should hoist the Union flag instead of his own. He replied coercion, brought a howitzer charged with slugs to bear upon the mob, and defied them.... If true, then Dan Rice's occupation as a showman is gone in the Northern and Western sections of the country."[14]

Circus people trouped at their own peril. So did the patrons, who took real risks and abuse on midways, populated by spectators of all classes, some of them eager to vent pent-up emotions and hostilities in the name of a good time. Others came with bias and hatred. "A Shameful Abuse," headlined an editorial in the *Daily Conservative*, reflecting on a visit to Leavenworth of DeHaven's Circus.

> When colored men, women, and children visit a circus, they pay their money like white folks, and we have always observed that they behave themselves equally as well. The badge of inferiority is made sufficiently apparent by huddling them together in a particular portion of the amphitheater, without subjecting them to the brutality of those fellows in stripped garments, who, being employed to play the fool, generally seem to be qualified by nature for that role. The sort of humor which delights in ridiculing a poor and defenseless people never excites the risibilities of the true lady or gentleman, and is scarcely ever met save with the loud guffaw of the shameless courtesan, and the masculine bodyguards who are equally shameless.... This is not the day, nor is Kansas the place for such exhibitions of contempt for the negro.[15]

Rice baited political adversaries spotted in the audience. The Civil War gave him a cause and a tongue, and only heightened the expectations of the crowd, hoping to hear verbal sparks fly. The hotheaded clown was once charged with making a secession speech in the South, which brought an angry mob to the circus's heels. In his defense, Rice claimed that he had actually raised a monument to Union soldiers in Girard, Pennsylvania.

William Coup observed such encounters with dismay. "I thought him rather foolish in those exciting times, and there appeared to me great danger in his action."[16]

Rice was given $32,000 by the U.S. government sometime after it seized his steam-boat, the *James Raymond*, for wartime use. He returned the money to President Lincoln, a friend, asking him to distribute it to wounded soldiers and their families. He also gave $35,000 towards a war monument honoring soldiers at Girard, and he helped build churches in the South for slaves.

In his prime, Dan Rice made the astounding salary of one thousand dollars a week. Was he box office gold or not? Adam Forepaugh, for one, paid the star wise guy a grand every seven days. So did Doc Spaulding. And still, the prince of topical barbs did not last long on any showman's payroll. Invariably, petty quarrels and misunderstandings hastened an early Rice exit. He broke contracts and deserted shows. He left Spaulding to organize his own circus. Now, the two men competed viciously against each other. Bill posting wars ensued over a fractious four-year period. Spaulding had his ex-clown arrested for slandering his show. Rice was made to appear in a Rochester court. After that, into the Blue Eagle jail he was thrown. There, during a two-week confinement, he composed a little ditty, "Blue Eagle Jail," which lambasted Spaulding. It added a crescendo of rowdy humor to Rice's popularity.

He was never so successful as a show owner. Following a number of ill-fated circus ventures, incredibly, Doc Spaulding hired back his old nemesis at the same salary. And how was the Doc rewarded this time? Oh, Rice ended up breaking another three-year contract. Once again, the foolish egotist went out on his own, this time floating up and down the Mississippi as Dan Rice's Great Pavilion Circus. Fatefully, it was seen during the spring of 1870 in the town of MacGregor, Iowa, by five young brothers named Ringling. The boys, too young to have an opinion about the show owner, only saw an utterly enchanting sight as, one by one, wagons and people came streaming down a gangplank onto the shore, to parade through the town and drum up customer interest. "The sight of the spectacle had so affected the brothers that they stood riveted to the spot, clasping each other's hands in speechless ecstasy."[17]

Little could they have known that the circus which ignited their young imaginations was just another ill-fated Dan Rice venture. The river boat opus hit the rocks within three seasons. And thirty-seven years later, when those five Ringling brothers, now circus kings, were rivaling the largest big tops in the country, Mr. Rice, who had long since fallen into decline and dissolution, a victim of his own reckless ways in collusion with the bottle, died alone at the age of 84. The year was 1900.

By then, the one-ring show in which Mr. Rice excelled was nearly a thing of the past. A newer, much larger form of tented entertainment now dominated the national landscape. Thousands and thousands of Americans lined up on midways daily to pack huge canvas arenas. Inside, the lone clown who once held court around a single ring could no longer be heard by the masses. Now he appeared in tandem with dozens of others, each prancing around the track with visual gags and goofy illusions while props for the next display were set.

The circus had mushroomed into something far closer to Pittsburgh 1956 than to Philadelphia 1793.

Rice lived to rue the demise of the one-ring format. So did a lot of performers and fans, who now

Circus owners adapted rapidly to changing technologies. Note, in this Dan Rice 1869 newspaper ad, the allusion to rail transport (Circus World Museum, Baraboo, Wisconsin).

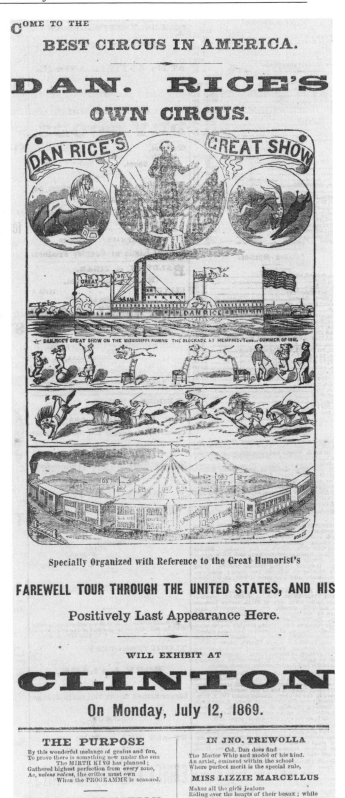

COME TO THE
BEST CIRCUS IN AMERICA.

DAN. RICE'S OWN CIRCUS.

Specially Organized with Reference to the Great Humorist's

FAREWELL TOUR THROUGH THE UNITED STATES, AND HIS

Positively Last Appearance Here.

WILL EXHIBIT AT

CLINTON

On Monday, July 12, 1869.

THE PURPOSE
By this wonderful melange of genius and fun,
To prove there is something new under the sun
      The MIRTH KING has planned;
Gathered highest perfection from every zone,
As, *nolens volens*, the critics must own
      When the PROGRAMME is scanned.

THE INTRODUCTION.

IN JNO. TREWOLLA
      Col. Dan does find
The Master Whip and model of his kind.
An artist, eminent within the school
Where perfect merit is the special rule,

MISS LIZZIE MARCELLUS
Makes all the girls jealous
Riding over the hearts of their beaux ; while

MASTER DICK CLARK

looked back on the old mud shows with warm nostalgia. Those were the days when spectators sat close and felt more like a family. The days before rings and stages and a wide hippodrome track separated the artist from a sea of barely visible faces out there in the seats. Huck Finn might have rued their passing, too.

Or might he have been dazzled by the ever-growing size and the sheer grandeur of it all? Progress, the American way, could not be stopped. Not in the cities growing taller. Not in the common households, the factories of innovation, and certainly not under the big top. The railroads were changing everything, offering sane, restful all-night relief from muddy and unreliable dirt roads. Circus men chased new technologies almost as quickly as they surfaced. In 1869, just 16 days after the historic occasion at Promontory, Utah, when a golden spike was driven to seal the marriage of fresh-laid tracks from east to west, Wisconsin circus clown and owner Dan Costello, in partnership with James M. Nixon, arrived by train in Omaha, Nebraska, to open a two-day stand. And from there, "Dan Costello's Great Show, Circus, Menagerie and Abyssinian Caravan" was loaded onto a special eight-car train to begin a journey of Western dates that would take it through Colorado and clear out to San Francisco. 1869: The nation was joined by steel ribbons of transportation unity — and by the first transcontinental railroad circus.

In the revolutionary aftermath of Costello and Nixon's historic journey, circuses were about to move up a distinctly American road paved with gilded glories and spectacular nomadic rituals enacted on a scale of mind-boggling magnificence never before witnessed anywhere on the planet. You've not seen anything yet, folks!

Dan Rice, viewing it all from a disbelieving distance, probably died of a broken heart.

3

American Heyday

The seeds of the 79-car train that ended in Pittsburgh in a way began to take root 83 years earlier in the mind of a young market-driven midway man — an individual who had never been a performer.

Time to bring out the dude himself who set the American circus on the road to glorious grandeur and overkill. Introducing one William Coup. Fooled you, didn't I? You were sure I'd say P.T. Barnum. Not to worry. He's back there, too, waiting for his turn to go. Let him wait.

First to Mr. Coup, born in Mount Pleasant, Indiana, in 1837. After spending some time apprenticing as a newspaper printer, and before that, working in his father's hotel and tavern, Coup set out on the open road to find his own niche in life. And he found it on carnival and circus grounds. He started out as a roustabout down there in the trenches. By 1861, at the age of 24, young William landed the sideshow manager's job on the E.F. & J. Mabie Circus, a position he held for five years. Shows then were one-ring basic, a fact you'll need to keep in mind.

Next up the ladder, Coup advanced to assistant manager of the Yankee Robinson Circus. By now, Mrs. Coup had tired of the glamorous mud-show life. She talked her husband into exchanging it for live stock breeding on a farm not far from Delvan, Wisconsin. Not the best place for a still-young circus man to retire to: Delvan was full of tent-show veterans who talked the business all day long. In fact, everywhere a trouper went, he was likely to meet up with another trouper. Down in Chicago, Coup ran into Wisconsin native Dan Costello — yes, that Costello. In recent years, the two had operated a floating boat show up and down Great Lakes ports. All it took was a little persuasion on Costello's part to lure Mr. Coup back into "the show business," as they then called it. The two restless vagabonds took out another floating attraction called Dan Costello's Great Show and Egyptian Caravan, which fairly followed the route of their earlier trick.

This led them to broader goals. You will recall that Mr. Costello managed the first transcontinental railroad show all the way out to San Francisco in 1869. He opened his run through the Golden State in Truckee on July 17, and closed in Redwood City, October 21. Drawing upon that success, Costello and Coup shared a vision as wide-reaching as the unfolding American saga, emboldened by a sense of manifest destiny as the nation's citizenry began to move more frequently — and fluently — between its two coastlines. They wanted to form a much larger show which would play to larger crowds and, of course, turn larger profits. Neither man's name was a household word. So Coup sought the participation of a much older showman whose name alone could draw a big crowd in a spectacular second. Yes, P.T. Barnum. And, yes, we're about to bring him out.

The 33-year-old Indianan took a trip to New York to start up negotiations with the ballyhoo genius, then in "retirement" at the ancient age of 61. When Messrs. Costello and Coup broached a proposed partnership, out of "retirement" old P.T. came, ever ready to face a new challenge. His eager young partners, not without their own savvy, believed the Barnum name alone would guarantee huge crowds — no matter the program.

Nor did it matter that Mr. Barnum's legacy was somewhat removed from big top happenings. Although, in his youth, young Phineas had spent a brief period working on a circus, his fortunes were amassed through the seeking out and exploitation of a bizarre succession of strange human oddities, freaks of nature, and various oddball illusions put over on a public which relished a good hoodwink. Barnum's dramatically-hyped "finds" were exhibited in the museums he opened in New York. Fire was a constant adversary, burning down one of them after another. After every calamity, Barnum managed to pull himself back up, rebuild, restock and reopen.

P.T. practically invented the art of ballyhoo as an amusing end unto itself, luring the multitudes time and time again to yet another irresistible hoax. Americans could not resist the latest jaw-dropper — be it a rare human deformity or an alleged historical figure, such as, respectively, the Fejee Mermaid or 161-year-old corpse Joyce Heth, touted to have been Washington's nurse. Patrons were especially intrigued by a sign which read "This Way to the Egress," sensing an invitation to check out another display. Once on the other side, though, they found themselves outside the building, being laughed at by others on the street. Egress means "exit."

Away from the museum, the peripatetic showman had also brought legitimate luster to his name as an upscale promoter of genuine theatrical talent. He set up a tour of U.S. dates in concert halls for Swedish nightingale, Jenny Lind. He hit more pay dirt through his masterful handling, here and abroad, of midget charmer Tom Thumb. And now he was being invited to lend his name to a circus about to be formed by two impressive young dreamers with a sketchy track record. Coup and Costello agreed to Barnum's terms — 3 percent of the proceeds for the use of his name plus the normal profit for his share of an investment in the new show.

Here, in a letter dated October 8, 1870, from P.T. to W.C., we can see exactly where old Phineas's passions lay, and what he was ready to contribute to the new "circus" being formed: "I will join you in a show for next spring, and will probably have Admiral Dot" — another version of Tom Thumb. "You need to spend several months in New York arranging for curiosities, cuts, calls ... we can make a stunning museum department ... you can have a Cardiff Giant that won't crack, also a moving figure, sleeping beauty or dying Zouave."[1]

The following spring, under a 5,000-seat tent in Brooklyn, New York, the "P.T. Barnum Museum, Menagerie, and Circus, International Zoological Gardens, Polytechnic Institute and Hippodrome" opened.

Spectators turned out in force to prove William Coup's marketing instincts right. In fact, the turnouts were so overwhelming that before the inaugural season was up, they had to enlarge the tent in order to accommodate the overflow crowds, hungry for a touring version of the Barnum magic from New York City. Customers were offered a first rate circus program, according to Earl Chapin May, besides which, in separate tents, they could stroll among the animals or ogle over "Barnum's favorite museum pieces"—freaks and wax works of the sundriest sort. The company paraded daily following the usual nightly mud-show trek over distances ranging from ten to thirty miles. They traveled through New York and New England, and hit a few towns to the west.

Having licensed the power of America's premier showman, Coup's next bold move was to focus in on the larger cities. The only way he could bring this off was on rails. And if he needed any convincing that this was the way to go, all he need do was discuss the idea with Dan Costello, who had plenty of experience. By train power, they could skip all the smaller hamlets and concentrate on mass population centers.

Prior to 1872, circuses had dabbled in rail transport to mixed, often inhibiting results. A show would ticket its performers on regular passenger coaches and transport the canvas, seats and props in baggage cars. This meant extra work unloading the equipment at the railroad yards onto "gilly" wagons, hauling it out to the grounds and then unloading the same stuff a second time. Ditto for the return trip back to the depot. Time-consuming, yes, though not nearly as muddy.

In 1856, Spaulding and Rogers, the first show on tracks, had ordered specially built rail cars of their own to eliminate the "gilly show" phase. But because track gage widths differed among the many different railroad companies, these cars were confined to the rails that matched their wheels. Good luck, Mr. Routing Agent. Worse yet, these over-the-rail troupes could ill afford to carry a sideshow or animal top, so they were tagged by their mud-show competitors with the degrading term "Railroad show"![2]

By the time that Barnum, Coup and Costello took to the steel ribbons at the outset of their second season in business, track gages were becoming more uniform. Still, Mr. Coup had to push—amazingly, against—the now conservative Mr. Barnum to win his approval for a sixty-one car train, specially built to move the circus into and through sixteen states as far west as Kansas.

The 35-year-old visionary from Indiana experimented with new ways to draw larger crowds, among them, a joint effort with railroads to put out special half-rate excursion trains which delivered customers from farms and villages miles away into the cities where the show pitched its expanded tents. The venture proved so successful that during the 1872 tour, even after adding a middle section to the big top, they still gave three shows a day—at 11, 2 and 8—to handle Mr. Barnum's fans.

This ever-expanding canvas arena led to unexpected audience alienation as patrons in the cheaper seats found themselves seated farther from the ring and straining to see. Some would get up and walk down closer to obtain a better view. Others in princely seats found their views ruined by these invading squatters. Mr. Barnum approached Mr. Costello about the unruly crowds. What to do?

Costello is alleged to have told P.T. that they would have to put in two rings. Or was it William Coup who though up the idea first, with Costello passing it along to P.T.? Did he know anything about a similar format that English impresario George Sanger (who would lease Astley's old amphitheater in 1871) had tried out in 1860, placing two stages on each side of a ring? Coup is famously credited for the revolutionary idea of blowing up the one-ring format and setting the American circus on the road to three-ring extravagance. Hear it in his own words, folks. Mr. Coup, if you please...

"Our experience with the vast crowds of the season before had given us the idea of building two rings and giving a double performance. This, of course, doubled our

The road to three-rings: At far right, the first three-pole tent, designed to feature two rings, as toured by Barnum, Coup and Costello in 1873 (Circus World Museum, Baraboo, Wisconsin).

company, but it kept the audience in their seats, since they were precisely as well off in one part of the canvas as in another."[3]

1873 was a year of profound change more far-reaching than perhaps any other season in the history of American circus entertainment. Reported the *New York Clipper* that year in reviewing the show's Boston stand, "The novelty of seeing three rings in action at once is alone worth the price of admission."[4]

Why three rings? The reviewer counted the hippodrome track encircling the new two-ring layout as a third ring. And that's just how Coup and Costello pitched their theatrical audacity in advance couriers sent out ahead to prospective patrons: "Three rings in One Vast Pavilion.... Two of these arenas or circus rings will be in operation by two different sets of performers, at the same time ... while the third vast ring, larger than either of the others, will be used exclusively for the Grand Entree Pageant, Tournament, etc., and other spectacular demonstrations."[5]

These business-minded innovators had not only addressed customer frustrations, they had made circus a more exciting spectacle. Listen to some more of what Coup had to say about the accidental creation of a totally new performance concept: "It at once hit the popular fancy, it proved a great drawing card for us and others. For within a few months smaller shows all over the country began to give two-ring performances. Indeed, from that time it seemed to me that the old one-ring show was entirely forgotten."[6]

A new era. A new format. A whole new road traveled with Yankee pluck and confidence. "Double show" became a trend. More — if not better — had infected the program. Can we not agree how inconceivable it would be for any circus performer with an ounce of pride to ever relish appearing at the same time next to another act?

William Cameron Coup, you will recall, never rode a horse in tights. Never walked a tightrope or juggled a single hoop. Never swung from a trapeze. The circus he had built up in size and grandeur cleared $250,000 in 1873. It put P.T. back in the spotlight, and it drew other showmen to his side, each seeking their own expedient shortcut to public patronage through partnership with the prince of humbug. During his 5-year tenure with Coup and Costello, P.T. leased the use of his name to at least one other character, the grifting John Pogey O'Brien, an operator who specialized in threadbare programs as an excuse to draw a crowd for fleecing purposes. O'Brien once put out a circus so bad, it inspired an elderly gent, on his way out of the tent, to pause where the owner was sitting in an arm chair, and comment, "I want to congratulate you, Mr. O'Brien, on having the poorest ring performance that I ever saw."

Pogey suggested the old chap had spent too much time inside purchasing bricks of popcorn and probably missed the best act on the bill.

"There's one thing certain," agreed the customer, "If there were any good acts in the show, I missed them."[7]

The appearance of Barnum's name on a second circus gave competitors a perfect reason to smear the number one operation: "Barnum's show is divided!" And it so disgusted Mr. Coup that at the end of the 1875 tour, he finally withdrew from the concern. From there, Coup went out on his own in less-flamboyant ventures, first opening the New York Aquarium on Broadway and 35th streets in alliance with Charles Reiche. Soon, the two were feuding; for

Hyping artistic conflicts during simultaneously presented acts, the cunning P.T. Barnum promised "two separate rival rings" in this 1874 ad (Circus World Museum, Baraboo, Wisconsin).

The World's Great Object Teacher's Culminating Triumph

P. T. BARNUM'S
Great Traveling Museum, Menagerie
AND
WORLD'S FAIR!

1874

BOYLANCE & PURCELL

In Canvas Colleges Canopying Acres,
COMPREHENDING
20 GREAT SHOWS IN ONE!
AND OVER 1,000 MEN AND HORSES,
Will exhibit, in all its Vast Entirety, at
Owego, Wednesday, May 6,
Giving Daily Three Full, Grand and Complete Expositions at
10 A. M., and 1 and 7 P. M.
100,000 CARDINAL CURIOSITIES!
1,500 Magnificent Representatives Animals, Beasts, Birds, Reptiles, Amphibious Marine Monsters,

Steam Engine Operated Automatic and Polytechnic Institute,
And Stupendous Inter-Continental Amphitheatre with Seats for 14,000 Spectators, and
TWO SEPARATE RIVAL RINGS!
In both of which appear, at one and the same time,
DAN CASTELLO'S

one thing, Coup did not want to operate on Sundays. A coin toss for the property they co-owned, at Coup's impetuous suggestion, left him the loser.

The luckless Mr. Coup put out the Monster United Shows, which failed to click, a victim partly of bum weather and of a railroad wreck. Then he tried his hand at a one-car show, and then at another museum. Both languished. Beaten down, he returned to his farm in Delvan. The instigator of multiple rings, Yankee style, ironically never achieved name-fame. He died in Jacksonville, Florida, in 1895.

The circus bearing Barnum's name, after William Coup withdrew from the concern, was reduced back to a one-ring layout when the Flatfoots managed it through the late 1870s. And six years after Phineas got dumped by Bill, he was courted and picked up by another young showman with first-rate management skills named James A. Bailey. The perfect partner for the Prince of Humbug, Bailey had the organizational genius to oversee the day to day operations of a big top behemoth, which was what Barnum & Bailey would become. In 1881, the two joined forces and went out as "The Greatest Show on Earth." And to prove they were the greatest, that year they added another ring. Now we had our first true three-ring circus.

The next season, P.T. outdid himself when he imported Jumbo from an English zoo. The cost: $30,000. In six weeks on tour, Jumbo is said to have grossed $336,00 for the circus. At the end of a 31-week tour, the receipts reached $1,000,750. During the three and a half seasons that Jumbo toured with Barnum & Bailey, P.T. claimed that nine million Americans saw him and that he was ridden by a million moppets.

In 1885, at the rail yards in St. Thomas, Canada, while the show was unloading, Jumbo was fatally hit by a locomotive.

While honest performers endeavored to reach the audience, more and more now it was spectacle and size that seemed to move it the most. Circus-goers wanted more Jumbos. More of everything. Bigger bigger bigger. Elephants became tokens of prestige by which the size and therefore the importance of a circus might be judged. In 1881, Barnum & Bailey toured four pachyderms; Adam Forepaugh, five; William Coup, three. Less than ten years hence, the combined titles of Forepaugh and Barnum & Bailey, temporarily sharing the rings at Madison Square Garden one spring, paraded *sixty* lumbering giants around the track.

Coup was but one of many innovators who read the public. Dan Rice was the first showman to use a press agent. The first American show to be illuminated by electric lights was a circus. The great specs that filled big tops at the turn of the 20th century were seen nowhere else until epic movies from Hollywood flickered on silent silver screens a few years later. Modern modes of advertising and promotion were pioneered by circus men in hectic, very ungentlemanly competition with each other.

In the land of free enterprise, bloody bill posting wars erupted between rival circuses, each fighting for coveted space on barns and building walls, on warehouses and store windows for the display of their posters and 14-sheet lithographs. Each fought to stay ahead of the other in a constant battle to reach the public first. One day, a town would be plastered with lithographs touting the Sells show, for example, on July 5th. Keep that date in mind. The next day, the date might have been altered to July 3rd — the skullduggery of a rival circus moving into town two days ahead of the other show, in effect stealing use of the already posted paper by merely changing the date. Routing agents had to shrewdly assess harvest times in various parts of the country in order to get their shows in just after the crops were picked. This was the critical moment — the moment when the locals had fresh, hard-earned money to spend and the urge to reward their labors with a good time. What better way than at a circus?

William Coup once estimated that one-half of his entire budget went into the advance advertising and promotional campaigns. In a typical town, bill posters might paste, hang and tack over every available space as many as six thousand sheets of colorful paper. Did we tell you how circuses virtually invented the art of image-making hoopla?

Dirty tricks abounded. On the mud-show trails, rival companies burned bridges to deny each other needed passage to the next stand. "Rat sheets" in the form of small, viciously derogatory handbills spread malicious rumors about the competition. On rails, the tactics of surreptitious sabotage turned ever more devious. Circus "agents" showed up at depots pretending to represent a competitor, asking to have a carload of its paper sitting out in the yard shipped to another destination under the pretense that it had been routed there by mistake.

"One of the many other shady tricks played on me by opposition shows," Mr. Coup wrote, "was that of equipping men with sample cases, and sending them in advance of my show in the role of commercial salesman." During the course of friendly chit-chat with local merchants, the traveling "salesman" would casually mention Coup's name and disclose that his concern had "disbanded and gone to pieces." This would set a rumor into circulation from town to town, in Mr. Coup's opinion causing him "irreparable harm."[8]

Bombarded with such drama and intrigue, the public developed an insatiable appetite for the next big pre-show buildup, ready to be teased by an avalanche of gaudy lithographs suddenly appearing everywhere and promising a circus of unimaginable wonders; ready to believe in the incredible and then be amusingly surprised over the next elaborate deception. Talk about spin. Circus-going Americans came to expect bigger and better things. Who came to town with the longest train? Who had the largest number of horses — well, at least the best looking horses? The most beautifully decorated band and cage wagons? The grandest free street parade? (One was said to have been three miles long.) Most of all, who carried the most elephants? Who, yes who, indeed, gave us the *mostest* show on earth?

When another crack showman, Adam Forepaugh, claimed in 1884 to have the whitest pachyderm in America, "Light of Asia," P.T. Barnum was provoked into answering back with an even holier specimen, the sacred white elephant. He claimed to have imported it from Burma at the cost of $100,000. According to Earl Chapin May, maybe not. Barnum's entry might have been killed by the Burmese before ever being allowed onto a ship. And if that was what happened, then Mr. Barnum had actually produced an understudy, secured stateside, which bore "pinkish spots."

The sacred white elephant war erupted. Forepaugh berated Barnum's pitiful imitation, claiming that it made his own Light of Asia look that much more angelic. Barnum cried fraud, accusing his rival of a literal whitewash by having applied a coat of house paint to a domestic bull. Fueled by the Fourth Estate, which at times turned out circus stories as fanciful as those penned by publicity hacks, the public took keen delight in this latest battle of the ballyhoos. Imagine, after a hard day's work on the farm, retiring to an easy chair to read about all this amusing nonsense in your evening paper.

The elephants from heaven enlivened the season of 1884. That was the same season when five ambitious brothers burst onto the sawdust scene with a remarkable vision of ethical behavior and with the pluck to sell it to the public as nothing less than a full-scale midway makeover. That spring, under a small 600-seat one-ring tent in Baraboo, Wisconsin, the Ringling brothers, in partnership with aging showman Yankee Robinson, opened their first circus. They had spent the previous two winters as homemade touring vaudeville enter-tainers. Al Ringling, who had already worked on a number of small shows, balanced a plow upon his chin. His younger brothers, Alf T., Charles, Otto and John, did simple acrobatic acts, played musical instruments, sang and danced and made themselves generally charm-ing. These were the same five who, 14 years earlier, had glimpsed Dan Rice's Great Pavil-ion Circus offloading onto the banks of the Mississippi at MacGregor, Iowa. On that magical day as later recorded by one of the five in book form, Charlie said "Let's have a circus!" Otto was already forming bold policy directives: "I would say to the big man with the loud voice, who bossed the fellows unloading the big bandwagon, not to swear like he did."[9]

The hurly-burly, graft-ridden circus world soon faced the daunting criticisms of five very virtuous-acting brothers righteously bent on cleaning it up. Determined to make their midway a swindler-free zone, the Wisconsin boys rose remarkably fast because of or despite this well-advertised mission. Many would attribute their early success to the loving care with which they treated the customer. The Ringlings were so effective in setting themselves apart in this regard, that the realities of other similarly above-board operations were nearly for-gotten in the blinding whirl of literary fictions posing as fact. Historian George Chindahl tells us about family circuses of the time which "gave good value for a small admission fee, were free of graft and objectionable conduct, and graduated competent performers, advance men, and managers to larger shows."[10]

For example, on the Whitney family show in 1882 (two seasons before the Ringlings got going under canvas), our young apprentice, Billy Fairweather, observed genuine com-passion for the customer. Mrs. Whitney (called "mother" by every man on the show) one night discovered that somebody, arriving late, had given her a twenty-dollar gold piece for a dollar at the front door. She had the ringmaster announce the error and state that the money would be returned that day or in the next town to whomever could properly iden-tify the loss. Wrote Billy, "A young fellow came to the next town and got his money back. The Whitneys were honest people."[11]

Nonetheless, the Ringlings advertised their ethical resolve as a main event in itself—as if they were the very first showmen to operate on the up-and-up. They played their hand with bravado, hiring Pinkerton detectives to comb the grounds for suspicious activity. They refused the then-customary practice of selling "privileges" to professional pickpockets, short-change vendors and card sharks for the right to ply their craft on the midway. Operating cleverly against the grain, the brothers stationed employees near the ticket wagon, shout-ing "Beware of pickpockets! Count your change, ladies and gentlemen!" Were they not on a genuine moral mission? If they weren't, they were five very accomplished actors.

So let's go out on a limb here, folks. It has been written in more academic quarters that James A. Bailey, about the same time, also had Pinkerton men monitoring his lot. Then we have to ask ourselves — did James do it because of the Ringling brothers? Or did he do it in order to separate favored lucky boys from those not wanted? If the Ringling brothers were not the first to engage detectives or the first to run a clean midway, one thing is cer-tain: they managed to bamboozle the press and the public into believing that they alone liberated the entire field from its sordid and crooked ways. Virtually every author since then has given the Ringlings exclusive credit for an ethical revolution. There was George Ade, who wrote this: "They found the business in the hands of vagabonds and put it into the hands of gentlemen."[12]

They fairly won the hearts of all Americans, and within six fast-rising seasons, their "World's Greatest Shows" hit the rails on eighteen cars. In five more years, they added another twenty, and in another five, the train increased by fifty percent. The Ringlings now traveled on fifty-seven flats and coaches. In 1905, they numbered seventy-six.

They indulged themselves in claims of artistic supremacy born of a youthful arrogance and a marketable disdain for the status quo: Hear them out in this 1895 newspaper ad they placed in opposition to a day-and-dater with Sells Brothers:

> The up to date show has arrived. The show that stands on its own merits. Does not divide.... Sails under no false colors — Borrows nothing from the past — Gives you the energy and the results of the actual living present — Is too big — Too Modern — Too generous — Too broad — Too liberal — too prosperous — too great to seriously notice the petty insinuations of concerns that cannot keep up with up with the march of progress.

Here's how up to date these bragging young showman were: In 1897 they invested in a cinematograph movie projector put out by Thomas Edison. They stationed it under a "black top" on the midway where patrons could marvel at moving images of a boxing match that had been fought that very same year between Corbett and Fitzsimmons.[13]

Even though the five brothers started out as music hall entertainers, whatever reservations they had about three-ring juggernauts — and at least one of them, Albert, had some — did not hold them back from competing for audiences everywhere who clearly preferred the new-style American circus program. Not until 1891, though, seven years after entering the business, and the same year when P.T. Barnum died, did the Ringlings finally add a second ring. Three rings were fast becoming the norm, even though single-ring shows still lingered on in the hinterlands. Many troupers and die-hard fans harbored a yearning for simpler times closer in spirit to Astley than to Barnum.

In 1894, Adam Forepaugh scaled back to a single ring. And at the turn of the century, as a number of small armories and arenas were being built, the circuses that played them could only fit one ring into the buildings. Ex–Ringling employee Edward Shipp went out on his own during the off-seasons through the Midwest, presenting solo acts. In 1899, he produced a week-long show, the Comedy Circus, at the Detroit Light Guard Armory. Fraternal clubs like the Wheelmen and the Moose Lodge sponsored indoor one-ringers. This takes us right up to a pivotal moment, to the very first Shrine Circus, produced by Shipp at the Detroit Armory in 1906. Credit the Moslem Temple of Detroit for launching a trend that would turn into a nationwide institution, as, one by one, other temples began to produce their own annual circus days.

Outdoors, three rings dominated. Listen here: In 1910 there were thirty-two circuses in Yankeeland traveling by rail on a combined total of 675 cars. Ten of them required anywhere from twenty-seven to eighty-four cars; another twenty-two, from two to twenty-one. Besides that, thirty truck shows moved over roads and highways. The Ringlings now ruled the field, having absorbed their principal competition — Barnum & Bailey, Forepaugh and Sells Brothers. Not for long would the brothers tour all three. Without competing owners, there was little incentive to keep them all out, especially when the Ringlings began passing away. Then came the Great War, which zapped the circuses of the manpower needed to move them down the tracks. All of these diminishing realities led, in 1919, to the grand amalgamation of all three titles into the giant of surviving giants: Ringling Bros. and Barnum & Bailey Combined Shows.

"New York has gone circus wild," wrote columnist David W. Watt. "Never in the history of the circus business has there been such a demand for seats as there is this season. The super circus is turning them away at every performance. On account of the tremendous

Fifteen acres of canvas for the city that moved by night: Patrons enter the Ringling Bros. and Barnum & Bailey lot in 1925 (Circus World Museum, Baraboo, Wisconsin).

business, the management of the Ringling Bros. and Barnum & Bailey show is obliged to give extra performances in the morning.... It is estimated that an average of about 2,000 people are being turned away at each performance."[14]

What did the actual program itself look like, you might be wondering? Picture, if you can, three rings and four interlocking stages forming a straight line down the center of a six-pole big top 600 feet long by 200 feet wide. Picture fifteen thousand people seated around it in portable wooden grandstand bleachers and chairs. They called it the Big One.

The sideshow pitched novel attractions to customers on their way to "the Big Show." Seen here are Daisy Doll and barker Clyde Ingalls (courtesy of the John and Mable Ringling Museum of Art, Tibbals Digital Collection).

The called it Big Bertha. They called it the Greatest Show on Earth. For sure, it was the Mostest Show on Earth.

The roaring '20s gave us performances on a scale unimaginable by today's modest standards. Well here, let the press agents describe it in the 146-page *Magazine and Daily Review*, which sold for 15 cents on the midway: "The names Ringling Brothers, P.T. Barnum and James A. Bailey have long been household words. They have stood for all that has been

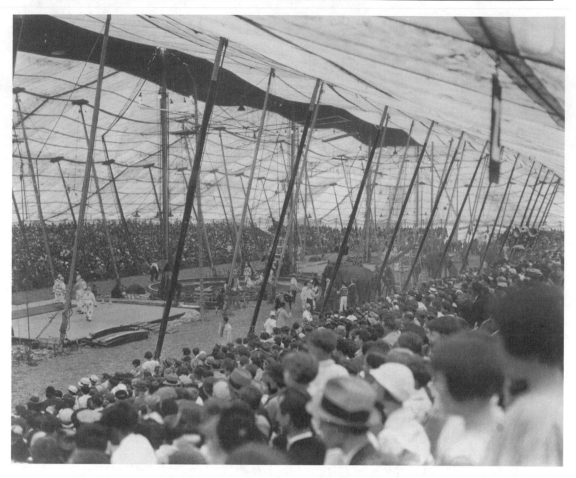

Under the nation's largest big top, fifteen thousand Ringling patrons witnessed action in three rings and four stages (courtesy of the John and Mable Ringling Museum of Art, Tibbals Digital Collection).

biggest, best and supremely novel in the world of gigantic amusements.... Thousands are daily astounded by the immensity and scope of this marvel circus which brings the most unusual, the most spectacular, the costliest and easily the most magnificent of all earth's entertainment.... The year 1925 finds the titan of the show world ever greater than before and sweeping all before it."[15]

In 1925, animals and aerialists ruled the big top. Of some 20 displays on the bill that season, nearly half of them featured horses. The first thing the audience saw that year was "Fete of the Garlands," an opening pageant containing, so promised the *Daily Review*, "the greatest number of horses ever presented in one display."

Audiences those years witnessed a royalty of circus stars, names like May Wirth, Lillian Leitzel, Con Colleano and...

"Ladies and gentlemen!" cried ring announcer Lew Graham, "The greatest aerialist of all time will now accomplish what no other person in the world can do — *the triple somersault in mid-air!*"

...the one and only Alfredo Codona. These superhumans were lionized just as would be the screen idols of Hollywood-to-come within another decade. They seemed to embody

Trapeze star Alfredo Codona thrilled audiences with grace and style (Circus World Museum, Baraboo, Wisconsin).

the jazz age. As our visiting scholar from London, Helen Stoddart, sees it, they had "good looks, romance, highly publicized lives and a blatant disregard for death."[16]

"The greatest show on earth thrills the Coligies!" announced a Path A newsreel in movie houses. "Washington: President and first lady attend the circus during its visit to the capital!" The clip showed circus king John Ringling, with cigar and straw hat, accompanying the nation's first family to their seats under the canvas.

Audiences sat through two action-packed hours filled with horse-riding stunts and aerial daredevils. Leitzel? High over the center ring at the climax of her act, she riveted the crowds with furiously fast one-arm gyrations, often numbering over one hundred revolutions. Bird Millman? In a long flowing gown with parasol in hand, the grand dame of rope walkers high-kicked her way across the slender strand with the flair of a flapper. Jorgensen? He had sixty horses going every which way, all carefully controlled in shifting carousel patterns, in one wonderful ring. Con Colleano? The program magazine described him: "From the Littlest Continent, Colleano the Great... Presenting the Australian wizard who, among many hazardous feats, somersaults backward and forward with naught to spring from or return to save a single strand stretched athwart the air." During a backward somersault, he removed his trousers in flight, landing perfectly on the wire in a pair of tights!

Alfredo Codona, the triple-somersaulting god who flew with swan-like grace, is still

Roaring '20s circus icon Bird Millman on top of the world over the New York skyline, circa 1922 (Circus World Museum, Baraboo, Wisconsin).

held in loving regard by those who never even saw him perform. On old grainy film clips, the man's lithe balletic reach is there to behold. Our very own Tito Gaona, who dazzled us in the here and now for many years, calls Codona "the greatest aerialist who ever lived." And says Tito, speaking of the time when Codona and Leitzel (who ended up married to each other) both soared like angels, "I believe in the style and the elegance of the 1920s. Back then, it was very difficult. Codona had everything — elegance and wonderful showmanship."

With so many rings and stages to keep occupied, the show had the time and the space to include all kinds of offbeat novelties. In 1917, the Ringling brothers featured a display of light industry at work: one ring was devoted to a wood-chopping contest between Australia's "mightiest axeman." In another, speed mechanics assembled the "intricate parts" of an automobile. Still another slot was held by an exhibition of California orange-packing.

Al G. Barnes one season put forty singing girls out on the track while a couple of dozen dancing horses showed off. Hagenbeck-Wallace, in 1928, had the young Clyde Beatty and his wild animals spotted between two rings of performing elephants.

Although most performers were, in essence, forced to compete alongside each other in these seven-act displays, still they loved being "with it and for it." After all, there was the obvious need to fill the tent with action so that everybody in the seats, especially those at the far ends, had something close by to watch.

"It was a fascinating life," May Wirth once told me. "You look forward to the next day — what's going to happen and who's going to come."

Lillian Leitzel, one of the chosen few, enjoyed the final minutes of her performance alone. The other acts had taken their bows and now the entire tent turned its attention to the star over center ring. With thousands of eyes directed her way, sometimes she found her "audience" in a single soul out there:

Miss Leitzel, if you please...

"It is frequent that one person — often, a child who seems tremendously appreciative of what I am doing, will be the only person in a tent filled with twenty thousand people who really has my attention. Manifestly, it is impossible to play to them all and the logical person to work for is the one who probably appreciates what I am doing."[17]

They trouped together, across muddy lots and grassy fields, through thunder and rain and heat. They were a veritable united nations under one canvas roof, working together in a rare harmony. Indeed, their day-to-day survival depended on such cooperation and tolerance.

Remembered Jackie LeClaire about life aboard the "pie car," where snacks were sold on the train: "Now, these elephant men had maybe loaded the elephants. The horse people had loaded the horses. So, when they came in at night, they didn't have a chance to shower before they got in there, but after a while you kind of got used to that and you could turn to somebody next to you who was maybe very very rich, and say 'Hi, how are you doing tonight?'"[18]

By the mid-twenties, even Shrine temples, now a big promoter of indoor shows, buckled under to the three-ring imperative when the Detroit Moslems took up quarters in the larger state fair coliseum. It was large enough to allow for a trio of rings. Once again, Detroit led the way. The American circus was in its heyday. A host of new titles from Sells Floto ("the show beautiful") to Al G. Barnes and Hagenbeck-Wallace gave the public plenty of choices and plenty of circus days to look forward to.

Four years later, and the stock market crashed. And the Roaring Twenties fell. And a great depression followed. It wasn't nearly so easy to keep a gigantic three-ring operation in business. Suddenly, the halcyon years were coming to a painful end. Midway through the Great Depression, one Shrine temple went back to making do in an unexpectedly big way with just a single ring. How novel.

Midway through the Depression, too, the cheap labor that had moved circuses down the rails was starting to demand decent wages and better working conditions. Of all times to be uncooperative, just when the Ringling circus was playing some days to hundreds rather than thousands. Just when they were wondering if they should do away with matinees altogether.

The American circus, forever reinventing itself, was about to take a turn up a long wrenching road to the grim realizations that awaited it in Pittsburgh. En route, the colorful, at times tragic struggles it endured to bring its magic to towns large and small under aging assumptions were something to witness. On a brighter note amidst all the oncoming heartache, just look ahead to our next canvas painting, folks. To Sacramento, California, 1935, where the seeds of a return to old-time simplicity were planted.

Dan Rice and Al Ringling, both long gone from the world, would surely have smiled that day.

4

Brother, Can You Spare a Ring?

Enter the Great Depression. Enter long downtrodden lines at community kitchens. Enter diminishing crowds on circus midways. Canvas men on strike. Too many three-ring shows bearing too many wagons, too many performers, and too few patrons in the seats. Enter the worst decade ever for American big tops.

Enter one hurdle after another, as circus owners faced a bleak economic landscape barren of the surging crowds they had hosted during the roaring '20s. Now, they were forced to crimp and cut back, to leave wagons behind and trim the payroll. Now, they were fighting against each other to reach a devastated market. To outwit competitors or face more empty houses around sadly ignored rings. A cunning breed of truck show operators, taking advantage of new highways and better back roads, made a nasty habit of beating out larger railroad circuses into cities by mere days to "trim" off the community's limited spending money. These motorized bandits cleverly obtained rail-show routes through a network of cooperating station agents on the take. As reported by *Variety*, "there's no way of telling which way the truck shows are going to head." The big rail outfits would come into a town, "only to learn that the 'trimmers' as the auto outfits are known, have played already in a spot some five or ten miles away."[1]

Bankruptcies and labor strikes wracked the circus field. 1931 is a good year to begin: The Royal Olympia Circus, playing Danbury, Connecticut, came to a sudden halt when a sheriff attached the show just as it was close to sneaking out of legal hot water across the state line into Peekskill, New York. Providers of livestock feed that day were demanding to be paid. So was the local newspaper for ads it had run. Royal Olympia fell into foreclosure. Only its animals were spared.

Also in 1931, on the cost-cutting front, live music became one of the first victims of bad times. The Ringling-owned Sparks Circus did away with its band. Charles Sparks hired a guy to play phonograph records, although he retained a real live calliope player and a drummer to add a touch of human warmth to his bold experiment. Surprisingly, according the trade-friendly *Billboard*, a weekly showbiz periodical, the new piped-in sound struck a welcome chord with audiences.[2] We have to wonder, though — was *Billboard* paid to say that, or did spectators really jump to the novelty of such crude cutting-edge technology? To be fair, the phonograph records did replicate huge forty- to sixty-piece studio bands.

The innovation was declared such a hit, that rumors spread about other Ringling shows gearing up to replace their bandstands with record players for the duration of 1931. How important was live music, really? Rosy *Billboard* reviews aside, Sparks did not return to the road the following season — or any season thereafter. Nor did artificial soundtracks accompany any of the other circuses as rumored.

Less manpower, of course, meant less burden on the kitty. And just at a time when circuses could ill-afford the mammoth payrolls they had routinely handled during better times, labor started to flex its unhappy muscles. In an effort to trim expenses during the 1931 season, John Ringling ordered a pay cut for his canvas men, seat men, drivers and grooms. They answered him back, en masse, by walking off the Brooklyn lot. Manager Carl Hathaway, seeking a middle ground in haste, promised the striking workers that he would make every effort to get their reduced wages restored. To a degree, he succeeded, bringing Mr. Ringling to a compromise, the wages closer to what they had been. The show went on.

It did not go on with John Ringling at the helm for very long, however. The last of the surviving brothers, Mr. John had by far the biggest ego of the bunch, and was the least capable of running the circus on his own. After his brother Charlie died, there was nobody left to counter Ringling's reckless tendencies. He alone now directed the destinies of the family fortunes, and he made decisions like a capricious king stupidly in love with power. He and the Depression were not meant for each other.

Shortly before the infamous "Black Friday" in October 1929 when the stock market fell, John Ringling stood up the officials of Madison Square Garden at a meeting to sign a contract for the show's annual spring engagement the following year. In Ringling's cavalier absence, Garden officials awarded the contract to the rival American Circus Corporation — owners of Sells-Floto, Hagenbeck-Wallace, and Al G. Barnes, among a slate of winning properties. When Mr. Ringling woke up to what had transpired while he slept, he was outraged. He had lost the coveted Garden date. Luckily, though, he had one costly ace in the hole: a few years earlier, he had taken out an option with American Circus Corporation to purchase its assets. Now, he was forced to act on the option if he wanted to reclaim the Garden spring contract. This meant his borrowing $1.8 million to complete the acquisition. And this he did.

A few weeks later, Wall Street hit the skids. Within three years, John Ringling lost control of the circus though another foolish omission when he once again failed to meet a simple deadline. He defaulted on an interest payment due on the note, throwing his heady empire into default. The note holders took control, appointing Sam Gumpertz, a friend of Mr. Ringling's, to run the circus. Ringling was demoted to corporate vice president and barred from active management. For the next five years, he foundered like an over-the-hill boxer licking his wounds in forgotten shadows, and he never gave up on a feeble quest to reclaim the throne of power. John Ringling died in New York City while trying to raise the funds to assume the loan on which he had defaulted.

At Ringling's demise, the American circus world was about to enter a new era of unprecedented showmanship. Enter Mr. John's equally strong-willed nephew, John Ringling North. In 1938, the 35-year-old recaptured family control of the circus. A natural-born innovator at heart with scarce regard for sacred traditions, North quickly made a name for himself by elevating the quality of the performance through improved lighting, color-coordination in costume design and the inclusion of "production numbers" at intervals throughout the regular program. These theatricalized flourishes lent variety and animation to the performance. They also promised novelty season after season.

North overhauled the physical layout by engaging industrial designer Norman Bel

Big top innovator John Ringling North, left, reviews plans by industrial designer Norman Bell Geddes, circa 1941, for a bold new menagerie layout (Circus World Museum, Baraboo, Wisconsin).

Geddes to redesign the big top. From white to blue canvas it went. Now, sunlight could not trickle in through the tent to invalidate any special lighting effects. Now, during the afternoon performances as well, theatre lighting could be effective. Box seats were added. Air conditioning was introduced — for a brief promising spell. At the Garden, the sawdust was tinted. Broadway's Miles White designed a decade of fabulous costumes for the shows produced by JRN. John Murray Anderson and Richard Barstow directed them. Original theme songs were composed for the specs and aerial ballets. North canvassed the world almost every summer for new acts, and he stocked his programs with scores of the finest artists on the globe.

A gift of the Depression: Like an Impressionist painter, North created a circus much more dream-like in character than the old hurly-burly, straight-ahead show. Slower? Maybe for the good. The dazzling parade of accomplished stars along with the brilliantly outfitted production numbers kept audiences enchantingly engaged for the space of two intermissionless hours. North's version of circus was a soft, surreal kaleidoscope dripping with color and animation, three rings all the way. It was a glorified metaphor for our consumer-oriented society that still applies. Today's "multi-taskers" who channel surf, incessantly check Blackberry and other assorted message gizmos are three ring addicts at heart.

North was not nearly so lucky with finessing labor. In fact, "labor," he would one day

North hosts Eleanor and her son John Roosevelt at the circus (Circus World Museum, Baraboo, Wisconsin).

state, was his worst enemy. It started his first year at the helm, when in 1938, shortly after the show opened in New York, the common workers went out on strike. North, along with other executives, found himself out on the hippodrome track, his sleeves rolled up during the opening parade, pushing wagons and floats around the arena, and being cheered on by the audience. The show made peace with its various roustabouts and elephant handlers, embarked on the road tour, and got as far as Scranton, PA. A series of walkouts and comebacks along the precarious trail to Scranton left North at the end of his Irish patience. He closed the show, routed it back to Sarasota, and sent many of his acts over to join another Ringling-owned property, Al G. Barnes–Sells-Floto. They played out the season. During the winter, the circus and labor once again reached a tenuous accord.

1938 was the worst year in circus history. Eight shows folded that season, and only two of them would return.

All of these nagging technical problems caused Johnny North to cast a critical eye on size and manpower. When Ringling Bros. and Barnum & Bailey returned to the road in 1939, it was scaled back a bit, the big top shortened by two poles. North replaced horses with tractors. He acquired automatic stake drivers. And, in the eyes of many, he was committing heresy.

A circus king in his private car, the *Jomar*, circa 1950. North's lavish lifestyle epitomized the sweeping artistic changes he brought to the circus (courtesy of the John and Mable Ringling Museum of Art, Tibbals Digital Collection).

At the end of five controversial seasons — certain members of the Ringling heirs did not like Mr. North's arrogance anymore than they had liked his uncle's — the bright new Ringling mover and shaker was thrown out. His five-year contract had run its course, anyway. In North's place came the totally unprepared Robert Ringling. At the end of a mediocre opera career, Robert was goaded on by his mother, Edith, wife of the late Charles Ringling, who had hated John Ringling and therefore hated his spitting image, John Ringling North. Robert led the concern into tragic misfortune through incompetent management. Recklessly, he brought back the old six-pole big top which required more equipment, seats and props and more men to move it. He did this during the middle of World War II, when the show was woefully understaffed.

Perhaps the only sane thing that Robert Ringling did do was to try out a one-ring version of Ringling at Madison Square Garden in 1943, called Spangles. By most accounts a lovely, solo-oriented program of top-drawer talent, tastefully directed and scored, Spangles was favorably reviewed, only modestly attended, and it closed after three respectable months.

Then came Ringling's date with tragedy in Hartford, Connecticut July 6, 1944, when the big top went up in flames, cutting short the lives of 168 people, mostly women and chil-

The elephant ballet, 1942, produced by John Ringling North (courtesy of the John and Mable Ringling Museum of Art, Tibbals Digital Collection).

dren who were tramped to death by the escaping mass. In the ashes, the callously sidelined Johnny North found a way back into management. Three seasons later, he had 51 percent ownership of the circus. North continued in his ways, making the program even more colorful and exciting. Labor, too, continued in its ways, never content with the paltry paychecks handed it. North and the Greatest Show on Earth were less than a decade away from Pittsburgh.

Robert Ringling's promising bid to simplicity, Spangles, may actually have been inspired by the lead set by two enterprising showmen, Louis Stern and Irving J. Polack. Enter another gift of the Great Depression. In the thirties, when games of chance sprang up around fly-by-night circus presentations, Stern and Polack joined forces. Stern was born and raised on 125th Street in a tenement section of New York city. When his father, a house painter, died, Stern, then only 12 years old, went out on his own as a "mutt" delivering telegrams for Wall Street houses. The kid got his boss to add two and a half cents per delivery, upping his take some weeks to eighteen dollars. Six months later, he found work at an amusement park as a chocolate vendor in a burlesque house. The next summer, he worked a "hoopla" booth — customers threw hoops over pegs for kewpie dolls and other cheap prizes.

By the age of sixteen, Stern and a friend partnered up to take out their own hoopla game on state fair midways. Barred in Brockton, Massachusetts, from booking the game at a fair which only allowed one such concession on the grounds, in quick make-do time Stern invented a substitute offering: the Pan Game. He bought some cupcake baking pans at a five-and-dime store, a bunch of rubber balls in a toy bin. Patrons tossed balls over the pan, hoping that one would fall into a slot and stick. It was an instant hit, bringing in $500.00 the best weeks. And its inventor began to sign his checks, "Louis Pan Stern." That's the story.

In 1916, the lifelong bachelor and nondrinker purchased all 18 concessions at the Utica

Irving J. Polack, right, seen here with two Shriners, teamed up with Louis Stern to produce stellar one-ring Shrine circuses (Circus World Museum, Baraboo, Wisconsin).

Amusement Park. For nearly 15 years, his concerns breezed profitably along. He was pocketing a few grand every month. He was coasting on his laurels. Then came the punishing returns of the 1930s, from which few men could escape. Including Mr. Stern.

Irving J. Polack had been operating his own carnival, the World at Home Shows, itself another victim of the 1929 Wall Street tumble, when Stern looked him up. For a couple of seasons, Stern had been following the success of a winter circus promoter, John W. Moore, whom he turned into a role model of sorts. Moore had been reaping hefty profits booking circus acts and presenting them under local auspices during week-long engagements. At the same events, Moore also ran carnival games, food stands and dime-a-dance concessions. A "circus" mixed up with a carnival was maybe not the prettiest sight to everybody. But for a promoter, as long as the cash registers rang...

Shortly after Mr. Stern went belly-up in Utica, promoter Moore retired with his fortune intact, wisely, it would appear, retreating from an oncoming economic train wreck. Stern licked his chops over the circus dates just abandoned by Moore, and looked up his carnie acquaintance Irv Polack with a timely proposal: why should not the two of them take over those dates and give it a try? Over a productive lunch, between entrees and desert, Polack Brothers Circus was formed. Why not Polack and Stern, or Stern and Polack, or, well, Stern Brothers Circus? There you have your introduction to the self-effacing Louis Pan Stern.

Using Polack's connections in many cities and towns where he had booked his old carnival, the new partners threw together enough "acts" to justify their business title. They came into towns under the sponsorship of civic organizations, who were given 15 percent off the top. Admission was 15 cents, another dime for a reserved chair. Once admitted, en route to the "show" the ticket holder confronted a maze of revenue-enhancing diversions — the Pan Game, the Hoopla, burger and popcorn stands.

Polack and Stern, nonetheless, were cut from slightly different cloth, for the latter seemed to have something of an esthetic conscience. Stern grew wary of all the merchandising gimmicks they had in operation to compensate for the poor profits they turned during 1932–33. The following year, he began pitching an upgraded attitude to his colleague: "It's got to have class, pal, or we'll milk it dry." Stern feared that an inferior performance would soon tag Polack Brothers as just another skimpy fly-by-night trick.

Now that was a rather daring position for Louis Stern to take in the depths of the thirties. How to put out an affordable show given the drastic drop-off in public patronage? How to revamp the extravagant and costly three-ring program? Without all the answers, Stern and Polack started pitching an idea to Shrine temples in 1935. They offered to produce something more noteworthy than a carnie circus. They heard the Shriners tell them that games of chance would not be allowed and that a first-class circus was expected — or else.

So, the central question became: how could they match a temple's higher expectations in an affordable manner? Certainly not, Stern reasoned, with three rings of action. The two devised a plan to reassure the Shriners. They would guarantee the temple against loss by assuming the risk themselves. To keep the overhead down, they would stay in a town for at least a week. No canvas or seats to carry. Shriners would serve as the sales force. And at a time when the temples were favoring three rings, Stern and Polack decided to pitch an older-fashioned form, promising every temple a more "intimate one-ring display in which every act was a star attraction."

Out west in Sacramento, Polack Brothers Circus landed its first Shrine date when it signed with Ben Ali, offering the group "famous and very expensive" talent.[3] The eleven-day engagement helped launch a return to something welcomed by many. In fact, a residual preference among patrons and performers for the solo turn had never completely died. Al Ringling himself had briefly broken ranks with his brothers during their early railroad days to take out a one-ring mud show of his own. It flopped out sooner than later, and Al rejoined the family fold. Dan Rice, in his twilight years, rued the demise of the smaller, more intimate circus. Wrote Earl Chapin May in 1931, when a new one-ring show, Leon

Among numerous star turns featured on the Polack show: Francis Brunn. Assisted by his sister, Lotti (Circus World Museum, Baraboo, Wisconsin).

Brothers, had just opened and was not doing well, "Personally, I much prefer a one-ring show, but I am of the great minority."[4]

Another voice in the desert was David W. Watt, who observed in 1918, "Thousands of people will be found today who, if properly approached, will declare without hesitation that for exhilarating music, for thrilling grand entrees, for spectacular bareback, balloon and ring riding, for high and lofty tumbling, for innumerable other things, the one-ring circus was head and shoulders above the three-ring enterprise in its palmiest days."[5]

It is safe to say — some of you will no doubt rise up and cheer — that no performer alive would disagree with what Karl Wallenda told me: "I'm against two and three ring circuses absolutely. A real performer can never show his act unless he's alone.... I can't understand it. This is the same thing: you take three tvs out there, each tv makes a different tone. What you gonna see now? This is the same in the circus. I always worked solo."

In fact, Wallenda did not always work solo.

"But I'm only talking about good performers. When I put a show on I put most of the acts alone. When you put acts together, you put them together because you don't care what kind of act goes in there."

Furthermore, stressed the famed high-wire star, "The people don't care either. They look from one side to the other, they get distracted from one thing to the other."

He spoke of countries like Japan, like China — "the whole word" where one-ring is king. "And when an act is on, you don't dare go in there and ask them for peanuts and popcorn and cold drinks.... I'd rather work in the European show, absolutely."

Today's Alex Chimal will tactfully state a natural preference for exclusive attention from the crowd. He told me that when he worked on Carson and Barnes, people are harder to reach because with five rings in virtual competition, they glance from side to side in an effort not to miss anything. Sometimes, ironically, they will miss a good trick while looking elsewhere. This makes it doubly hard for the performer, explains Alex, who reveals how disheartening it can be when you sense you do not have the audience. You are inclined not to put out as much. Conversely, Alex believes that because the one-ring format puts all the attention on the solo performer, it provides the incentive to try harder — to turn in the perfect performance.[6]

Many fans, as well, prefer the singular focus. And some of them even prefer a *smaller* spread of canvas, believe it or not. Historian Joe Bradbury sighed, "There's something about a small railroad show on the lot that's just almost indescribable. When I was growing up, frankly, I'd rather be on a small show like Sparks or John Robinson ... than even Ringling-Barnum."[7]

The first Polack Brothers–Shrine Circus to play Sacramento was such a success — the temple made a nifty $25,000 — that world quickly spread to other temples: Polack is a class act; these guys are above-board operators. No hanky panky. No clever excuses. The bills all get paid on time. And in no time, other temples throughout the U.S. were rushing to ink contracts with Louis and Irving. This Shrine association gave them an almost immediate prestige that it might have taken them years to acquire in other ways.

In 1948, when John Ringling North's Greatest Show on Earth made its first appearance in San Francisco's new Cow Palace, turning them away by the thousands, Polack Brothers was another household word in the city — as it had become in other cities from coast to coast. There were now two touring Polack units — the Western and the Eastern — each playing a year-long string of dates in their respective regions. The majority of engagements in California were sponsored by Shrine temples. In San Francisco, each spring Polack Brothers appeared at the civic auditorium downtown for eleven days. It enjoyed steady repeat business from thousands of avid fans, holding its own against other shows in the field including Ringling-Barnum.

With its prestige now well established, Stern and Polack were able to attract the cream of circus royalty to their single ring of honor. Many headliners off the Ringling show went out with Polack the following season: Juggler Francis Brunn, aerialist Rose Gold, the Flying Palacios and La Norma, Lou Jacobs and the Zoppes, Harold Alzana — and many, many more all brought luster to the Polack programs. The Wallendas performed their draw-dropping seven-person pyramid, not with Ringling, but with Polack. "In many ways, working in this show was like appearing at the 'Palace' in vaudeville," said Buckles Woodcock, who managed the Polack elephants in the mid-'60s. "Consequently, it enjoyed the cream of circus talent."[8]

Robert Mitchell, who ringmastered for Louis Stern during his last season in business, remembers a no-nonsense boss of few words. "Very quiet. Didn't compliment you or anything." Nor did Stern ever tell Mitchell how to do his job. "When I joined in Albany, he gave me a list of the acts and said, 'Here, lay out the show.'"

Mitchell was thrown off guard. "Always, the owner of the show always laid the show out."

Only once did Stern take his last ringmaster to task. On occasion, Mitchell would ask the audience at the end of the first half, "How do you like the circus so far?"

After one of these spiels came the boss. "Hey, kid. Don't do that, because one time they didn't like the show and we got booed."

At its zenith, the two touring Polack units helped the Shriners nationwide raise over $100,000,000 a year for children in their hospitals. And the one-ring model it set so handsomely, with added production touches supplied some seasons by director Barbette, reopened the eyes of America to the artistic benefits of such fare. Indeed, it may have inspired the birth of other such presentations around the country. In 1948, vocally gregarious John Strong, continuing in the tradition of his father, went out under a charming little tent, booking himself onto county fairs, where his mini-programs were offered to fairgoers as a free attraction. Student circuses favored simpler formats. The Sarasota Sailor Circus opened in 1950. Paul Pugh's Wenatchee Youth Circus began in 1952, Circus Kirk in 1968.

An even more spectacular argument for the way circuses were staged virtually everywhere outside the United States was the Moscow State Circus, which began sending shows to select American cities in 1963. Spectators were mesmerized by the perfection and polish of the Soviet artists. Their acts seemed choreographed, the entire performance directed more along the lines of a ballet. In place of a band, there was an orchestra. In place of hoopla, refined artistry. Every single moment of action seemed to draw greater scrutiny and respect from the audience.

In 1966, the first pro–European U.S. troupe to pitch a one-ring tent in the modern era was Famous Bartok, "America's largest circus in the round." The tent, inherited from the disbanded Hunt Brothers Circus, was red, white and green. Also known as the "freedom circus," the equipment was painted in red Hungarian hues in honor of the ex-Ringling performers appearing with Bartok who had defected to hide-out points in Sarasota and later managed to gain U.S. citizenship. Among them were aerialist Kurt Szmansky, Ryzard, and bear trainer Jan Perez, who wed Bunni Bartok, daughter of the show's owners, Milton "Doc" and Betty.

Bartok's band was placed above a performers' entrance. Las Vegas–style showgirls "opened the curtain and shut the glitzy door," recalls Bunni. Ringside chairs allowed patrons the suave luxury of resting their feet on the full-size ring curb. With a touch of crusty pride, claims Bunni, "This circus brought forth a totally new concept for American tented circus.... The reason was the performer would feel like an 'artist' being the center of attention. They would try harder.... The Famous Circus Bartok always asked 'How great is your act?' — not 'How many minutes can you do?'"

A year after Bartok, took to the sawdust — or polyester — trails, the magnificent Moscow Circus made a return visit to the states, adding additional cities and wowing thousands more with its ultra-refined mode of execution. West Coast critics cheered. Crowds jammed the turnstiles, in Oakland leaving thousands more stranded at the gate without tickets. Sold out, sir. Sorry, ma'am!

The same season, John Ringling North, whose indoor version of the show his uncles founded was now playing to millions and turning profits once more, was ready to retire after years of triumphs and setbacks and the never-ending feuds with family members who held 49 percent of the stock. In the fall of 1967, North sold the show to outsiders, opening the door wide to fresh blood. A very different vision of what our nation's most beloved entertainment tradition should look and sound like lay ahead. Demographics and marketing were about to push the circus into a more democratically outgoing, audience-friendly direction. And you, Mr. and Mrs. ticket holder, were about to be invited down onto the hippodrome track to join in the parade.

Who said not anybody can be a clown?

5

Spectacles Unsublime

Once upon a season circuses were otherworldly. They had secrets. They had foreign tongues and faraway rituals. And magical ways. They gathered a cross-section of humanity under a big top of the world. They slipped mysteriously into town at dawn, spread their tents and pitched their wonders — then, just as mysteriously, slipped away into the darkness of night. Back of gaudy bannerlines you beheld the bizarre and the incredible, exotic creatures from Africa, whirling wizards from Asia, intrepid pole vaulters from Europe. The pageant came so irresistibly close, and yet, as the great ringmaster Harold Ronk once said, you could never quite touch it.

"Strange and glamorous is life under the big top," wrote circus owner and press agent Floyd King, penning a catalog of promised qualities for an advance herald sent out to communities weeks before the circus arrived. He wrote of "the entrance of strangers into strange lands ... our astonished eye will gaze on the gorgeous pageant and the parade and returning to the grounds will peer freely and familiarity about the place of strange sounds and entrancing sights."[1]

Freak shows were waiting there to startle and seduce. Wild animals were dangerously close there. Acrobats of all stripes and motions thrilled the masses. Unus stood with imperial aplomb on his forefinger. Gargantua the Great, a snarling photogenic gorilla, held court in his "jungle conditioned" cage. Antoinette Concello flew triples under a star-laden canvas heaven. The Cristianis thundered with gusto on their horses. From start to finish, through the final days of glory under canvas, costume king Miles White painted the spectacle in feathers and sequins brimming with unconventional color. Johnny North turned the canvas from white to blue, spread tinted sawdust over the rings, added more lights and more floats and made it so wonderfully surreal that Ernest Hemingway was moved to describe it as "the only ageless delight that you can buy for money ... a truly happy dream."[2]

When Mr. North retired from producing in 1969, the new big top boss who took his place was so determined to make you like him and his circus — so eager to share his delight in running it — that you were practically invited down into the rings to perform with it yourself. Introducing Irvin Feld, who, in concert with his brother, Israel, and Judge Roy Holfheinze of Houston, purchased the circus from North in 1967. From that moment forward, the old "strange and glamorous" atmosphere gave way to a more democratically-pandering vision of Mr. Feld's. Give the man his due, folks; never, with the possible

Exuberantly in charge, Irvin Feld reveled in Ringling power and publicity (courtesy of the John and Mable Ringling Museum of Art, Tibbals Digital Collection).

exception of P.T. himself, has a show owner taken more satisfaction in being seen as the show owner. Feld reveled in the role. It's a shame he didn't live long enough to write his memoirs; like Phineas, who did, Irvin might have loved sitting out where the crowds gathered — or, better yet, down in the center ring before the show — perched proudly behind a pile of books, autographing copies for fans.

We will not dwell too long on Mr. Feld's colorful bent for rewriting circus history in order to lend the erroneous impression that he managed the circus ten years before he actually managed it. This he did in order to cast himself in the role of "savior" of Ringling Bros. and Barnum & Bailey by striking the tents in Pittsburgh and moving the show indoors. We could, in fact, present a whole annex of his numerous fictions. We will only note how shrewdly successful Feld was in getting people in high places to embrace his rewrites, clear up to the Museum of Science and Industry's Circus Timeline Web site before the fantasies were recently removed.[3]

Feld is here, front and center, for he too made a lasting impact — good or bad, depending on your taste — to the vanishing American circus scene. For a time during the early years, our modern-day Barnum looked infallibly successful. He opened a second unit of Ringling-Barnum. He built a gigantic circus theme park in Florida. He planned Ringling retail outlets in shopping malls, snapped up ice shows and signed new rock singers to recording contracts. Before most of these grandiose ventures failed, it looked as if the entire amusement field might end up under Mr. Feld's pillow. "Everything that has circus on it, I want to own," he told Paul Binder.[4]

The old tent-show mystique? Forget it. Strange and glamorous? How about cheerful and bland as Bozo? Entering the arena after Mr. Feld took over, you'd first notice a festival of concession stands everywhere, upscale in design, and very pricy, loaded with high-end sweatshirts and jackets, coloring books and mugs, every possible circus-looking artifact imaginable. The circus magazine itself, which sometimes would cost you more than the cheapest seat in the house, was so bulky (and still is) that — consumer alert — you might need a mini-cart to wheel it off. In it, many of the articles dropped the name "Irvin Feld" dozens of times. You were bombarded with slick images of a circus designed at every turn to win you over, up close and in your face. This we will grant: those concession stands did and still do lend a much-needed semblance of the older-fashioned atmosphere to the sterile indoor arenas that replaced the big top.

"The merchandising is wonderful," says Norma Cristiani. "You can't walk anyplace without falling over something, which is a good idea."

Inside the arena, Feld fairly broke down the invisible barrier which previously separated spectator from performer. If the circus of John Ringling North was elusively surreal, the one of Irvin Feld was hyperactively reachable. Hold on. We're about to explain.

First from the audience to join the parade were the recent graduates of Mr. Feld's well-publicized Clown College. Here came men and women from all walks of life posing as professional funsters. They could be your next door neighbors. After spending a couple of months in the Florida sunshine dabbling in the science of slapstick and getting Feld's nod for a contract to tour with the show at dirt-poor wages, our sigma cum clowns donned pretty faces to enliven the program with very safe, very generic mischief. A few excelled. The majority did not last beyond the standard two-year stint. You see, Mr. Feld had to make room for the next year's graduates so that he could keep his clever PR mill (aka Clown College) in operation.

A clown is, first and foremost, a character. A clown is not a pretty face. The makeup extends and exaggerates the character, but can't create it. Behind the gloss of the assembly line joeys, there was little character. Little mystery or hardship. Little mystique. Bandmaster Merle Evans, who fronted the Ringling windjammers for nearly half a century, complained "Those homemade clowns they got, I can't go for it!"

The old-time clown was a little subversive, a little bit threatening to some kids; offbeat and off kilter, loners and losers seeking a shred of respectability in stolen spotlights. They were charming misfits hungry to be noticed. Commentators on the human condition, down there on sawdust mimicking and mocking the airs of accomplished jugglers and horse riders who enjoyed real acclaim. Stuck in the shadows between the rings, the jesters can only pretend, and in the old days their quirky attitudes and faces formed a part of the mystery. Mr. Feld let the shady brigade all go to make way for a brighter, giddier procession of silly sanitized faces guaranteed not to frighten the meekest moppet.

The kids out in the audience had to be played to, respected, honored. Our P.T. Feld even invited them down from the seats into the actual show itself. Before the performance began, staff members pre-selected the requisite number of children to appear. At the proper moment, they were shepherded onto the track and into the floats for spec. Strange and glamorous, that? Dozens of kiddies round the track waving to us in the audience? The parades passed by — and by — and by, consuming fifteen minutes or more, endlessly rehashing a theme or two or three — Mr. Feld had so much he wanted to say. So much he needed to share. What was the point of it all? Mr. and Mrs. America, we are the circus! This is the greatest show on earth! It's a three-ring world after all!

And say it he did, mainly in the color red. Bright red. Purple red. Light red and pink red. Red red and just red. Off red and on red. Variety? Contrast? Counterpoint? Even "center ring" suggested something undemocratic. Something old school. Maybe they considered it an affront to the artists in the outer rings, equally important in the Feld universe. So the term, long used to honor the headliners, was retired. In its place came the ignoble-sounding "ring two." And for a weird spell, the word "circus" no longer showed up in the title. For a spell, you would read Ringling Bros. and Barnum & Bailey Sears.

How else to remove all traces of a bygone era rich in traditions that were more honest and strange? Nothing would undermine the circus so much as allowing for the use of mechanics — long ropes attached to the performers to save them from dangerous spills. This practice had already been condoned to a small degree by Mr. North when he began importing troupes from behind the Iron Curtain, where lifelines were regularly engaged during the program. However, the rapid proliferation of these rigs under Irvin Feld's stewardship only further tarnished the integrity of circus art.

During pre–Soviet era times, mechanics were confined to practice sessions, particularly by young artists in training. Let's ask Norma Cristiani, who should know a thing or two about this controversy, what she thinks. By the time she was five during the depths of the Great Depression, Norma was woken up by her mother to take part in the swinging ladder routine on the show. And sometimes she fell off, hardly aware of what was going on. As she learned to master the more risky tricks higher off the ground, she never performed with a telltale wire around her waist. Norma?...

"You went up the web and you put your foot in one loop. Well, we didn't even have a safety on it, and the idea was, it wasn't to scare people, but we had to keep our foot a certain way when we were working so we didn't fall out. Well, now there's two, three loops on every web. You just don't get the type of people that really devote their life to performing or are committed."

"Everything is gassed up," she says. "We never used them.... I think you can do a lot more tricks if you know you weren't going to get killed."

Karl Wallenda had little respect for the unschooled performer rigged to safety. "You can make a ten-high if each one is on a cable. When they fall, they hang like puppets."

This modern-day obsession with security over daredevilry turned the circus of Irvin

Feld on occasion into an outright embarrassment. We're thinking of the year 1976, when Mr. Feld booked the Tzekovi Troupe from Bulgaria, to perform on *double* high wires. One of their stunts involved a Russian swing stationed on the end platform, from which a man was sent into the air to land in a chair at the top of a pole held by two men, each of them portioned between the two wires with one foot on each. Both the chair and the man landing in it were rigged to mechanics. In another stunt, the top two performers in a three-high pyramid were both rigged to lifelines. Since occupational safety came first up there — where, as the ringmaster used to cry, "Angels fear to tread!" — might our Bulgarian daredevils have been better off working from a couple of wheel chairs rolling along the twin cables? Ladies and gentlemen, I invite you to wonder along with me in a state of utter disbelief: What in the name of circus were those human marionettes doing up there in the first place?

Down on the ground, the same amateurism marred the show. One season, a group of horse riders wore mechanics. Most seasons, all of the teeterboard acts wore mechanics during their most difficult feats. Many single-trap aerialists wore them. In 1976, *six* of the displays on the program were rigged to lifelines. The greatest show on earth had turned chicken. And it had turned to selling its soul out there in the seats, seeking volunteers by the dozens to give the parade a neighborly face. To assure everyone in the audience that we are you. You are us.

Into this sinking morass came the redeeming Gunther Gebel Williams, a true star who never used a mechanic, who never threw himself at an audience for extra applause. He came from the old school — strange and glamorous. Feld turned the slight, blond-haired, German animal trainer into one of the greatest circus celebrities of all time. He did it, we might add, with more than a little help from the production team left behind by a departing John Ringling North. In fact, the last show that North was credited with producing was the one that introduced Williams to America.

Make no mistake. It was P.T. Feld who persuaded the 37-year-old Circus Williams headliner to make the journey from Berlin to Sarasota by agreeing to buy out and import virtually the entire show. He built a second unit of Ringling around it. Even then, who could have guessed what a transformation was about to occur when Williams entered the Ringling spotlights. I'll share something with you: I had once seen the German star at work on a quasi three-ring Italian tenter, Circo Americano, and forgot all about it until, years later, I discovered a black and white photo of him in the program magazine that I had saved from the date. There he is, a nice enough looking young guy, pictured with the elephants wearing a traditional uniform. Only a few years later and, as produced and staged by the bisexually flamboyant Irvin Feld, Gunther was now a tanned sex symbol in flashy, flesh-revealing attire. Feld got more than his money's worth by spotting his prized possession six or seven times during the program — opening parade to spec and closing parade, tiger act, elephant act, horses and other animal novelettes. Gunther once led a giraffe, supposedly "trained," around the track. Another time, he caught a leaping leopard in his arms.

He drew from the gentler Alfred Court school of animal training, which shunned whip and chair and the shoot-'em-up gun. His elephants, stationed throughout the entire arena, executed sit-ups and turnarounds, starts and stops at the mere sound, it appeared, of Gunther's voice commands. The tigers jumped over pedestals, reared up on their hind legs, lay down together and rolled over in creamy unison for the charismatic trainer, who held a long, rarely used whip with casual elegance. The man's laid-back ways lent an air of effortless showmanship. And it made him the perfect symbol for youthful anti-establishment sentiments of the peacenik era. Then, the undisputed master would blast off around the track

Reigning Feld-era superstar, Gunther Gebel Williams (courtesy of the John and Mable Ringling Museum of Art, Tibbals Digital Collection).

while the pachyderms were being coached into a roaring long mount or out the door. That was the quiet understated glamour of Gunther Gebel Williams.

If only there could have been more Gunthers and less of the rest. The late John Hurdle was so awed by the German's overwhelming contributions to an otherwise lackluster program that he remarked, "If one of those tigers decided to eat him, they haven't got a show."

Williams was so critical to Ringling's image and success that he amassed remarkable clout backstage. His self-defined nice-guy image concealed what a petty tyrant he could be. Williams pulled rank whenever something displeased him — for example, if he did not get the best parking spot for his trailer. And his puritan work ethic was easily offended. "He did not like people weak enough to become addicted to drugs, and saw all human problems as deficiencies of character," wrote Kristopher Antekeier, who ringmastered for Ringling-Barnum during the 1986 tour of the red unit. The neophyte announcer got a good dose of Gunther's prudery close up while playing a game of cards between shows once with assistant performance director Sarahjane Allison ("SJ"). Their deck shuffling had evidently been noticed by Gunther's daughter, Tina. The next day, SJ faced the animal trainer's wrath. "You will not play cards anymore! It isn't ladylike or right for a director!"

SJ held her ground, shouting back, "A card game is not moral degradation! We're playing between shows, and we're not playing for money!"

Gunther inhaled angrily, glared at SJ for a minute, and stormed off.

Antekeier was astonished and "irked" by the audacity of Gunther's trying to dictate what people could or could not do on their off hours. The Williams family, he recalled, "were the saddest bunch, unable to care enough about their fellow workers to show sympathy."[5]

The ultra-glamorous Gunther Gebel Williams could not stay young, suave and novel forever. In ten years, Mr. Feld's circus was no longer quite the drawing card, no longer playing to packed houses on some of the better dates. And Gunther was no longer able to compensate for the many second-rate acts that filled out the programs. A younger generation of circus-goers began to question a stale Ringling formula. For one, there was author Joanna Joys, who rued the mixed results: "During their halcyon years, their superiority could only be aspired to by rivals but never really attained." The Ringling circus, she wrote, "was the best, bar none. It served as a constant challenge to even its toughest rivals.... Now, when the old excellence returns almost in blinding flashes — as in Dolly Jacob's number — you can see for a few minutes what a true circus star is, can imagine what a circus made up entirely of stars is like, and it makes it even harder to accept the ho-hum acts, and inexcusable mechanics."

About Mr. Williams, she observed, "When we watch him we still catch some of the verve of old, and we only wish for one more really winning season — one more smash of originality and daring."[6]

Okay, Ringling itself was one of two big reasons why the 1970s were so naggingly inferior. Some of the younger generation who saw the show in their youth left with empty souls. Although John North's indoor conversion had been touted as a welcome departure for the average customer from the occasional discomforts of tent-show accommodations, many of the older buildings in which the circus now played in smaller towns were anything but comfortable or flattering to the program. Air-conditioning might be nonexistent; sight lines, bad; ceilings, too high or too low. In his crusty, tell-all book, ringmaster Kristopher Antekeier, who survived but a single year as a Feld announcer, remembers some pretty dismal places, one being the Dorton Arena in Raleigh, North Carolina, whose huge picture windows erased all lighting effects during matinees. "The old arenas in the south kept getting worse," he writes, recalling that in Little Rock, the clowns had to dress in "a smelly livestock building down a hill from the arena."[7]

At least under a tent, the show could sustain near-identical performance conditions from day to day.

Not just fans, but showmen, too, were beginning to question where Ringling had gone, and how they themselves might better compete to draw away its growing number of disillusioned customers. One of the professional doubters was Cliff Vargas, who had never accepted what happened back in Pittsburgh. He believed, so he would later claim in press copy, that the circus belonged under canvas. He professed a burning desire to restore the three-ring, tent-show traditions "as they once were in America."

Enter, now, a second reason for a decade of mediocrity: Boiler room big tops. Before turning his dream into reality, Vargas had worked his way up from the inferno of back room calling centers where highly skilled telephone solicitors pitched blocks of free kids' tickets to local merchants for a "charitable" cause. Keeping the show on the road had never been easy for anybody. Once, they operated crooked concessions and games of chance, shorted customers at the ticket windows and picked their pockets on the sly. Now, so many decades later, they were working the phones with a vengeance, exploiting so-called humanitarian goals to raise millions for the needy, the "needy" being mostly themselves.

All a typical circus promoter need do was land a sponsoring contract with the local policemen or firemen, the Jaycees or the Chamber of Commerce, set up shop and start ripping and tearing over the phones. Merchants were reluctant to say "no" to an unseen voice calling on behalf of the sheriff's department, and so thousands of tickets got sold in books that got tossed in waste baskets. The "circus" came to town and few people turned out to watch it.

Art Concello once put it to me this way: "When grift went out, the phones came in."

When it came to making hay in a boiler room, Sid Kellner, who went out as James Brothers Circus — until he changed the name to George Matthews Great London — ranked with the best. And he even managed, now and then, to produce a fine performance. Another ace operator was James Hargrove, who fronted for John Strong, reaping millions in the act for a circus that sat only a hundred or so! Hargrove ended up touring courthouses, not by choice, having to answer numerous complaints alleging that most of the money he had raised for charity actually ended up in his personal bank account. Hargrove had no feeling for circus art whatsoever. John Strong was just another account. And John Strong, who had once told me that he was in the business for "the love of it," became a party to one of the most flagrantly profitable boiler room scams of all time. Laws were passed through the shabby, shameful '70s mandating how much from every dollar raised must be turned over to the sponsoring organization. James Hargrove eventually took his life down in Arizona.

Sid Kellner's sons, Matthew and George, continued on in their father's ways for many more years, fronting for mostly non-circus ventures. In 2004, they ended up in a Santa Clara County criminal trial, accused, along with an ex-sheriff and with their own mother, Lovie, of raising $3.6 million between 1993 and 2000 for various quasi law enforcement groups and keeping all but less than $50,000 for themselves and their phone room cronies.[8] Did we tell you about the shady collusions between city hall and less-principled circus owners?

Now here's where the tale takes a spectacular turn. In a burst of late-blooming showmanship beating all odds, Cliff Vargas overcame his phone room addictions and found his destiny building up a first-rate performance. Born on a farm in central California, he drew some inspiration from his dad, who had worked horses on a circus in Portugal. Pittsburgh haunted the younger Vargas all his adult life. "It was almost twenty years ago that the professional prophets of gloom pronounced to all who would listen that the tented circus in America was dead."[9]

At the age of 19, Vargas hitched a ride to Chicago. There, he took odd jobs to support himself. Still a buff, he took in the Medina Shrine Circus, attending every one of its night shows during the entire 21-day run. He got a job working for the man who promoted the date. Vargas worked the phones and sold advertising for program booklets. Two years later, he returned to California, doing essentially the same thing for four different circus companies. He ended up on Miller-Johnson with mounting doubts. What was the point of it all other than to turn a fast buck? Was he a circus fan himself? And if so, did he not wish to participate in a more meaningful way?

Miller-Johnson's owner, Charles Germaine, was doing it, according to Vargas, "the cheap way — get as much money as you can." Vargas grew increasingly uneasy with the meager programs they offered the public in exchange for its support. Vargas and Germaine devised a new form of advance telephone sales aimed directly at homes rather than businesses. All of a sudden, the tickets they were now pitching to families were showing up at the door, and the seats were actually being sat in. What a novelty, selling tickets to people who intended to use them. Maybe our Portuguese promoter was touched by the sight of so many people wanting to see the show. Maybe he was moved to wonder, "Do they deserve something better than what we are giving them, something we can afford?"

Suffering his own Louis Stern moment, Cliff Vargas faced his expedient, profit-driven partner with an ultimatum. He was no longer willing to tolerate the status quo rip-off.

"Look, if we're going to be in the circus, fine. If not, let's put our hat in the ring and get out of it."

The next day, Vargas listened to Germaine on the other end of the phone offering to sell him the show. A house in San Francisco, owned by Mr. Vargas, was put up for sale. The proceeds enabled him to become Mr. Vargas, circus owner.

"I rented some trucks and started buying some animals, and that's how the whole thing became what it is today."[10]

On the road to showmanship, Vargas put out some very unremarkable shows, erecting large tents and underpopulating them with solo turns. He trouped like a madman (some of his most admiring fans are convinced that he was), routing his dream into the mud and slosh of Northern California winters. Sandy Dobritch, a likeable enough presence, was one of his first ringmasters. For music, you might hear one season, a trio, the next an accordion and trumpet. "Great traditions" on the rebound? We went. We sat. We watched. Most of all, we waited in vain.

Our foundering, rhetorically ambitious showman promised the public not only what the American circus had looked and sounded like in its heyday, but one free of contemporary taint. "It is of primary importance to Cliff Vargas that the circus which bears his name be just that — a circus! There has been and will be no attempt to turn it into bogus Broadway or ersatz Las Vegas. Cliff Vargas is, quite simply, the biggest and the best real circus in America today!"

Now, just when did he come on with this grandiose boast? Oh, in 1974, during the inaugural season of Circus Vargas (succeeding the Miller-Johnson title) when the show offered only *one* three-ring display and *no* clowns at all. When only *two* young musicians named Vynn and Wynn — one at the Yamaha EX-42 organ, the other on drums — made up the rinky-dink Circus Vargas "band." On the program were Wally Naughtin's bears, the showmanly Pat Anthony bringing high drama to a cage full of lions and tigers, Semon's chimps, Yaski on the high-wire, from Morocco the Hassani tumblers, the Flying Farias with 10-year-young Julio, and other acts of general merit, all helping to round out a good old-fashioned one-ring offering in a sprawling three-ring tent.

Vargas was chasing a much costlier vision, one musician at a time. At one curious point during his erratic climb to credibility, he added even more canvas and set up a six-pole big top. Why? Only the gods knew. In it, a one-ring performance proceeded apace. At least it was nice inside to gaze up at all the cloth and dream of Ringling in the twenties.

In 1975, the band was enlarged by a third with the arrival of the Parker Trio. Two tours later, Circus Vargas pitched a sideshow and a petting zoo out on the midway. On the bandstand, there were now eight men under the sure-fire direction of James Gibson. The show was starting, at last, to take shape. Nothing pushed it as far ahead, though, as an epochal moment in the San Fernando Valley down in Southern California. Faced with a last-minute pullout of the sponsor for a Devonshire Downs date, Mr. Vargas had to make do on his own. Without a charity pitch. Without phones. He would have to rely on individual tickets sales through advertising and other means. We call this a "cold date."

A local circus fan and rock promoter, Douglas Lyon, was appealed to by performance director Parley Baer to lend a last-minute hand with publicity. The quick-thinking Lyon dispatched an elephant through a car wash. That night across television newscasts all over Los Angeles, the audacity of it all upstaged coverage even of a Henry Kissinger visit to some foreign capital. The next day, thousands of people turned out at Devonshire to patronize the circus the old-fashioned way: they stood in long lines to buy tickets with their own money. And Cliff Vargas had a career-changing epiphany. Soon, he was playing all of his dates "cold." No more phones. Bring on the ballyhoo, build up the show itself, and watch them come.

Learning to survive away from his boiler room addictions, Vargas turned himself into a bona fide showman. Driven first by a dream of revival, then by the blinding light of what a good ballyhoo can achieve, he now desired to produce a top-level program worthy of the public's patronage. For a time, his madness seemed an asset as he joined the ranks of true circus kings and moved promisingly ahead into a new decade.

So let's say good bye, folks, to the seedy seventies. To schlock showmanship and pathetic promotions. About to appear out here is a new breed of young street performer, equally disillusioned with the era. They're set on doing something very un-Vargas and even more un-Ringling. Stick around for this next display on our vanishing midway. There's still much more — excuse me, much less — to come.

6

Mavericks on the Midway

They grew up juggling on street corners with a hat nearby for donations and flower-power smiles on their unscrubbed faces. They glimpsed the three-ring juggernaut in their youth and saw tacky parades. They watched in dismay as performers worked side by side in multiple rings. They hoped for a personal connection to the artist and saw only overproduced spectacles. They gazed at clowns who spent more time selling coloring books than raising laughter, at intermissions that grew longer for elephant and pony rides.

They felt assaulted by a promoter's get-rich machine. One of the disenchanted was Paul Binder. "When we started in the seventies, people in the country said, 'circus is dead!' Heard it everywhere we went."

Binder thought he saw a dying institution that insulted him on two fronts: First, he likened the public perception of it to "seedy traveling people with carnivals ... promoted as something other than performing arts." Second, he was put off by the way it was sold to the public as a modern-day version of the old Circus Maximus from Roman times — "a promoter's idea, not history."

Brooklyn born and raised, Binder's childhood years had not enamored him of big tops. In the late '40s, his mother took him to see Ringling Bros. at Madison Square Garden. She whisked her little boy quickly past the sideshow curiosities into the main arena. All he would live to remember were the fat lady, the smell of elephants, and one performer who left him spellbound: "In a bright white costume, tails, gloves, standing on his finger on a marble ball, the image has remained with me. This kind of stark moment. Unus was the image. The most powerful and single image I had of Ringling Bros. and Barnum & Bailey the first time when I was a kid."

Now that's a pretty tough act to follow. Maybe the kid saw the best too soon and turned prematurely jaded. As the years passed, circuses held little sway for Binder, who went to Dartmouth, graduated with a degree in business administration from Columbia and landed a succession of jobs in tv production. He served as stage manager for French chef Julia Child. He was a talent coordinator for Mike Douglas, booking serious guests onto the program. Came the restless revolutionary sixties, and Binder itched for a lifestyle change. Out to San Francisco he went.

About that time, other young people of Binder's age and education were finding little inspiration from the circus. They saw shows thrown together by phone-room promoters on

66

His first trip to the circus at Madison Square Garden in the late '40s left Paul Binder with one haunting memory: the singular image of Unus (photograph by Ted Sato/author collection).

the backs of bogus sponsors. They saw the once-stellar Polack Brothers Circus in sad decline. They saw Circus Vargas pitching acres of old-world canvas, inside which a not-yet impressive performance was given. They saw tawdry mud shows, like the notoriously chintzy Hoxie Brothers, peddling crumbs of nostalgia and little else to a diminishing fan base. They had a hard time finding a tent to believe in.

They might have seen Sid Kellner's latest incarnation, George Matthew's Great London, down to a dozen or so performers during one particularly bleak tour in the '70s when there were only two good acts on the bill to write home about: wire walker Herbie Webber and Moore's Mongrel Dogs.

Circuses from hell? Here's where you'll find them. And if you want to go out for a concession break from the tyranny of if all, folks, that's quite okay with us. Otherwise, brace yourself for a nauseating onslaught of subpar entertainment. They're handing out free kids' tickets galore. They're serving a good cause, too — think Elks or Jaycees, volunteer firefighters or Daughters of the Revolution milk fund. Think of the cops, phone-room kings of indoor swindles. Out there in San Francisco at the Cow Palace during the '70s, some of the worst circus programs ever foisted on the public were sponsored by the Police Athletic League. Sorry, Sir Officer: You serve a great purpose protecting us from ourselves. Around a sawdust circle, you should have been arrested on countless occasions for contributing to artistic malpractice.

Looming above this sad state of affairs with a profound respect for authentic artistry was juggler and New York University professor Hovey Burgess. He cast a spotlight of high respect on the primacy of the individual circus artist. And he, a big top Buddha of sorts, would influence a handful of young protégées to question what was happening to our circuses and shake things up for the better — maybe. Burgess taught circus skills to acting majors at the university. On the side, he did his own juggling act at the Electric Circus in the East Village, a night club and dance hall where such talents were highlighted each evening.

Working the lights at the club was a young dude named Larry Pisoni, who had done acrobatics in his youth, and who was struck by the professor's skills. They started talking, and one night, Hovey offered free training. "If you want to come by my class, you're more than welcome."

Says Pisoni, looking back, "And that just changed everything."

A new Burgess student was learning to master an ancient art, and then some. The two became friends, and they wandered together all over the map to view circus skills as practiced in commercial settings. Explains Pisoni: "Hovey was my mentor. If there was a circus within a hundred mile radius of Manhattan, we went and saw it, no matter what the size it was. And in those days, no Internet, no route cards. We followed the arrows."

What Pisoni grew to appreciate the most were the spectators themselves. "It was really an enormously mixed audience generationally, linguistically, class-wise. And it was a wonderful mixed program and mixed audience. That was an audience I wanted to play to."

Pisoni felt a desire to reach them in a more direct, heartfelt manner. To do this, he concluded it would be essential to remove layers of tradition and hyperbole that separated patron from performer. The times, they were a-changin.' So, why not the circus?

Paul Binder was another maverick on the frayed and crumbling midway, ready to take on the purveyors of schlock: "In America, the counter culture issue empowered a generation of people to say, 'Hey! Circus is not something that only you can do,' which I think was a very important empowerment. That freed up the minds and the souls of a lot of people."

College students who went out with the all-student summer show, Circus Kirk, also had issues with status quo big tops. They especially were not thrilled with Ringling. Charles Boas, son of Kirk's founder and manager, Doc, regarded the Big One as "an ice show without ice."

Too much glitz, complained he and his cohorts, back when I talked to them on the Clymer, Pennsylvania, lot. "Hard to find the acts among the glitter. So much flash, you get dazzled."

Another Kirk guy, theatre major Bernie Collins, did not consider Ringling to be "a circus anymore." Nor was he much amused by its cookie-cutter faces behind cute red noses. "The clowns do not have a chance to express any individuality on Ringling."[1]

Although Circus Kirk ran out of money and determination after 10 years of summer tours (after Doc Boas suffered severe health problems), the spirit of what it stood for only added to the growing movement in this country towards smaller, more intimate circus programs.

Also motivating Larry Pisoni were the metaphors he attached to the acts. Jugglers symbolized "keeping multiple projects going," while the trapeze artist gave welcome wings to our flying dreams. Hovey Burgess instilled in his protégée a conviction that, in fact, all circus skills bear a core relationship to each other. To a student wishing to master a particular skill, Burgess would typically reply, "That's all well and good, but if you want to do that you need to learn how to juggle."[2]

Having learned how to, Pisoni went west bearing the Burgess torch. He fell in with the politically left-wing San Francisco Mime Troupe, to whose members he taught the skills he had just been taught back East. One of Pisoni's students was Paul Binder, who had gone out to the city by the Golden Gate, drawn to incense and beads at the height of the hippie era. And here he was, about to be infected with the same enthusiasm for juggling that had bitten Pisoni under the Burgess spell. As Hovey had done with Larry, so did Larry with Paul: Let's go out and see circuses.

Same intent. Same zealous sharing of notes ringside. Same result. Person by person, convert by convert, a new way of looking at an old American form was starting to spread. Binder credits Pisoni for taking him to shows in the Bay Area and teaching him how to spot in the most mediocre programs the occasional rare talent — or rare trick well done.

Binder started to look beyond seedy trappings, and he discovered authentic artistry here and there. At the same time, he was becoming a good and confident juggler himself, now ready, he thought, to try his luck on European soil. Maybe over there he could juggle on street corners, if not professionally. Would Larry like to go with him? he asked. Larry was not ready, Larry replied. So, instead, Binder hooked up with another San Francisco Mime juggler, Michael Christensen. The pair booked flight, clubs in hand, for London, and ended up in Kent. The year was 1974. Little could they have known that the path they had taken would lead them from being paid circus performers abroad to being the founders of their own show back in the states.

The same year, Larry Pisoni and his life partner, Peggy Snyder, founded the Pickle Family jugglers.

One of the local circuses that Pisoni had seen in San Francisco gave him confidence in his own minimalist vision. "An awful lot of people came through the John Strong Show. It was very modest, but I liked the fact that his son was involved. And he had a German father-daughter act [the Wendanis] that I liked very much. Free head-stand balance act that I liked. And it was small and in large measure the small shows convinced me that it was possible to do my project."

Under John Strong's humble little tent, the chatty ringmaster talked to and joked with his audience like a room full of friends. In that intimate setting, Pisoni may have seen and felt something magically similar to what our forebears saw and felt when Dan Rice came out to trade barbs with the ringmaster and joke with folks in the seats.

Twelve months later, Pisoni, now 24 years old, and Snyder advanced from the Pickle Family jugglers to the Pickle Family Circus. They pursued local community groups for low-key sponsorship, very unlike the high-powered boiler rooms then running rampant on

John Strong's folksy one-ring format gave Larry Pisoni added incentive to create the Pickle Family Circus in 1974 (author collection).

larger shows. We're talking health clinics and arts collectives, such as the Lobero Theatre Foundation in Santa Barbara. The sponsors sold advance tickets, helped secure the grounds, served as house ushers, sold refreshments and shared a percentage of the gross.

They performed under the open sky. A bright canvas sidewall served to establish an enclosure. Portable grandstand risers gave the crowd decent raked seating. A jazz band of about six men played standards the first season, thereafter original compositions. For jazz lovers, the fine music was a plus. The Pickles never carried a traditional ringmaster. Most of the modestly accomplished acts were announced by members of the band. In the laid-back setting, they were a sunny pleasure to watch. The program always built to a rousing finish with the "Big Juggle," in which most of the company participated.

So what made the Pickles more than the sum of their unspectacular parts? A down-home feel stripped of cliché overkill. In a way, the anti-circus. In a way, more like a party with talented friends. No place here for prima donnas. Pisoni's Pickles proceeded to charm at a sauntering gait. Take time to savor the moment—to study the art of the acrobat in slower motion, they seemed to stay. We're in no hurry, are you? San Francisco crowds, in small grateful numbers, came out to agree. However, there is no escaping the fact that modest showmanship begets modest attendance.

On a more impressive note, some inspired first-rate clowning gave this new circus a superior edge over many of its bigger competitors. Statuesque Bill Irwin, fresh out of the Ringling Clown College (but without a job offer from the Felds), put on a face for the Pickles and proved himself over and over again with hilariously inventive bits. So did Geoff Hoyle, who snuck through the ring between acts as the precocious Mr. Sniff. Pisoni himself, forever lugging around a trunk full of this and that, made up the trio of stellar Pickle buffoons. The show could deliver laughs in spades.

Hoyle's Mr. Sniff was not born out of a trunk, but out of many, and over a period of a year or two. Hoyle grew up in England, admiring comedians such as Norman Wisdom, whose movies his mother took him to see, and other slapstick talents like Laurel and Hardy and Buster Keaton. He professes a strong preference for what he calls "reality-based clowning" (as opposed, we will assume, to the assembly line). For example, Hoyle praises a personal favorite, Otto Griebling, the long-time Ringling hobo who would wander through the audience with what looked like a roll call in hand, pretentiously checking off names. Griebling's famed prop, a motley package loosely tied together with "lots of string and plastered with shipping labels," as Hoyle fondly describes it, is now displayed at the Circus World Museum. It was the tool of a gifted comedian much admired by Hoyle.

"You knew that was going to be hilarious, this thing looked as though it had been shipped around the world seventeen times and back again, through every single post office."

Can you tell us, Mr. Sniff, what in your opinion marks the genuine jester?

"What a real clown does, he subverts established reality. And subverts propriety. But he also reveals human feebleness and weakness, which is so reassuring to everybody watching. And you laugh to me mostly because you recognize it, and it's very affirmative. It's therapeutic, it's curative. And most of all, when it's well done, it's accurate."

Back to the creation of Sniff: Hoyle first engaged in long discussions with Larry Pisoni and Peggy Snyder. They pored through articles and illustrations for ideas. "Any kind of a visual material that we could lay our hands on that sparked our interest," he says. One of the books they examined covered French acrobats and mountebanks, and in it they discovered a picture of a guy in a very long coat. Hoyle's imagination was stirred. He began sketching out a character based upon the image.

"Either I or Larry, or somebody else, said, 'Why don't we try a large nose?' We looked for some clown noses, and we found this big long nose in a makeup shop."

Hoyle secured the thing over his own nose. He donned an extra long coat, and they made it bright yellow, "to conform more to the Pickle Family Circus color scheme."

Mr. Sniff was coming into his own. On the outside, he appeared to be a very simple character of silly airs and intrigues whom you find endlessly amusing. On the inside lurked a very intellectual actor paying tribute in his own mind to classroom philosophy. "I like to work off the idea of the exile — sort of Kalfkaeqsue. Someone who has everything he needs with him. He has a suitcase and a long coat. Whatever else do you need?"

What a riot was the sniffy Mr. Sniff. And you didn't have to know anything about Kafka to be thoroughly entertained in his wry, wacky presence. He was that perennial child in us all, the one we are when we have learned a few words and think we can speak every language on planet Earth, the one we are after learning to walk and believing we can now police the entire neighborhood. Whenever Mr. Sniff paused to sniff out the air like a would-be detective, we laughed.

"Mr. Sniff was born that particular season," says Mr. Hoyle, unsure of the exact date, placing it around 1976. "The nose was very prominent, and I started smelling things, and I have a very active sense of smell, and it seemed to be mirth-making."

The Pickle Family Circus, circa 1977. At the left, Bill Irwin in top hat and jugglers Peggy Snyder and Larry Pisoni (other performers not identified) (Circus World Museum, Baraboo, Wisconsin).

The Pickles gave us excellent original comedy. They gave us fine juggling, some buoyant acrobats, a tightrope walker now and then, and they gave us a "circus" we had never before seen. A circus the world had never before seen. A circus without a *single* animal. Not one elephant. Not a horse or a bear or a dog. Not even a kitty cat.

Only humans. Because they were so small and new, there was little reason to even notice the omission. And in bohemian San Francisco, this very young, rather avant garde troupe hardly had to justify the departure. They did not ask to be judged by traditional expectations. They only asked to be given the chance to entertain as best they could, in their own way.

"We prided ourselves on being a circus that showcased human skills," states Mr. Sniff.

Were they purposely thumbing their noses at the sacred roots of the American circus?

Answers Larry Pisoni, looking back — not exactly. Heck, let's bring him out here to speak for himself on this momentous matter. Mr. Pisoni! ... if you please...

"I really didn't know anything about training animals, for one thing. I knew the animals had to be an element. I just didn't think that I needed to actually have real animals, that given this notion that the value rests in the metaphor, that I could put people in animal costumes and have the suggestion of animals, and not carry them."

You were *not* trying to prove that circuses can do fine without animal acts?

"That certainly wasn't my initial thrust, but it was definitely part of it. I used to say to people, 'What I want to do is create a circus that satisfies everyone's conceptions of what a circus is, and then go someplace else with it.'"

So there you have it, folks, in his own words from a true modern-day innovator, Larry Pisoni, who was perhaps as truly radical in removing the animals from the show as was William Coup in adding rings.

And while the Pickles are out here, Mr. Sniff has something he'd like to add concerning those early days of change that may have sparked a silent revolution. Mr. Sniff?...

"Oh, I remember that one of the big selling points, that it was no animals. It was a great relief not to have animals, partly because they're very difficult to take care of when you're moving around a lot. They require enormous amounts of care and attention, and then there's the abuse problem."

A Pickle policy born of San Francisco politics?

"I don't think anyone said, 'Okay, we're going to start a circus, and the main thrust of this circus is it will have no animals.' I think we're interested in all aspects of circus, but we're interested in a circus that is intelligent and not demeaning to anybody or any creature. And the way to do that is to showcase spectacular displays of human prowess and skill and achievement and not dress up a dog in a tutu and have it walk around on its hind legs after a piece of kibble that someone's holding in their hand."

Those latent political underpinnings, however, would, in the years to come, be codified into a more strident language bordering on a manifesto. Here are the words of Jon Carroll from his and photographer Terry Lorant's 1986 book, *The Pickle Family Circus*: "It was considered important, even necessary, to create a satisfying unity between work and art and politics.... A redefined circus meant no scantily clad chorines dangling from long ropes. It meant no animal acts; putting a creature in a cage and taking it on the road is obviously cruel and unusual behavior. It meant no artificial division of labor, with low-paid roustabouts endlessly toiling so the stars could sweep in and garner assorted kudos. It meant an organization that was, if not precisely a collective, at least a vigorous democracy."[3]

No airstream trailers for this crowd. In their egalitarian backyard setup, the Pickles made their most pronounced political statement. There, you would come upon a sterile-looking spread of small tepee-like tents in which they lived. And still, they will admit to the petty tensions and conflicts that now and then wracked company morale. Larry Pisoni's saddest memory of his days at the Pickle helm was the toll it took on his marriage to Peggy. They would eventually divorce.

So, here's the question of the moment: Did the Pickles actually set off a counter-revolution in the ring? Hard to say, for a lot of their peers around the world were also, about the same time, experimenting with alternative visions of what "circus" might mean. Three years after the Pickles formed, in 1977 Australia's Circus Oz got going in a far more subversive way. Kafka, come back here! Oz was really a theatrical delivery system using circus skills to help make big political statements about the darker side of life. Nuclear war was one of their pet issues, addressed in the morbidly funny "Holiday in Harrisburg." In it, a whimsical computer malfunctions, unleashing a scene of social chaos. We need to keep in mind that it was an Australian novelist, Nevil Shute, who wrote the book *On the Beach*, about the end of the world following a nuclear war. Send in the clowns for cleanup? "Holiday in Harrisburg" was set to some pretty ragged music played by angry-looking rock guitarists.

You're wondering, where is the "circus" in this? So was I while I watched it. On safer ground, Circus Oz had a guy walking upside down, his magnetized feet attached to the floor of an upside down lounge in the sky. He is a lonely drifter of sorts (who might not even know he is lonely), in search of a good time with another upside down type. The hoped-for hook-up does not happen, so the best our loner can do is find another loner to share the fare for an inverted taxi ride out of the place. Home to more post-nuclear alienation.

The Aussies' view of circus was darkly hilarious. They were all things anti-establishment. We were still in the gender-bending seventies, and in the seventies, as in Oz, women bore unshaved armpits. A sexy bombshell is the butt of all humor. And she who once posed dumbly in the shadows of a male circus star is now the star herself, and he, the one posing dumbly. She is the one who now hoists him into the air. Otherwise, what an offense to feminism that would be.

As good as were some of the circus tricks on Oz, it was still a dramatic vaudeville show favoring satire and also shunning animal acts. Other less pessimistic visions were also taking root around the globe. Paul Binder, a survivor of San Francisco politics in the hippie era, decided that the circus did not need to be reinvented or deconstructed or revived or recycled. Or, what else? No, it only needed to be restored to its original European form. On the continent while performing with his juggling partner, Michael Christensen, the two made a fair name for themselves, ending up on the bill of Annie Fratellini's Novo Circus in Paris. And there, they experienced a life-changing epiphany.

Declares Binder, "I was totally taken, because the tradition is still alive in Europe. Families still create great circuses in Europe."

Profoundly engaged, Binder became a convert to the form first established by Philip Astley in 1770. Over two hundred years had passed when, in 1976, Binder and Christensen returned to New York, intent on starting up their own show. They called it the Big Apple Circus.

"One of the reasons we started Big Apple," explains Christensen, "was to reclaim and bring back and celebrate the one-ring format, which had been waning here." The bigger three-ring shows, in Christensen's view, had "really played havoc with the art form of the one-ring circus."

Their single-ring conversion became almost a religion for Binder, who argues, interestingly, that the ring actually predates Astley himself by a thousand years, to a time when people sat around circles to engage in theatrical rituals necessary for their social survival. Hear him out...

"What I mean is, there are roots in this tradition that go back to the earliest primal instincts in time, that the form we present is the original theatrical form. It is connected completely to the original tribal rituals out of which all — and I will say again — *all* of the performing arts grew."

Opera, too, Mr. Binder?

"Yes."

"The circus is the closest thing to the original form that was — the community came together in a circle to reassure itself through ritual about its survival, and it spoke to all of the most primal instincts, so that the primal instincts could come to the surface, so that they could be reassured that they knew how to survive."

What about *Astley's* circle?

"That was the modern circus."

The first Big Apple programs came with a split personality, good enough for a split decision from the judges. Rarely is a circus performance from start to finish the perfect moving mechanism that we dream it can be. Binder's earnest first efforts were no exception.

Paul Binder, left, founder, and Michael Christensen, co-founder, of Big Apple Circus (courtesy of the Big Apple Circus).

Seen by yours truly in 1978 (their second season out), Big Apple's first half shimmered with novel acts cast in a no-frills showcase, one at a time. After the intermission came a different sort of a thing, clumsily disconnected in style from that which had preceded it. A bicycle act, for example, was decked out in schlocky Vegas-like costumes. A cradle act, too similar to one already seen in the front half of the program, hardly distinguished itself with its conspicuous reliance on mechanics.

So, Binder and Christensen took us from the remarkable to the humdrum in the space of a couple of hours. Let's give them some slack, though. They were just beginning their restoration.

Among the newer, never before seen acts they presented, there were the energetic, in-the-rough Back Street Flyers, six dudes from the inner city who had trained at Big Apple's New York School of Circus Arts. This bold experiment in producing home-grown talent was born of an impractical dream that would not last long.

On more sounder footing, Binder and Christensen built up a nonprofit organization along the lines of a civic-based philharmonic or ballet company, with a board of directors and a list of corporate and individual donors. One of their initial supporters, David Balding, would ten years later attempt the same thing in St. Louis, where he founded, with Sheila and Sam Jewel and Alexandre Sacha Pavlata, Circus Flora. Balding's eclectic offerings mixed up circus skills, animal acts, dancers and actors, story lines and original live music. They too claimed to celebrate "the classical, European style circus."

The Pickles out West. Flora, mid-country. Big Apple in the Big Apple. All three outfits, so it appeared, were up and running with promise, each to a different muse. They shared one thing in common: one-ring intimacy. None came close to turning a fortune, and none ever would. The artists they employed were treated with a type of respect we will call "collegial." None to our knowledge was ever expected to sell coloring books or pitch pony rides.

Binder, a natural diplomat and organizer, led the pack. Season by season, his fan base and subscriber lists grew. Within a few years, he was pitching his tent at Lincoln Center each holiday season for a nearly three-month engagement.

By the mid eighties, Larry Pisoni was still not pitching a tent anywhere. His dream had stalled, only halfway realized. "Our little sidewall arrangement suggested the big top, but we really needed to have a big top, and we needed to have a little more control over the environment. There were acts that couldn't work because of the wind."

Had he been able to afford the canvas and poles, Pisoni believes that he could have gone a lot farther artistically. He told me, "It clearly would have changed the show. Not so much in spirit, but in content. We could really do the kind of different things for aerial acts.... We could have gone to another level of production if we had lights. It wouldn't have seemed quite as innocent as when you saw the show."

With a ring, some seats and a sidewall, the Pickles managed to tour as far east as Iowa. To the south, they played dates in Southern California, erecting their teepee dressing tents in the backyard in which they lived as a "collective." Friendly ovations greeted their exuberantly good-natured offerings.

Out in Santa Monica one season, a band of performers from Circus Oz took in the show, and went backstage afterwards to offer cheers and say hello. "We were thinking," remembers Pisoni, "Wow — something's happening globally."

Also that same year in the Los Angeles area following another performance, a trio of Canadians from Montreal made their way into the strange Pickle backyard. The visitors were high on the program and eager to share their enthusiasm with the director and his troupe. Unknowingly, in the hands of those three young French-speaking artists, a momentous new epoch in circus history was soon to unfold.

"They introduced themselves," recalls Larry Pisoni. "They said they loved the show. They said they were from a project called Cirque du Soleil."

7

Cirque du Invasion

They came down from the northern heights like a band of brightly clad sorcerers from another planet. They came down from across the Canadian border with attitude, and with a small yellow-and-blue tent. They were young and brash. The best of them came from Europe. They claimed to reinvent the circus.

They headed straight down to the entertainment capital of the world. They chose an exotic spot in the City of Angels in which to perform: Little Tokyo. They did it during the city's 1987 Arts Festival, opening on September 3. You could get the best seat in the house for only $17.50. You could go in there and witness a burst of something very new rooted in something very old. You could glimpse the dawn of Cirque du Soleil.

Before the performance commenced, you'd have little reason to expect anything much out of the ordinary. Two old-style clowns, Benny Le Grand and Catitan Cactus, traipsed through the hot tent as if they owned it, unloading tons of water on unsuspecting patrons in a variety of funny ways. The boisterously bawdy pair suggested a far more traditional show than the one waiting in the wings to blast off.

Into the tent walked a gaggle of grotesquely masked average-looking mortals on the humble side, not unlike the hordes of homeless out there in the real world only a few urban blocks away. The masked souls looked more curious than hungry — charmingly touched by the circus images as children are touched. Once inside, they were met with kindness by the Cirque gypsies, who invited them to live out their fantasies by turning them into performers themselves. One became the ringmaster. And the show was on.

A line of eight young gymnasts attired in black and white as corporate penguins strutted on with business briefcases in hand, up to the teeterboard and into the air — into the eccentric sphere of Cirque's unusual rhythms and stunning stage pictures. From Circus Knie, where she had first appeared at the age of six, came Masha Dimitri, who had studied at the Gruss National Circus in Paris and later appeared with the Pickles in San Francisco. Dimitri bounded across a slack wire on one foot while the other balanced the tip of an umbrella. And while she worked, the Three Children and a magical jester played by actor Marc Proulx danced and cavorted below. Proulx postured triumphantly each time a high-point in the routine was achieved, as he would for each succeeding act on the program.

A four-person chair balancing number produced by Poland's Christopher Suszek was another of the early charmers. Up to this point, the young, average-talented company had executed some highly inventive moves to exciting new-age music played by two men on synthesizers, one on sax, another on the clarinet, and one playing drums. The entire cast was candy-wrapped in colors both subtle and bright. This visually beguiling show looked designed by Dali.

After intermission, the mood intensified as Cirque's most accomplished artists proceeded to capture our emotions and drive them skyward. First to win the highest kudos were head and hand balancing wonders Eric Varelas and Amelie Demay. They had met while both were enrolled at Annie Fratellini's circus school in Paris. They ended up performing together in Fratellini's show, then broke up and went their separate ways into cabaret and film. Varelas and Demay reunited for Cirque du Soleil, and weren't we lucky. Let me tell you, it rarely gets better than this. Their terrifically difficult tricks were executed in seamless fashion. Not one moment of wasted motion. The band accompanied their mesmerizing sensuality with a torrid cabaret tango.

Varelas and Demay rated a standing ovation.

Comedian Denis Lacombe, his feet anchored to a flexible base, played a mad orchestra conductor who becomes so carried away and caught up in his emotional attack at the podium, that his body tips hilariously from side to side without falling to the floor.

Then came more heart-stirring turns: a breathless cradle act of surprising invention brought off with clean dash by the English duo of the Andrews — Andrew Watson and Jacqueline Williams. From whence, them? From ordinary day jobs to Gerry Cottles' Circus School in London, followed by stints with the Cottles Circus itself and with English and West German shows.

The Andrews climaxed with a standard cloud swing breakaway in which it appears they are headed straight for a crash landing over the sawdust — until the last moment when they are suddenly spared by wires attached to their feet.

Bring on the three-person Zhao family of trick bike riders direct from communist Beijing. They turned zippy tricks in whirling motion. The two men and a woman were joined by another six riders from the company to form an exhilarating pyramid of nine souls. The audience was nearly on its feet in euphoria. And it was over — the end had arrived, heart-stoppingly to the point.

Amidst the cheers, it is not really over yet. Those outsiders who have spent a couple of magical hours indulging their circus dreams are now being gently returned to their former selves, waved goodbye by the cast. The "ringmaster" is given the red hat to keep as a souvenir. One more time, the visitors turn to wave good-bye to us all and to their hosts. And they are gone.

What was it about the simple little story that moved us nearly to tears in the end? Was it a shared dream of tinseled glory? The pathos we felt for a group of downtrodden souls likely confined to a menial existence, given a second chance in life? A terrible sadness for the reality of their humdrum condition outside the yellow and blue top? For their humble gratitude?

Or was it the rapture of the circus itself that had turned our blood to fire and set our spirits tingling?

The entire performance glistened with a rare woven-together quality — as if each action was an intricate shard in a carefully controlled kaleidoscope. You viewed, in essence, a more refined form of the Russian circus that had so impressed us in the 1960s. The music, too, all seemed as fresh as these nouveau performers pushing to create new modes of expression for old tricks. About the production style — was it ballet? a live MTV video? a circus? It took you by the gut to a place both familiar and hip, earthy and erotic, played upon your emotions like a master illusionist, and left you sitting there in awe. And on your feet cheering, you wanted to reach out and touch these gifted artisans. The standing ovations continued minute by minute. They bowed and retired behind the curtain. More applause. More lusty cheers. Once more, they returned. More bows. After five minutes of hand-clapping euphoria, they were gone.

Cirque du Soleil, let there be no doubt, offered the jaded American ticket holder dazzling proof that circus can be an infinitely superior art form unto itself.

And the next Los Angeles morning, the town woke up to the news of a fantastic troupe in its midst. Good morning, Montreal! And, the same to you, L.A.!

Cirque's real ringmaster, Michel Barette, was thrown into instant duty as interviewee-designate to speak with members of the media, rapidly forming around the back door with all sorts of buzzing questions.

"We were really surprised," he remembers. "We didn't know what to expect.... They were waiting for me the day after the opening night.... The *Entertainment Tonight* microphone was under my nose. As soon as I set foot on the site, our people from communications got hold of me and said, 'You need to do these interviews!' The first one was *ET*."

Only the night before, Barette and his fellow performers had been all eyes, peering through the back curtain to study the faces of many "well known actors in Hollywood" out there in their first U.S. audience.

"We were a bit impressed to see the guys that normally you see on tv you never meet, to see what we were going to do."

The critics were thumbs up all the way, from welcome pleasure to all-out raves. "Here's a circus like no other," reported Polly Warfield in the *Hollywood DramaLogue*.[1] *Los Angeles Times'* Dan Sullivan compared it to its U.S. counterparts and declared, "We've had it with tired elephants, unfunny clowns, sullen trapeze acts and morbid side shows.... I never saw a circus that showed me why Toby Tyler wanted to run off to the circus. This one has it.... Le Cirque du Soleil molds its performers, throws rainbows on them, back lights them ... interesting that Cirque's directors Guy Caron and Guy Laliberte think that their show has 'demystified' circus. Actually, they've remystified it, without taking out the fun."[2]

The Los Angeles Festival's overnight star attraction caused the reviewers to haul out some musty old adjectives they hadn't found reason to use in years. At the *Herald Examiner*, 40-year-old Richard Slayton wrote, "Beware: they succeeded beyond our wildest dreams."[3] Next door in an adjoining notice penned by 14-year-old Dan Adler, the kid critic took pot shots at the competition, admitting never to have been much of a fan of the town's principal spring visitor, Circus Vargas, the only other tent show he had ever been to. "I didn't see most of the things I generally associate with the circus, such as mangy camels and sawdust on the floor."

What Dan did see, said the tenth grader from Santa Monica High, was "a careful blend of comedy and drama, more than once jumping from death-defying acrobatics to hilariously funny comic routines."

Adler, too, like Mr. Sullivan at the *Times*, could "understand why a kid would dream about running off to join the circus. There was something about seeing that show, a feeling I got, that I have never experienced in a movie theatre or watching television.... The show as a whole changed my entire opinion of the circus."[4]

There were many more Dan Adlers in the crowd who walked in as skeptics and walked out believers. Business exploded. Soon, Cirque du Soleil was packing and jamming them daily into its 1,700 seat tent. It became about the hottest ticket at the Arts Festival. Ovations rang out night after night after night.

Barette fondly recalls those triumphal receptions when only one or two ovations might leave the cast with the feeling that maybe they had not gone far enough. "What we were aiming at was more than two. We got one, and sometimes we got two. And then we said, 'Okay, we need more than two to make sure we did a really good performance.' And it was some sort of a standard we were looking for, because if we had only one, it was like an okay performance."

So thoroughly satisfying were the all-human acts offered by these invaders from Quebec, that many customers did not pause at first to consider something daringly missing from the tent — that same something missing from the Pickle Family Circus: animals. Pisoni's troupe, though, was but a modest beacon next to the stratospheric acclaim accorded the troupe from Montreal. Nor was Cirque's omission nearly as political a gesture. Actually, in one of its early programs, a duck got into the program by fluke and expressed itself to the music of one of the acts by bobbing from side to side. The "dancing" duck ended up playing out the rest of the season.[5] In another program, they are said to have included a live rat. But by the time they got to L.A., they realized what a marketing advantage they would enjoy by going along with the anti-animal sentiments which were driving a growing legion of organized protestors to harass American circus lots. And they ran with their newfound all-human purity.

Soon, the guard dogs that Cirque had employed to patrol their grounds at night were quietly retired — a not so welcome sight to Cirque's emerging fan base of yuppies with big bucks to blow on cutting-edge diversions.

Not everyone stood up and cheered. Down at the Paul Eagles Circus Luncheon Club, a mixture of professionals and fans who met on Monday mornings at Philippe's restaurant near Union Station, a mile or so from Little Tokyo, the mood was muted. "Not traditional" is what a number of them said. Some were quick to note the absence of animal stars. They had a point. The public at large, however, did not appear at all bothered by the lack of a menagerie.

Comparison shoppers might compare the fresh Cirque magic to humdrum Vargas clowns, ill-assembled Shrine shows, the overproduced Ringling Circus, or the underproduced fly-by-night phone room shows.

Victoriously acclaimed in tinseltown, Cirque du Soleil went out to Santa Monica and packed them in. And then up to San Francisco, where the critics jumped cartwheels of cheer. "More youthful élan than Ringling brothers ever dream of," gushed Scott Rosenberg in the *San Francisco Examiner*. "The traditional circus will never be the same."

Wrote Bernard Weiner in the *San Francisco Chronicle*, "The show makes the blood race with its artistry and excitement."[6]

Whence this audacious troupe? In the beginning, core members of the company consisted of a band of street performers from Bohemia, unlimited. One of the more outlandish ones was stilt walker Giles Ste-Croix. He picked apples on stilts. On one occasion, he stilt-walked from Baie-Saint Paul to Quebec City — a stunt undertaken to snare free newspaper coverage for a street theatre Ste-Croix ran which featured puppets. He patterned himself after the famous St. Alexis Le Trotteur.

Members of Ste-Croix's circle lived in communes and survived, they claimed, on Kraft dinners and on hat donations. They took part in an annual festival of street artists outside

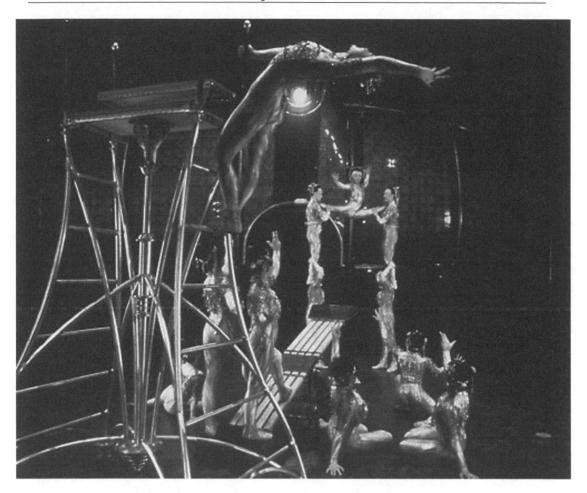

The teeterboard act in Cirque du Soleil's *Dralion* (Photofest).

Quebec. Hundreds of other like-minded souls came to join in, to party and to hold workshops. And to show off their talents to tourists. Among the group was one Guy Caron, the man who would later found the National Circus School in Montreal.

In preparation for the 450th celebration of Jacques Cartier's arrival in Quebec and discovery of Canada, a fire-eater in Ste-Croix's troupe named Guy Laliberte talked the organizing committee into funding a tour of their street theatre. He went out and raised $1 million. From there, the fledgling group acquired a tent, and Cirque du Soleil was born in 1984. The first show was rehearsed and directed by Guy Caron inside the school he had founded in Montreal. Some of its students became Cirque's first performers. The bold originality witnessed in Los Angeles three years later was not the exclusive work Caron and colleagues. In fact, they had drawn inspiration from European and Russian circus movements.

In France during this period, President Mitterand granted large sums of money to the Ministry of the Arts for the purpose of funding many small circus companies and street performers. He wanted to bring these more populist forms of entertainment "as close to the general audience as possible," in the words of Michele Barette. Mitterand's gift was also intended to encourage and foster a quicksilver exchange of ideas between theatre, circus and ballet. "You could find theatre in which dance would also be part of the theatre show, and vice versa.... In that moment in show business in Europe, a lot of different genres were influencing each other. They would borrow from one to each other to integrate that into the one they were in, so that's what happened in the circus."

But France, let us argue, was only a sideshow to Russia. In communist-bloc Hungary, where advanced Russian ideas about circus education and performance were followed, Guy Caron had studied at the Hungarian State Circus School. While there, he took in a number of eastern-bloc circus troupes, and he was impressed by how many of the acts told little stories. Also, six years before he arrived in Hungary, he had attended a performance of the Moscow Circus in Montreal. Following the eye-opening experience in 1970, Caron exclaimed, "*This is it!*"[7] He became an instant convert to the Soviet-style circus. Upon his return to Montreal in 1977, Caron formed the national circus school, intent on passing down the artistic values he had absorbed in Hungary. He believed the circus should change with the times.

So, essentially, Cirque sprang from Soviet soil. Caron sought to bridge circus and theatre in newer, more dynamic ways. The concepts he and his cohorts shared in the beginning said "no" to many of the things they had seen under U.S. tents — or heard about. They blasted the multi-ring affair without mercy. Caron told a Canadian magazine, *Equinox*, that when he was eight years old in the late fifties, he was left totally unthrilled on Yankee sawdust. "I detest the circus.... I saw an American circus with three rings. I didn't like it and never went again. Around the world the circus is dying. It is boring everybody."[8]

Left out of the press kit when Cirque came to California was a snide poster it had put out up in Canada, said to have parodied an American type circus with mug shots of two circus managers, "Ding and Ling," along with allusions to a celebrated show slogan. Guess who?

We've not seen such cheek since the Ringling boys, in their first flush of dominance in 1895, blasted their rivals, as we've previously noted, calling them such things as "outclassed, overshadowed and overwhelmed."

Still, L.A. was a big gamble, and it was the money man, Guy Laliberte, who rolled the dice, banking everything they owned on a break-out success in Southern California. Michel Barette will tell you that, had they gone belly up in Little Tokyo, they might have returned to the humble ranks of struggling street artists once again. "If we had not been a success in L.A., I don't think the circus would exist anymore. We were very very deep in debt, and we didn't have enough money to come back."

Credit the suddenly go-for-broke Laliberte, who carried on like a marketing genius. He was a take-charge boss who quickly and self-servingly canonized his control of the kitty and turned himself into something of a modern-day Astley or North — or both. The Canadian either had a prophetic vision, or he saw one appear the morning after the first standing ovation in lotus land. He set out to turn his little tent into a many-tenacled empire of bigger tents roaming the globe in search of greater acclaim and profits.

Who is this Guy Laliberte? He was born into a middle-class family in Quebec city. His father was a public relations executive for Alcan Aluminum Corp. His mother was a nurse. In his teens, he hung out on Montreal street corners playing an accordion that he had found in his dad's closet. Commercially centered, Laliberte mastered the instrument as a means to lure tips from passing pedestrians. He dropped out of college to hitch rides across Europe. Along the way, he met jugglers and stilt walkers. What to do? He took up fire eating. Back in Montreal, he fell in with his future Cirque colleagues.[9] The first year

Soviet artistry rooted in ballet inspired Cirque du Soleil's founding artistic director, Guy Caron (author collection).

out, in 1984, they were subsidized to the tune of 97 percent. In 1985, by 50 percent. The next season, it was down to 32 percent. And in 1987, their fast-forward year, Uncle Canada chipped in only 17 percent. A juicy corporate sponsorship from Canadian Airlines has also bolstered the treasury.

In quick order from there on out, Laliberte amassed enough profits to help fund, were he so inclined, practically the entire Canadian health care system.

In the early Cirque years, Laliberte did not conceal his contempt for most of the competition south of his own border. He told Harriet Swift of the *Oakland Tribune,* "I hate traditional circus." He stopped short of naming names. He tossed a crumb of respect to the Ringling show for "what they are doing for the public that likes that sort of thing."[10]

What else? He presented himself as an aloof outsider, arguing that his show had "nothing to do with traditional circus. It is created the same way as Broadway shows are created." Not quite. It was created off a repeating assembly line. If Laliberte could set one tent in the same location for a few months and pull in enough people to keep the seats lucratively occupied, then why not add another two — or ten — tents, hire more acts, play more dates and make more money? Circus producers love attracting larger crowds. Love owning more shows. Think Bailey or Ringling, Polack or Feld.

Guy Laliberte was immediately courted by showbiz producers who saw lush subsidiary ventures trading on Cirque's rising name and identity. Columbia Pictures head Dawn Steel thought she had a deal with Cirque's quixotic boss to make a movie based on some of the show's characters and manners. So Ms. Steel threw a victory party to celebrate her good fortune, at which the other half of the circus-film partnership was nowhere to be seen.

Well, it was on the premises, sort of—just hustled off to a side table with lesser lights of filmdom, away from the hottest hotheads.

"I was basically put aside," complained Laliberte, who got up and walked out in pique before he could be announced and the pact applauded (assuming they knew he was there). "They just wanted to lock up our story and brand name and walk around me like they owned Cirque du Soleil."

After ditching Hollywood, Laliberte placed a call to his lawyer. "Get me out of the deal."[11]

The show world would soon realize that this Laliberte would not play second fiddle to anyone. God, beware! The ex-accordionist, instead of advancing to the *Lawrence Welk Show*, ended up remaking the big top on a global scale unimaginable to anyone at the time. Unimaginable probably even to himself.

There is the story of a shouting match in Las Vegas between Mr. L. and Vegas investor Steve Wynn. It took place a few years later, after the two had signed a pact giving Mr. L. complete artistic control to create a show, which would be titled *Mystere*, for Mr. Wynn's new Treasure Island hotel. As opening night neared, nerves frayed. Wynn tried to exert himself with suggestions in the manner of a co-producer, assuming in vain that his huge investment would count for something. It didn't. Cirque's owner would have none of it, and he exploded on the spot.[12] Nobody but nobody was about to tell Guy Laliberte how to put together—excuse us, reinvent—another circus or Vegas thing. They didn't then, and they haven't yet.

He had the growing infatuation of the critics and the crowds on his side, and he moved daringly ahead, driven by an evolving concept far more focused than that of, say, a Cliff Vargas or a Kenneth Feld. What Laliberte was chasing turned into an amalgam far more complex, more moody and operatic in reach, and eventually more darker, too, than what most of us had thrilled to when Cirque first blitzed the City of Angels in 1987.

Looking back, maybe my disillusioned friends at the Paul Eagles Luncheon Club had seen something that I hadn't. Cirque, say what you will, became a producing machine of spectacular success. Its special effects grew questionably more elaborate with each passing show. The artists it could afford to engage became ever more disciplined, to the point almost of a heartless perfection.

At the same time, Cirque callously distanced itself from circuses in the states, the one exception being the Pickle Family, to whom, during a rough patch, Cirque gave money and assistance.

Elsewhere, a lot of feelings got hurt. "They came on the scene of being street performers in Canada," recalls Paul Pugh, "and said they're going to reinvent the circus. They're going to show the world how the circus should really be. Well, that takes guts to make a statement like that when you're just coming on the scene. Well, Cirque du Soleil is basically not a circus, but it's a very beautiful, well crafted, technically superior show."

Norma Cristiani was taken aback by how Cirque snubbed its U.S. counterparts. "They don't recognize anybody in the circus business. When they first started, one of the men went over and told them who he was, and they said, 'We don't care who you are. Nobody comes in the tent free.'"

Circus Report, a trade weekly then edited by its founder, Don Marcks (now deceased), rarely saw a circus it did not have something nice to say about. And Marcks gave Cirque plenty of important coverage, pro and con. A review by author Herb Clement scathingly took Cirque to task for its haughty airs and cavalier disdain for tradition:

"Cirque is not a circus... claiming to reinvent the circus, the Quebec-based outfit appears, on second thought, to have done much to demolish it. Among the more cardinal of its sins against the circus is the fact that the two-year-old edition offered in New York in 1988 offers audiences not a single animal — not even a horse, upon which the very circus as we know it has been solidly based since its creation by Philip Astley in 1768."[13]

Circus Report columnist Billy Barton vented his own disgust with Cirque's arrogance, drawing references to Guy Caron's dissing of American shows. "It's easy to be disdainful of the North American circus when you don't have to fight or struggle for existence, when you have government support and private business funds as a nice fat cushion.... No one resents their presentation. What we resent is their attitude, and their rude unwarranted remarks. They are a guest in our country, and Quebec, after all, is a short trip north across the border. Let's face it. We have the Big Apple and Circus Flora, both of which are theme circuses with music and real circus acts, and animals!

"I say, Cirque du Soleil, go home. We don't need you."[14]

The Laliberte machine grew colder and more calculating. In only a few seasons, a number of the artists from the original company that had taken the states by storm decided to leave. One of them was Michel Barette, who here speaks of a fallout between the disenchanted and Laliberte: "We were very close, we were involved in the decisions, and at a certain point when money came a lot in the organization, then he decided that this company was going to expand and do something very important, which he succeeded in doing. I respected that very much, but this was not the way we though this could go, so we decided that we would move away. And then he could do whatever he wanted. Since he was the most important part of the business, we wouldn't have enough power to overcome that kind of thing."

Increasingly, Laliberte's staff treated the performer like a disposable pawn to be used or discarded depending upon the needs of a particular show in creation or question. Extreme bike riding champion Chris Lashua, after touring Japan with Cirque's *Fascination* and while working props for *Mystere* in Las Vegas, started rehearsing a new act inspired by a photo he had come across of a German wheel. He built his own wheel and taught himself to do tricks inside it. He hoped to impress the organization and get accepted into *Quidam*, then in rehearsal. Lashua spent two years self-training on the rig — from one to three-thirty most mornings.

"They saw that I really had an idea about something, and was very committed to making it happen, and people would stay late and help me. They would come in early and help me."

He regarded the wheel as "the kind of thing every kid wants to jump in and try."

Lashua's dream was thrown an icy cold shoulder when director of creation Giles Ste-Croix, who had been expressing potential interest in the act, instead of offering Lashua a contract to do it, went out "looking for somebody else."

They found their man, they thought — used to having their way with people — in the world champion of the sport, Wolfgang Bientzle of Germany.

Fortunately for Chris Lashua, the German was not at all interested, so Cirque talked him into coaching Lashua.

"I felt like, 'hey, I brought this to you, I had the kind of foresight to see this thing could be really cool, I've been working my butt off and you're going to give it to somebody else?' I was ticked off."

Cirque du Soleil certified: Chris Lashua survived a grueling rehearsal process to tour with Quidam for five years (photograph by Andy Espo, courtesy of Chris Lashua).

They sent Lashua to Germany for six weeks of training with Bientzle. Upon his return to the Montreal headquarters, Lashua now had to face choreographer Debbie Brown. The two did not click. "I wasn't a dancer. I can't count music. She got pretty frustrated. She didn't have patience for people who don't know their bodies, and I didn't."

Brown came close to tearing her hair out.

Lashua got Ste-Croix to let him go it alone, *sans* choreographer. He developed a role for himself, and it pleased Ste-Croix.

The hurdles Lashua had to surmount were hardly over. *Quidam's* director, Frances Dragone, was the next one. Unimpressed with the routine that Ste-Croix had passed on, Dragone pushed the German wheel guy into yet another direction. Chris was directed to try looking like a character out of *A Clockwork Orange.* "But I don't want you hunched over," qualified Dragone. "I want you to be proud and kind of goofy."

So proud and goofy he tried. Lashua was further instructed to "stand up and wiggle my head back and forth, and do this really kind of what I felt, a silly bow. And he said, 'That's your bow!'"

Remember, folks—are you still with me?—the enterprise behind all this fussiness was founded by a band of certifiably French street performers.

They kept working on Lashua's "character" until it consisted of several parts, as he tells us: "A bit dainty, a big just cuckoo. Like the bow, what he wanted me to do was like the guy that was a bit crazy, almost like somewhere between a gentlemen, a ballerina and an absolute nut ball."

Finally, an act was born. Despite his initial discomfort and misgivings, Chris came to enjoy the role over time. "The act kind of grew. I would be kind of shy, then I would get a little cavalier, till I was absolutely out of control, wacky at the end, and then back to this gentlemanly little guy look for my bow."[15]

As time rolled on in Cirque years, the shows they put out became less innocent, more intensely theatrical. In 1990, they offered the darker, slower moving *Nouvelle Experience.* It was not the effortless masterpiece that *We Reinvent the Circus* had been. *Nouvelle* was more self-consciously arty. Many of the acts, on balance, were superior to those sent down to L.A. in 1987. Too much time, though, was handed over to a comic character from outer space finding himself alone on planet earth and luring out of the audience stand-ins for a silent film he wishes to make about it.

Too much of the music turned mournful. Too much of the action was slow and point-less and overly detailed. Cirque had shown some of us what circus art could be; now, it was starting to show the world what circus is not.

It hardly mattered at the ticket wagons, where lines without end formed. Cirque had nearly conquered the upscale market with its intriguing creativity, with the stellar acts it could now easily afford to engage, and with its cutting edge special effects. "Cirque du Show"—yes, as Dale Longmire puts it.

"In addition to dealing a body blow to the traditional expositional nature of the American circus," wrote Herb Clement, "they have (at least in New York city) tapped the mother lode of upscale, Wall Street trendies (who don't recognize anything real unless they see it on ticker tape) and have insured themselves a vociferous, if mindless, audience for decades to come."[16]

Guy Laliberte's incredible producing wonder was moving unstoppably ahead. His tents circled the globe, each with only one ring, each with not a single animal to its name. So step right up, ladies and gentlemen, and get your cold bottled water! How about a low-carb candy apple? Or a bio-degradable muffin? Step right up and have no fear—you who are made uneasy by the smell of elephant dung, the shock of aerial daredevils risking life and limb, the roar of lions or the sight of grizzly-faced barkers lurking in the shadows. That big bad show that once entertained your mom and pop is not about to begin any time soon.

It almost makes you want to run away *from* the circus.

8

Encore for the Eighties

Before the big show — what's left of it — becomes a ghost of glorious seasons gone by, let's go back in time to pure circus. Before Montreal replaces Sarasota, let's talk about the acts, the artists and the programs that needed no fog machines or unidentified crawling objects to lure a crowd into a tent.

First stop: Long Beach, California, on a hot August night in 1981. August 19th to be exact. At about fifteen minutes before midnight in the Convention Center, 17-year-old Miguel Angel Vasquez and his brother, Juan, are working out on the trapeze after the night show of Ringling Bros. and Barnum & Bailey. Once again, they are striving against all odds to master a feat that has never been done before: a quadruple somersault from the bar to the hands of a catcher. Yes, four revolutions in the space in a speeding second. It is a feat dreamed of by many flyers.

One is Tito Gaona, Ringling's star of seventeen seasons. He had flown towards the elusive Big Trick during the 1978 tour when his attempts at history were announced at every show. Before anxious spectators, Tito flew out, flew high up, left the bar, hurled himself— one, two, three, four spins — and narrowly missed locking wrists with Eduardo "Lalo" Murillo on a withering fall to the net. Another epic try. Another epic disappointment.

Tonight in Long Beach on the nineteenth of August, the Vazquez brothers are once more dreaming of the impossible as they go through practice motions. Maybe this time?

"I swing away and back in," remembers catcher Juan. "Miguel, tall and slender at 124 pounds, made a powerful leap. I watched him swing back above the platform where Felipe stood. He rose above the parallel bars of the flying frame, lifting his legs in front of him as I swing away. Then he began his back swing, dropped his legs and drove high into the air. He pulled his knees against his chest in a tight tuck and somersaulted upward.

"I reached toward him as he unfolded his lithe powerful body. He reached for me...."

"Slap!"

"I felt the hand to wrist contact."

"My fingers closed around his wrists and his around mine."

"I felt a sharp pull, not a jerk exactly; harder than the pull from a triple somersault, but not as hard as I had expected."

"I had him!"[1]

Miguel Vazquez, angel of flight, prince of circus flyers unmatched, hero over sawdust — had just turned the first caught quadruple in circus history!

Stand up and cheer, if you wish, everybody. Savor the blood-tingling moment. That fateful night in Long Beach, Miguel Vazquez flew four somersaults—perfect, graceful, smooth, quiet and complete—into the hands of a big top miracle, himself into pure greatness. And he did it flying in a city where Spangleland's two most honored legends, Alfredo Codona and Lillian Leitzel, lie in peace beside each other.

After Leitzel took her tragic fall in Copenhagen, on Friday, February 13, 1931, her husband, Alfred Codona, buried her ashes in a Long Beach cemetery, fulfilling a promise. Six years later, Codona, who had not flown since 1933 when a torn ligament ended his trapeze career, shot his wife, Vera, who had filed for divorce, then turned the gun on himself in suicidal despair. He was laid to rest beside the ashes of his beloved Lillian. And nearly fifty years later, in the city where the one flyer fell to self-willed darkness, another rose to self-willed triumph. It was as if the younger was now honoring the older. As if a glorious reincarnation of kindred souls had transpired. Long Beach: Leitzel. Codona. Vazquez. Long Beach: Alfredo's dark fall. Miguel's transcendent flight.

Death and birth. The end of a season. The start of another. Like, in a way, the cruel-beautiful rhythms of a circus forever on the move through storm and sunshine, triumph and stress. Playing to packed cheering crowds one tour, near-empty tents the next. The circus: how to reinvent itself over and over again in order for the public to believe that it is always changing despite never really changing at all? How to invest its magic with surprise?

Its brightest stars usually start out when they can barely walk. Inspired to fly by the 1956 film *Trapeze*, at the age of 15, young Miguel was already turning the now fairly common triple—a feat considered extremely rare in Codona's time. During his teenage years, Miguel completed thirteen of the greatest trapeze tricks, including being the first to bring off a full-twisting triple somersault. And now, two Miguel Vazquez birthdays later...

"The quad! The quad! You caught the first quad!"

"How did it feel?" asked brother Gina, throwing his arms around Miguel.

"Like a high triple," answered the flying prince. "Faster spins, though, and a little more jolt to the shoulders when Juan and I locked arms."[2]

After the Long Beach breakthrough, Miguel struggled for almost another year of vexing failures to connect before he finally turned the first quad in actual performance. In Tucson, Arizona, on July 10, 1982, the first circus audience beheld the impossible. By then, the brothers had been practicing their act three times a week, and during each practice session they shot for the quad up to fifteen times. They had been videotaping their work so that they could study it and experiment with minor adjustments. On tape by the time they reached Tucson were six recorded miracles.

From the moment they reach their rigging until they are back on the ground taking final bows, circus flyers are the kings and queens of the big top. They leap, soar, spin like streaking meteors, catch and release and return to their tiny platforms to prepare for the next flight. Between their airborne travels, we can still feel the pulse of the act coursing like the subtle undercurrents of an ever-rushing river. Can still feel the imagined tricks forming in their minds while they rub more rosin into their hands and wrists, stretch limbs, and reach up with bar in hand to fly out again.

The ebb and flow of circus action in a top-notch program is much like a flying trapeze act. Everything feels connected, even the dramatic pauses, so that the show never really stops but moves continuously forward. You'll hear a lot of different ideas from this person and that on the subject of what makes for a great circus program. After all, on paper it's just a hodgepodge of different routines, isn't it? How to create the illusion of something much

Prince of the quad — trapeze star Miguel Angel Vazquez (Circus World Museum, Baraboo, Wisconsin).

more? How to fashion a finished performance? Paul Binder will tell you that it's all about the "virtuosity" of the individual artist. Kenneth Feld has called it "a giant, grand, gripping and glorious pageant of prodigious proportions." Some show people simply point to an all-star lineup; others will say that pacing is everything.

Ah, yes, pacing. Now, there's an old word overlooked by today's new-age theatre-circus gurus, who fancy telling stories that impart trenchant themes. I mean, unless you can compete with Shakespeare, your wire-walking skills don't amount to beans. These folks love the artful pause — the pause that is supposedly pregnant with hidden meaning known only to a chosen few. Let them contemplate their navels. I'll put my money, any day, on pacing over pausing. Sometimes, somebody down there on earth needs to crack a whip, the surest way to turn a bunch of acts who can't speak each other's language into a well-connected adrenalin rush of a parade from blastoff to tear down.

Ever ride a good old wooden roller coaster? Think back upon how it possessed you over every single tie of the track, not just the big plunging drops from the highest peaks but the screeching turns around corners, the rickety rolls up and the clattering dives down. You felt connected to the ride from heart-fluttering departure to breathless return, right? Of course you did. So, too, should you feel connected to a circus program from first whistle to final bow.

Of course, we can't expect every circus show to move like the Cyclone at Coney. Some rattle wildly while others just gently rock. We only ask for a sense of pacing and a style that holds throughout the entire show. To judge a Ringling program by Big Apple Circus standards would be foolhardy. Likewise, to look for Circus Oz at Carson and Barnes. We only ask that the furniture matches, that the music has a single soul and that the performers stick to a rhythmic game plan. We ask for a consistent vision and feel from the owner, the direc-

tor, the ringmaster — whoever can step forward to make it happen. Beyond this, I'm now going to offer you some high points from the eighties, a decade of remarkable variety in circus programs worth honoring.

Let's first go to the Pickle Family Circus, a poetic little roller coaster high on pure youthful innocence, comedy and charm. Director Larry Pisoni deserves lasting kudos. The opening charivari never disappointed, nor did the closing "Big Juggle," bringing out sometimes the entire company in a whizzing, high-energy exchange of clubs. They reached their peak in the early eighties, even without their two star clowns, Bill Irwin and Geoff Hoyle (Mr. Sniff), now gone. Pisoni now cavorted with his son, Lorenzo Pickle.

Most of the company juggled and tumbled. Wendy Parkman, Rebecca Perez, Judy Finelli (wife of Hovey Burgess), Marc Jondall and Gypsy Snyder all contributed winningly to the unpretentious Pickle

Larry Pisoni's Pickle Family Circus was the first to exclude animals from the lineup.

mystique, which felt as much like a playground of practicing young acrobats as a circus. In 1982, the troupe numbered just eleven people, and nine of them worked in the Big Juggle. None better exemplified the show's purity of spirit than Jay Laverdure, one of three trampolinists who bounced and flew higher and higher with a joyfully infectious smile. It seemed as if he and his co–Pickles had found the perfect place to be exactly who they wanted to be. And on warm summer days, yes, you could kind of feel their love.

Typical of the average Pickle artist, Laverdure came up through high school gymnastic programs. He won tournaments in springboard diving, joined the Washington men's gymnastics team, later worked with the Floating World Circus, the Wacky Waco Brothers, and the Bosco Boys. After a stint performing in cabaret revues, he landed in the Pickle show, and in the hearts of its fans.

Another Pickle plus were the five jazz musicians led by Jeff Gaeto. They played original charts composed especially for the acts by members of the band. They cut a more restful soundtrack which invited the audience to relax, settle down and go with a slower flow. Savor the moment, if you please. It's a nice day, isn't it? As we like to say in show biz, it was "all of a piece." Pickle perfect.

The Big Apple Circus scaled higher peaks up a larger coaster — without making the most of the ride. In 1986, Paul Binder's no-nonsense one-ring valentine to old Europe at Prospect Park in Brooklyn offered some of the finest acts in the business, if in modest supply: Only the year before, school-taught Barrett Felker and Jim Strinka had teamed up to create the Dynamotion jugglers for a Big Apple premiere. The Trampoline Guys — two men and a woman from Canada — were simply sensational. Ben Williams worked the elephant Anna May, the Flying Gaonas flew high with Tito. Swiss-born David Dimitri, who had trained in Budapest, performed a low-wire act with grace. The Wozniak Teeterboard Troupe, which had started out in 1975 at the Moscow Circus School, turned to a Russian swing act for Big Apple. Tisha Tinsman flew solo in the air. Jim Tinsman did hand-balancing maneuvers, a la Alfred Burton, Jr., on stacked chairs. Katja Schuman held court with a circle of liberty horses.

Was this a great circus? Not quite. It was a very good circus, sufficient, indeed, for the discriminating fan. To its credit, the somewhat rambling performance exuded a feeling of a high respect for circus art. A first-rate band led by Rick Albini supplied fine music. Perhaps Paul Binder himself, who filled the role of a traditional ringmaster with a passion bordering on the religious, was the heartbeat of this show. He shared his knowledge of circus history with the audience by lacing his introductions with brief facts and anecdotes; in so doing, Binder turned his tent into a temple of sorts. And if his program did not move to a distinctly circus beat or bear a compelling rhythmic style from opening to closing, it achieved quiet respect with its deference to a clean, gimmick-free format.

During the eighties, if you wanted more razzle dazzle and a more rickety old coaster of a ride, you'd be sure not to miss the unpredictable Carson and Barnes five-ringer, which varied wildly from one year to the next. Dory Miller, who ran his circus like a "toy," harkened back in outline to the high-flying twenties when the huge Ringling show would send out six or seven acts at a time to fill up the rings and stages in their 15,000-seat big top. Miller's tent, which on a good day might accommodate one-fourth that many customers, tried to recreate the heyday years when every ring was occupied by a live performer doing, well, something.

Just to get a slight impression of what the Big Show had once been, a ticket to Carson and Barnes opened musty canvas doors onto a golden past. Everywhere there were props and aerial apparatus, ring curbs and pedestals. And, oh, the many-fangled seats on wagons of all sizes, shapes, and curious configurations. You waited for the show to begin, hoping that this would be *the* one. Sometimes, Dory Miller delivered by design or accident in a wonderful way. Sometimes, the live band that particular season made it sound absolutely real. Sometimes, three trapeze troupes flew simultaneously, and where could you see this on any other circus? And always, there were plenty of elephants to supple jungle power.

In 1984 — we will kindly overlook a certain lack of program unity in style or pacing — at Carson and Barnes there was plenty to enjoy in slightly haphazard form: Bareback rider Lucy Loyal circled the ring like a ballerina on fire. Patricia White worked lions and tigers. "The Golden Age of Chivalry" brought on a generally colorful procession without arty pretense. They put up a nice aerial ballet showcasing the head-balancing tricks of Gloria Marquez. "Lullaby on Broadway" mixed up "Men, Maids and Mammoths." The show had camels and pooches, and more camels, and mules. It had jugglers aplenty. It had a seven-act display of balance and contortion. And, best of all, it sent four flying return acts into the air at once. Patrons attending the Friday night show on September 14 in Troy, Ohio, witnessed a breathtaking first in circus history: all *four* flying acts — the Vargas, the Randalls, the Rodogels and the Morales — landed the *triple.* Thank you, Dory. Charles Stevenson led seven crackerjack musicians through a breezy score, and the show, snapped, crackled and popped despite a rambling roughness.

Though rarely in recent years had it ever wowed in a big way, Clyde Beatty–Cole Brothers sparkled with smooth professionalism in 1988. This was one of the most polished shows ever to be seen under canvas. By 1988, they had been on the road so long that things usually went well, on cue and apace. That season, owners John Pugh and E. Douglas Holwadel engaged four thoroughly entertaining animal acts. The Amazing Marcan was making his American debut working with lions, tigers, and "ligers," the latter born of lion fathers and tigress mothers — all together, now, "for the first time ever!" A German veterinarian before turning to big cage theatrics and cross breeding "unique to the cat kingdom," Marcan brought a glib style into the tent, and his charges moved with unusual animation.

Other animal stars that season: Petite's Poodles, "the Mammoth Monarchs of Asia" supervised by Captain Fred Logan and family, and a nice round of Arabian thoroughbred horses drilled by Trevor Bale and daughters Gloria and Dawnita.

Jimmy James ringmastered to the point. James Haverstrom directed the eight-piece band. The clowns were another asset — funny and brief as clowns should be. The show simply sparkled. Nice to watch. Nice especially to see the animals holding their own in high form.

Ringling-Barnum: Following his father's death in September 1984, Kenneth Feld displayed exciting producerly promise in his first opus out. We are in 1986, and Feld has brought to America the Shanghai Acrobatic Troupe, and they alone are worth the price of a ticket. They offer fabulous hoop diving, jar juggling, vaulting and risley, contortion and hand balancing. And, of course, the lion dance. Feld glorified the Chinese infusion with an exotic pageant, "Eastern Expedition." Massed formations of paraders and dancers moved ingeniously around the track, in and out of the rings in complex, crisscrossing patterns staged and choreographed by Bill Bradley and Crandall Diehl. The fluid composition of it all was rapturous. Rarely had something so sophisticated in design and execution been presented by a circus.

After the conclusion of the Shanghai troupe came the far less convincing "An Oriental Odyssey." More splendid floats, yes — along with some garish costumes, clashing in ways that did not advance the exotic imprint. This part resembled a sleazy, multi-themed Irvin Feld production number from the senseless seventies.

Still, the '86 edition had plenty to talk about: Wade Burke's white tigers, the extraordinary high-wire Quiros, Marco and Prolo on the gyro-wheel, Captain Christopher and Commander Henryk out of the repeating rocket. Is that not enough? How about Miguel Vazquez turning quads?

Would Kenneth Feld follow in this more creative direction? Would he 86 his aerial marionettes, cookie cutter clowns and ersatz Disneyland parades?

Two years thence, Feld delivered another marvelous spec, "African Safari Fantasy," built around the audaciously old-fashioned Takahar, "the Marocain master" who faced an "awesome assemblage of angry alligators." It was as if Clyde Beatty had returned with congo hat, white uniform, boots, chair, gun and whip to stir up the sawdust, big time. Jim Ragona blew the whistle and announced it all with bombast. You could almost smell mud-stained canvas, sawdust and hay, popcorn and lemonade.

In 1987 came Cirque du Soleil to Los Angeles, and this was another big reason to celebrate the multi-faceted, many-circuses-to-choose-from 1980s.

Then came the Russians in a blaze of inspired creativity. The year is 1988. The place, the Los Angeles Forum. We are only one year away from the fall of the Soviet Union, and so the Russian Circus is still an empire consisting of a total workforce of 14,700 people. It operates some sixty permanent circus buildings throughout its fifteen republics, still employs roughly three thousand performers, each and every one of them guaranteed a regular paycheck whether they perform or not. And "Soyuzgostsirk," as the central administration calls itself, is still sending out its best acts on foreign tours. This stateside one were we are reviewing was produced by Steven Leder. Remarkably, only a few of the acts on the bill send the audience into orbit. At the top of the heap, two of them are flat-out show-stoppers.

Number one: the indisputably accomplished Digit horse riders from the Caucasus, led by the dashing Tamerlan Nugzarov. They charge through and around the ring with fierce agility, hurling themselves over and under their steeds in rapid motion, galloping on with a raw, powerful poetry. To toast international peace between the two countries, they raise high Soviet and American flags which unfurl like sails in the wind as the riders circle the sawdust. Nugzarov's commanding presence at the center of things lends the aura of a mythological figure traveling through an eternal loop, leading his ageless riders from one distant universe to another.

The second highpoint are the Flying Cranes, who give us another spellbinding vision unlike anything we have ever witnessed. Working from a complex rigging of multiple swings, cradles and platforms, the Cranes enact a ballet in the air to commemorate the spirits of fallen soldiers, their souls seeking release from death. Lena Golovko plays the last of the fallen, who is rescued by the Cranes and sent skyward so that "peace might prevail." Produced by Petro Maestrenko and directed by Vilen Golovko, the ten-member troupe of flyers were inspired by a Russian song commemorating World War II. They spent five years in rehearsal, and they are top-drawer trapeze artists: Included in their repertoire are double backs and *quad* somersaults which we might easily miss. In order not to detract from the flow and mood of the sacred story being told, the quad is not announced. Here is another reason to cheer what visionary circus artists can achieve.

When veteran trouper Robert Mitchell first saw the Cranes, he was profoundly moved. "The greatest circus act of all time. It is the only act that gives you thrills and can bring almost tears to your eyes with emotion for the dead soldiers."

Big top revivalist Clifford Vargas, at the outset of a remarkable rise from phone man to showman (Circus World Museum, Baraboo, Wisconsin).

About that Moscow Circus that played the states in 1988, Mitchell calls it "the best circus I have ever seen.... It wasn't just the acts but the way in which they were presented. The speed. No stalls. Don't trip over your high heels or you will miss your cue. Very little time, a couple of seconds really, for applause."

On all–American tanbark, no act quite dominated the mid-eighties, at least in the minds of Southern California circus fans, like the brief and fascinating, madly erratic journey into near-greatness of one Clifford E. Vargas. When the eighth decade arrived, Mr. Vargas was ready to make his mark on a dying circus world. He had begun reaching out to "cold" markets beyond the phone rooms in which he started out. He would begin to invest his line-ups with production flourishes and better music.

Vargas advanced a few important steps in this direction when he hired Dale Longmire, a Ringling clown, to inject more parades, ballets and costumes into the show. Longmire came over with his "life partner," animal trainer Ted Polk. In 1980, at Longmire's urging, Vargas staged his first aerial ensemble, "Look to a Star." Other production numbers followed, and soon Circus Vargas was looking more like a modest reflection of the old under-canvas Ringling show when John Ringling North produced it. Each edition came with an elaborate spectacle to close the first half, an aerial ballet, another costumed dance number focused around elephant routines, and a finale. Mr. V. installed *eight* follow spots, and he added enough extra illumination to make his programs the envy of the tent show field. He spent a great deal more money on frills. In the better spec parades which he assembled, Vargas sometimes had performers in all three rings executing their specialties, and this extra generous touch infused the air with festive animation. And he went after high-end acts. His operative word for performance values was "clean."[3] And it wasn't mere spin.

The madly engaged, obsessive, hands-on Cliff Vargas paid top dollar for acts, and he expected results, day after day. Unlike any circus producer we can think of in the history of this crazy profession, Vargas was known for hiding out in the seats to monitor the performance and make mental notes. Sometimes between shows, Mr. Forty-Second Street of the sawdust would hastily assemble the entire cast in the big top to critique and badger and complain. "He knew everything that went on in that show," recalls Ken Dodd. Why was a particular stunt left out of the routine, Vargas wanted to know. Why were smiles missing from faces during spec? And why such a sloppy pause between the horse act and the high-wire troupe?

Circus Vargas realized its glory days in the middle of our honored decade. In 1985, about the best show Mr. V. ever produced opened with Ted Polk and the tigers. After a clown walkaround came the aerial ballet, "Can Can." Wally Naughtin had three rings of bears. The flying Espanas dazzled with sassy, sexy showmanship. William Baker supervised a ring of well-paced horses. The Zamudos scaled the wheel of death with rare bravado. The Wilsons and the Rosays displayed fine control from cradle rigging. The three Bzarros executed a trio of swinging headstands in full arc. On terra firma, the Osmani Sisters from Holland offered nifty displays of first-class juggling, exchanging clubs that glowed in the dark. Oliver's Gauchos flung capes and ropes and pounded feet against special floorboards with clacking gusto.

Vargas was now talent-scouting the globe for an occasional find. He mined gold in South Africa when he imported the outstanding Ayak Brothers who did a double trap act without net or mechanics. This was as classy as it got at any circus anywhere.

Circus Vargas set-up mornings were promoted — come out, watch the tents rise, and get a free glass of milk and some cookies! At one point, the best seat cost more than the best seat at Ringling. Splashy Vargas posters went up in bus kiosks throughout the greater Los Angeles region, where the show pitched its tents for three months, moving from mall to mall. At the annual spring opening in the parking lot of the Hollywood Bowl, they packed them in. Box seats circled the track. The crowds expected to be entertained, and they were, even if not all of the basic parts which we expect of a great circus performance were there.

Looking back at the best Vargas years, what made them seem so good? In truth, how do we account for the man's success with the public when his clowns too often resorted to tired old gags like the balloon chase? When his production numbers tended to be more routine than original? When ringmaster Joe Pon's graciously rendered one-tone-suits-all announcements added little variety? When there wasn't even a program magazine to purchase early in the season (but only a one-page program sheet to rely on), for it had not yet arrived from the printer?

Despite what wasn't there, much that was there was wonderful. Circus Vargas delivered impeccable satisfaction, period. Its programs were straight ahead to the point, and that in itself can be refreshing. It offered high class acts. The tent was lavishly illuminated, and, best of all, through the mid-'80s the programs were brilliantly orchestrated and excitingly paced when James Miller ran the bandstand. Miller's music was steeped in driving Latin and jazz rhythms—nonstop tempos most of the way. It all worked on older fans, and it worked on younger ears, too.

And it was under the big top. It looked and sounded like a real winner. In a strange, ironic way, maybe because the action under canvas was so much better lit than it had ever been in the old days, Cliff Vargas was honoring both the solo artist and the three-ring format at the same time. And it worked. People paid top circus dollar to enjoy it. Free and discounted tickets brought a stampede of budget-conscious families to the door. Once inside the tent, smitten by the atmosphere and the promise of a major old-fashioned circus about to begin, many gave up their grandstand planks for pricier box seats. This brought them eerily close to the action when the elephants came roaring around the track and threw themselves up onto each other's backs in the dramatic, show-ending long mount. Front-row patrons could almost reach up and touch the trunk of a pachyderm and feel the primal power of something that destiny would soon enough mock and outlaw.

Within mere seasons, Cliff Vargas would see his great dream fall onto hard times. He would experience what too many circus owners have experienced down the tricky and punishing tanbark trails of time as he struggled to stay on the road. Circuses come and go with depressing frequency. Our next display may leave you with a profound appreciation for what Mr. Vargas—and Larry Pisoni, too—did manage to achieve in a relatively short period of time.

Both took questionable detours off the paths of their original journeys, and both were about to pay deeply. Exit the excellent eighties.

9

Vanishing Visions

Like the great Alfredo Codona without wings — like his swan-like form that lives in memory — when the creators of circuses vanish, so do, eventually, their distinctive styles of showmanship. Only John Ringling North could produce the kind of circus he produced. Likewise for John Strong ... or Louis Stern in his prime. And so on down the line. Legion are the big top lords who have had their day in the sun and then lost their way or their luck, ending up like John Ringling, with tears in his eyes, watching the parades of other men go by.

Such was the tale, sadly, for the still young, still gifted Larry Pisoni, who had set himself apart by being the first to present a show without animals, one of the first to enlist a group of jazz musicians to create original music for the acts. And surely one of the first to slow down the tempo and nurture a more intimate connection to the audience.

By 1987, the year when Cirque du Soleil first took America for a dazzling ride, Pisoni made a move he lived to regret, for that move set in motion an irreversible course away from the wagon of power. "I got fried. I left. I just couldn't do it anymore."

Only a few soul-searching seasons later, and Pisoni wanted to do it some more. But now he faced a board of directors — those entities that founding directors form at their own peril, for boards of directors have a way of amassing power for themselves and quickly losing respect for the Pisonis of the world. And they weren't smiling. After another Pickle personality, juggler Judy Finelli, directed the circus for a season, the board went out and hired the more traditional Don Jordan, who did not last for a single year. They then engaged theatrical dynamo and egotist-at-large William Ball, ex-head and founder of the San Francisco–based American Conservatory Theatre, to stage their annual holiday show at the Palace of Fine Arts theatre. Another victim of board-of-director discontent, Ball was now living down in Hollywood, where he was struggling to break into the movies but, instead, being treated like another wannabe. The alcoholic, couch-casting Bill Ball committed suicide shortly before his little moment in the fading Pickle sun.

Whom to the rescue? Larry Pisoni was there, anxious and ready to lend a hand, to do anything as a way back through the door. So he was hired "on a conditional basis." He now faced an audition for the post he had once owned, and he failed the test. This 1990 stage version of the Pickle Family Circus was full of artistic questions and administrative holes. Here was the Pickle's founder himself, to a degree directing as if Cirque du Soleil — or a

Cirque-obsessed board — was breathing down his back. The show offered some marvelous acts, to be sure. However, they were too awkwardly anchored to an obtuse and time-consuming storyline which bore a slavish devotion to another very new circus from a country to the north. Nor was there much of the comedy we had come to take for granted from a Pickle show.

Internal conflicts surfaced in unpleasant public disclosures: Stated the frustrated Pickle founder to the press, "I feel like my company has been stolen from me."[1] When Larry and I spoke about this incident, he told me that the powers in suits and ties "thought they had a better idea as to how to run" the operation.

That idea excluded the outdoor setup. Pisoni told the *San Francisco Chronicle* in his bitterest hour of rejection, "They wanted to make the Pickles more like Cirque du Soleil, to do circus theatre with plot and narrative. I believe the elements in each circus act are expressive in and of themselves, that the poetry of each act is where the value of the circus lies. To impose a plot and character on the circus is like trying to turn a piece of sculpture into a symphony."[2]

Pisoni had also run up against the naval-gazing limitations of the city itself, a place compulsively driven to be with-it and hip, forever in fear of falling out of style. You can almost hear the Pickle board smarting over the audacity of that troupe up in Montreal turning cartwheels around their little circus and leaving them back there in the dust. "Why, if only we had a few more million, *we* and not *they* would be leading the way!"

Board chairman Marc Snyder, defending their decision not to go with Pisoni, in effect slighted the very man who had created the whole thing: "We're interested in exploring the connections with circus, theatre and dance. We have to find new directions instead of doing the same old kind of things.

"I'm sorry Larry wanted to air his dirty laundry in public.... We didn't like his style of direction, which was too informal. We needed more material and he wasn't providing it."

Nor was Snyder keen on the old Pickle politics. "Larry wanted to go back to a '60s worker participatory democracy, but that won't work in the '90s.... We have to live with a certain amount of higher archy. We hope it's worker friendly."[3]

The company, then operating on a $1.2 million annual budget, was one hundred thousand dollars in debt. Want to guess how long the new capitalist-friendly version of the Pickles stayed on the road outside the city limits of San Francisco? It didn't last but a season or two. This particular entity, we'll propose, was never designed or destined to operate on a national scale. From the very beginning, its spirit was low key, minor, modest and intimate. At best, ultimate maturity for the Pickles would have been the tent that Larry Pisoni regrets they were never able to acquire. Had that happened, then they might have become the Big Apple of the West Coast.

Today, Pisoni looks back with bittersweet pride: "I'm very grateful to have been part of American circus history.... It would seem that I am, and that's not bad. Down the line, if I'm fortunate enough to have more grandchildren, and so forth, and if I don't get to see them, their parents can say, 'Well, he had a circus.' That's pretty cool."

Compared to Pisoni's minor slide into irrelevance, Cliff Vargas's decline was the stuff of grand opera. Many would call it a far greater loss to the traditional American circus, which Vargas had dedicated his life to reviving. Only a few seasons after taking Los Angeles for a wonderful under-canvas ride each spring through the mid-1980s, Vargas started to act oddly unsatisfied, as if he was restlessly in need of new horizons to conquer. He had broken free of the phone rooms with alternative promotions, discounted tickets and old-fashioned publicity stunts. Other circus owners were following his example, among them the Beatty-Cole show, which also shucked aside the boiler rooms and, in their place, hired marketing directors to bring the circus into towns on a "cold date" basis. Vargas had proved to his colleagues that they did not need to pitch charity to make a buck. They were better off pitching the show itself.

Wrote *Circus Report* columnist Billy Barton, "He not only rekindled public interest in the nation's big tops, but single-handedly resurrected a fading industry and instilled it with a glamour and excitement heretofore lacking."[4]

Norma Cristiani, like many of her peers in the business, looked up to Vargas with awe and admiration. "He did big promotions, not over the phones so much. He did things that nobody else did. He did a lot of beautiful advertising, and he had ideas that he could put across to groups, and he could get things done. He was just fabulous, and I think it was because he really loved it. That was part of him — what he wanted to do."

What Cliff Vargas wanted to do did not, unfortunately, proceed in a clear direction. What exactly was his vision? Perhaps he, having in his mind "revived" the great traditions he held dear, hungered yet for something more or better or different. Or maybe too many unpaid bills were finally catching up with him. Into the late '80s, he was already cutting back and skimping on the style of performance which had attracted strong patronage through his turnstiles. Worst of all, the wonderful band was gone. Doug Lyon, who had played a critical promotional role in the early years, had not been around for a long time. Vargas foundered in many dates outside of California as he fought to establish a name for himself in fresh markets. Chicago, no respecter of circuses, was hellishly inhospitable the first couple of seasons, and was by some accounts finally starting to pay attention and even buying a few tickets.

Getting the crowds into a four- or five-thousand seat tent was never an easy thing. And now, it was harder to find lots large enough to accommodate the show. Vargas played malls when he could and when the price was right. In some places, either a suitable space was not available or the cost to rent it too prohibitively high. Was our American circus revivalist coming up against the same logistical obstacles that had rendered the much larger under-canvas Ringling show a thing of the past? Was he, in fact, en route to his own Pittsburgh?

Whatever he was chasing after, Clifford E. Vargas carried on more irrationally than ever. In a way he was his own worst enemy. Some of those who worked for him saw a madness to the man. Just another manic-depressive? And they endured his volatile mood shifts from one day to the next. Vargas would take the wheel of one of his trucks, if need be, to help haul the show to the next stand. He was up ahead on promotions one week, and back on the lot the next selling tickets and concessions. Sometimes he even served as his own ringmaster.

When Doug Lyon was on the payroll dispensing advice on how to promote the show away from phone rooms, Vargas would call him up in the middle of the night with more ideas and questions. "What do you think of that?" And they would talk. "Well, how about doing it this way in the next town?" And they talked some more.

Vargas's pursuit of a circus dream bordered on the neurotic. Around the lot, somehow everybody knew when "Mr. V." was there; as I've told you, he was known to hide out under the seats, just to make sure that not a single trick was omitted from any of the acts. "I knew he loved it," recalls clown and production director Dale Longmire. "He did not miss anything that went in that tent. He would tell you how good you looked. He respected me for the fact that my wardrobe was spectacular."

The man's mood swings could be punishing. "Some days he liked you. Some days he didn't. That's just the way it was. You understood it. He was only as difficult as you allowed him."

Difficult, indeed. I had my own close encounter with Mr. V. And it was not on a good-mood day. He had agreed to let me ask him some questions on the Hollywood Bowl lot. When I showed up, I spotted him just inside the tent at a concession stand waiting on a couple of customers. At the opportune moment, I tried introducing myself, and what a nasty stink he made. His arms flailing about in utter annoyance, Mr. V. growled, "I'm busy. I'm busy!" The impression conveyed—go away and don't talk to me, for you're a nuisance—was brutal.

Months later, I tried again. Another phone call. Maybe a different contact in the press department. I was instructed to call the big top boss at a certain time, and when I did, he himself took the line. Cliff Vargas was as nice as anybody could be, calling me by my first name. And this, after he had just returned from a bleak tour through the unfriendly Dakotas. Perhaps humbled, he was more inclined to answer a few questions. Or was it the simple fact that nobody was around him just then, wanting to buy a Circus Vargas souvenir?

Mr. V. told me all about the bum business the show had done up through North Dakota. He called it "the death trail."

I could almost hear a wry trace of gleeful pride under his voice. Another misfortune overcome?

When I asked him to explain the key to his remarkable success so far in the better-attended cities, he replied: "Me. I don't give up, and I stay in there fighting. There is a real Mr. Vargas."[5]

His show was forever rumored to be financially in trouble. Every season, fans wondered if he was headed for bankruptcy. How could he afford to produce such formidable programs considering that the houses he played to were not always filled, that many dates outside of L.A. went belly-up? Some fans floated rumors that Mr. V. was getting extra help under the table by laundering Mafia money. Well, he had once lived in Chicago, and there was something shady and shifty about him. He was said to be attracting a growing parade of creditors seeking payment for past services rendered. Some were filing claims in court-houses.

And the show carried on, sort of. The programs offered in 1988 and 1989 went pro-gressively downhill in quality. An air of stagnation set in. A tape of the music, which only reminded one of better years gone by, had worn thin. The clowns were falling on their faces, and that was not meant as a compliment. Program magazines, as usual, arrived months late from the printer. The same production numbers were repeated for two or three seasons in a row. The show looked spotty and directionless. Had the man behind it lost his touch or will? Or was he struggling to keep a precarious empire built on plastic from falling?

Mr. Vargas reached erratically into new markets—maybe more death trails to test, as if he needed more vexing challenges to make him feel alive with agitation. More indifferent towns to seduce. In a way, he seemed to crave trouping onto more rainy lots in February, setting up the tents over a muddy morass and somehow getting a crowd to fill up half of the seats. Nothing was ever easy for this man.

Mad, maybe he was. Vargas fostered conflicting visions—a deadly recipe for losing your public. A return to the great traditions as they once were in America? In a strange betrayal of that relentlessly-publicized vision, Mr. Vargas started to return the show to its own roots under the hard tops of indoor arenas. He even went to some of the towns that Mr. North's circus had played (like El Paso) when it experimented with indoor dates in a similar way forty years earlier. During the 1989 tour, Circus Vargas played about 15 engagements inside buildings. What sort of a vision was that?

"He wanted to be like Ringling," as Ken Dodd recalls, leaving us to ponder the wisdom of the producer's scatterbrained modus operandi. And if that's what Vargas now wanted, how would he then ballyhoo his indoor venture? "Well, that would have had to have been changed," surmises Dale Longmire with a chuckle.

Nearing the end of the indoor segment of the '89 season, which the *Circus Report's* Billy Barton termed "a failed building tour,"[6] the phone man–turned–showman suffered a massive heart attack. He died on September 5th in his Hollywood Hills home. Vargas was only 64 years old, although his days were already numbered, for a deadly cancer was eating away at his liver.

Two months before his passing, on a down day, Mr. V. fired, first, Ted Polk, and then Polk's partner, Dale Longmire. They had been with the show for nearly ten years. "Vargas's biggest problem," advances Longmire, "was, he had a lot of people that did not produce ... that were there that caused problems for people that did produce.... And then after we were gone, they were gone."

Some did not hold up their end of the bargain, as Longmire saw it, and did a lot of petty things "to make themselves look good."

Given the boss's capricious moods, it's easy to imagine a trickle-down effect on the ranks.

Longmire says that he does not know exactly why he was fired. "I could kind of feel it. I could tell something was not right for three weeks. Vargas had been ill that whole year."

In fact, others have speculated that Vargas, a known homosexual who lived in a gay fast lane, actually died of AIDS.

There is a lingering image in my mind of his coming onto the Farmers' Market lot in Los Angeles during the best years, one spring morning in the mid-eighties. The big top was just then going up. Mr. Vargas had a briefcase in hand, his trusted general manager and life-long friend, Joe Muscarello, by his side. They chatted quietly as they approached the midway area. Vargas looked terribly exhausted. He looked like he had been on a campaign trail for many years and had to keep on going, no matter what, for this was, finally and at last, the only way he knew how to live.

That morning, I felt a rare admiration for the mysterious Mr. Vargas, observing his weak gait and wondering how much longer he would be with us.

Perhaps we should say this: as for the circus he so briefly and brilliantly produced, when he betrayed his passionately ballyhooed dream, possibly reaching for greater profits or just plain solvency, Vargas lost his way. The show he gave the public the last year he lived (touted as the 20th anniversary tour) was numbingly mediocre. Worse yet, bland. Lackluster in the air, pitifully inadequate along clown alley, the music a well-worn tape of richer seasons gone by. Pedestrian and redundant. Something that should have been there was conspicuously missing.

Clifford E. Vargas was so profoundly revered throughout the American circus community that no fewer than twelve full-pages ads in the *Circus Report* were taken out by colleagues and fans honoring his tinseled legacy.

How to sum up his story? For a few magical seasons, he gave us a circus much closer to the American three-ring heyday than to the typically half-baked phone room show of the time. Maybe his death was a blessing to his image, not yet tarnished by the unflattering setbacks that can befall a circus owner. Mr. Vargas, you see, had been trying against all odds to move the circus backwards in time when too many forces of modern economics and culture were pushing it forward. My hunch is that, had he lived, Cliff. Vargas would likely have met his own Pittsburgh.

Can you feel a sad quiet vacancy out here on the midway, ladies and gentlemen? Yeah, those '80s took us on some heart-stirring rides around the rings. And when they came to a close, gone forever were many icons of excellence: ringmaster Harold Ronk, who retired at the end of the 1981–82 tour; Gunter Gebel Williams bidding good-bye to the world in 1989; Larry Pisoni's Pickle Family Circus, and the Circus Vargas of Mr. V.

Things are slowing down out here, getting smaller and more discrete. The band is not so brassy anymore, the barkers as loud, or the tents as dirty with life. Nor are the seats so strewn with peanut shells and lost popcorn. And pardon us for not selling candy apples anymore, but we can't risk another dental lawsuit. So say farewell, then, to one dazzling decade when the old met the new, when for a time, yesterday's stars — both human and animal — held their own against today's nouveau darlings.

> The ringmaster waved the crowd farewell
> and whistled down the drums
> His magic kept us dreaming still
> of a season that never comes...

> Lights out, all of you who thrilled us under the old big top.
> Au revoir, Mr. Vargas...

10

Laliberte Latitudes

Say good-bye, great American three-ring spectacle! Say good-bye, Ringling Bros. and Barnum & Bailey — you who for over a hundred years ruled the big tops.

Say hello, Montreal, and enter the new circus king, Guy Laliberte. He is our new Barnum & Bailey rolled into one singular force. Behind his new-wave tents, he's out there auditioning raw talent, thinking up new concepts like a cutting-edge computer nerd, repainting the parades, badgering his guest directors to dig deeper and go farther. Since Cirque's Los Angeles invasion in 1987, American shows have been shaken to the very bedrock of the traditions they honored. Twenty years later, only two of them regularly present three-ring displays, and even then, who knows, both may soon be selling a surplus of discarded ring curbs on eBay.

Today, virtually all stateside shows bear tell-tale signs of the irresistible Cirque mystique. Most feature fewer animals, and several have 86ed their animal acts altogether. Not since the artistic revolution of John Ringling North in 1938 has another producer exerted such profound influence over how circus programs in this country are put together and sold to the public. From Astley to Coup and Costello ... from North to Laliberte.

Still not convinced? Maybe you will be when you see the Greatest Show on Earth perform without a single ring.

Guy Laliberte hawks his wares to an upscale market with a combined total of millions to spend on amusement. When last we checked, his ticket prices range from a charitable $40 to $195 for the V.I.P. experience, and the prices continue to rise faster than the national debt. Seven million people saw a Cirque show in 2003.

How big is the Montreal machine? For tidy comparisons, in its heyday before the Soviet Union splintered apart, Soyuzgostsirk employed some 14,500 souls. About three thousand of those were ranked as performers. Mr. Laliberte writes out paychecks to a work force of two thousand, of whom 750 perform. And, of course, each time he adds another tent to his touring division or creates another permanent attraction for Vegas or elsewhere, that means more paychecks.

Remarkably beating the odds against long-term success after being in the business for more than two decades, Cirque is still drawing boffo crowds. An old rule in this country held that, on average, if a circus could fill up half the seats, the show was probably breaking even. From our informal sources out there in the field, Cirque far surpasses that paltry

Cirque du Soleil in Atlanta, November 1991 (photograph by Richard Reynolds/Circus World Museum, Baraboo, Wisconsin).

benchmark. (Have you ever seen a Cirque audience that didn't blanket most of the seats?) Chris Lashua, who toured for five years with *Quidam*, told me that he rarely played to houses below 80–85 percent capacity. "Seems like we were full all the time."

Record breaking turnouts day in and day out? Not quite. "There were mistakes," conceded Lashua. "We played one week too long. It went down to 60 percent for a couple of shows. But it was very rare that you'd have a half house, almost unspeakable. But, sure, it happened." Occasional routing errors would send one Cirque into a city too soon after another had left. "Sometimes your team gets shortchanged. You have to go to a certain market at a crappy time of the year, because so and so went there six months earlier."

With its shows geared to stay two or three months in many cities, Cirque can afford to stay out of a major market — like it did San Francisco — for up to three years; hence, when it does return, the public is more likely to feel a renewed desire to shell out more money for the next Cirque du Soleil. And, so far, Laliberte's flair for creative surprise has convinced the public that each new show he sends their way will bear a distinctive enough imprint to merit return patronage. Are we dealing here with a master illusionist? There are people, like the Big Apple's Michael Christensen, who contend that any new Cirque show is actually quite predictable in style. Maybe so. The acts, however, are not, and that is what distinguishes any circus from the next.

One of Laliberte's smartest marketing ploys is to build up each new show around a whole new title and image. These changing elements get top billing, while the Cirque logo is relegated to secondary status in much smaller type size — a subtle signal, that, yes, this was produced by Cirque. Yes, you can count on another surprising sit. And yes, let your imagination dance. It all seems engineered to sustain the sort of mystery that once rumbled into the early morning darkness when a circus train arrived. And it all comes out of the magic hat of our childhood accordion player and former fire eater who raised the money for the first Cirque du Soleil tour in 1984, seized the purse strings for himself, held on tenaciously, and never looked back.

From Sarasota to Quebec. Heck, from Moscow, too. Up in Montreal, the National Circus School, founded by Cirque's first artistic director, Guy Caron, has put Canada on the map. Through its doors go aspiring young acrobats and jugglers to hone their skills or develop new acts. Through its doors, a Cirque audition may lead to a Cirque contract. And, at least one other show which originated in Montreal, Cirque Eloise, has made a name for itself in theatre venues. Dozens, if not hundreds, of young would-be circus artists and directors intermingle and collaborate on new projects up that way. Some of them are banking on a little Laliberte luck. *Good luck...*

With the tremendous worldwide fame and prestige that he enjoys, Guy Laliberte easily attracts some of the best gymnasts, raw or finished, in the world. And, alas, those bodies bend to Cirque's capricious designs. No room here, with rare exception, for the established performer unwilling to be recycled at the hands of coaches, "creation" directors, choreographers and designers, ad nauseam. The idea of a Lillian Leitzel, a Cristiani or a Gebel Williams submitting to the forces of Montreal is quaint if not laughable. In fact, Laliberte has failed to lure any number of stellar circus acts into his womb, assuming he has tried. Instead, working often from the ground up, he recruits gymnasts from the sports and Olympic fields, the occasional younger circus artist, and students from the schools. A few of them, to the man's credit, are molded into first-rate offerings.

Preparations for a new Cirque show were just getting underway. Auditions for a singer had turned up dozens of hopefuls. A crusty old guy who might have once hoofed on Broadway, bearing the number 135 on the back of his shirt, sang, "I should have been a dentist, a Seventh Day Adventist, the guy that paints the tie on mickey house!"[1]

No thanks.

Number 138: A young woman full of bluesy anger, belting, "You better think, think, think about what you're trying to do to me! Think, oh freedom! Oh, freedom!"

Not you either.

Andrew Watson, director of creation, spoke frankly: "So many people want to be involved in it, and a lot of them are going to be disappointed."

The unique, tediously long rehearsals, which will last as long as your standard pregnancy on planet earth, were laid bare before Bravo television cameras. It all took place behind the guarded gates of Guy Laliberte's compound, which itself resembles a shady industrial plant in a James Bond movie. Here, we are allowed to sit in on the elaborate shakedown process by which pliable bodies who make it through the first phase of auditions are bent, pulled, twisted, joined and painted into Cirque characters. Their individual personalities will be merged into a collective collage behind masks and exotic makeup, behind fog machines and laser lights, into a fantasy thick with allusions to some other place.

"We're actually entering the phase of the immediate preparation for the creation," announces Watson.

Oh, really?

"We're not going to avoid complexity. It's complex. Second, we all accept that it's not clear. That's your reality, and that's our reality. If for you life has got to be simple, forget it. And if for you, the expectation is you'll get all of your answers from us, forget it."

While the chosen few limber and stretch and practice, directors from other mediums intervene to observe, then to make suggestions for novel variations, and to push, push, push. The "twins," Kevin and Andrew, from Manchester, have arrived with medals from gymnastic competitions in England and with plenty to offer in the air. Never enough up in Montreal, though. And that suits them just fine, for they see this gig as a "vehicle to go farther." They will redevelop their strap act with the streetwise input from hip-hop choreographer Bill Shannon, in from New York to make cool suggestions. Due to a degenerative hip condition, Shannon moves about on a skate board and crutches, resembling, himself, something of a new Cirque act in the making. As he labors with Kevin and Andrew, we watch a very good aerial routine evolve into something more intricate and soaring in design.

From Russia come six Russians. Among them, the "old man" in this new Cirque troupe, 35-year-old Oleg. He says he had grown tired of the Mexican circus for which he was working. "I found there is nothing interesting going on there, and I don't like it anymore. Then Cirque invited me and I came here ... so many things I can do here. Different directions. So it's something big for me, and at 35, with another big move to another big creation."

Oleg has been teamed up by the staff with Tatiana Gousarova of the Ukraine, and they are about to craft a stylishly fast-moving, very fluid acrobatic number. Despite the management's strange decision, when the time arrives, to exclude the duo from a special upcoming premiere for invited guests, the act they develop proves to be one of the new show's stellar moments.

Director Dominic Shampoo sits by, observing the rehearsals and watching the parts come together. It will be his sole responsibility to shape the entire production. He will decide how to mold the characters, and how to impose a vision over the entire affair.

One night before a run-through, he exhorts the cast, "You just—yaaaaa! We're the best, okay? You're just yelling something. Show off a little more, okay? Let's feel it. I want you to feel it, okay? 'I'm powerful! I am in the top circus of the world! I am a survivor and I want to make it tonight!' I want to see it in your eyes!"

Another English duo with a track record in local sports, Gareth and Ashley, are being taught to perform a risley act. Gareth's mother is stricken with cancer, so Gareth is often miles away in his mind. He has a hard time concentrating. The coaches remain unimpressed after weeks of inconsistent executions despite constant grilling. "Am I positive about it?" asks one. "Am I negative about it? I don't know."

At intervals every so often, the company's progress is monitored by the man at the top, Mr. Guy Laliberte himself, checking in to take a look-see at each act and deliver his approval or reservations. These personal appearances are hyped by Bravo as something akin to God coming down to earth to measure the creative health of the human race. Some examples:

"They gear up for their first appearance for the company's powerful and exacting owner, Guy Laliberte."

"In a closed performance behind an ominous black curtain, Stella and Raquel get a final chance to impress the circus owner."

"As usual, the audience consists of just one man, Cirque du Soleil's powerful founder, Guy Laliberte."

Behind the "closed curtain," Raquel, a trapeze artist from Rio, and five other women are put through their paces on a cumbersome new rigging called the multiple trapeze. It looks like something dug up from an abandoned industrial site, so useless that even a Salvation Army pickup truck would reject it. This is a Cirque experiment to fashion something totally new in the air, and what the women are doing from it, theoretically airborne, is about as ethereal as half a dozen Mack tractors dangling from a helicopter.

Our powerful and exacting owner grimaces in childlike displeasure at the sight of the thing and the women struggling to give it and themselves cosmic redemption. The boss's face turns away in professional embarrassment. "The structure looks like a pile of scrap metal," he pronounces. "I'm sorry. Sometimes you're brilliant, but I'm not engaged by this act at all. It's not just one or two people inside the structure. There are six of them. I won't have six people in an act unless it makes me say 'wow!' Do something fast or find another act."

Gone.

Meanwhile, in the casting offices Cirque scouts are on the phones, furiously scrambling to find the right vocalist for the new show. Dozens have been auditioned. None have made any kind of a cut. After rejecting a total of one hundred singers, they settle on Romania's most popular vocalist, Adrian Berinde. He arrives in Montreal with high hopes. He sings a chord or two from the new score. Faces of authority do not smile. He is allowed to rehearse, but he will not see opening night. A setup for Bravo to ensure the drama of cold stark rejection?

Show titles are being tossed around. They agree on two semi-finalists: *Kisali* and *Varekai*. Director Dominic favors one over the other. "I find Kisali too weak for the show. I love the sound of *Varekai*. I like the 'ka' sound — like an explosion. Hats off!

"Exactly what I wanted: It takes off then explodes!"

The Twins, Kevin and Andrew, who have been impressing everyone on the premises, talk themselves into believing that they are worth a lot more than the standard contract offered them. And, without representation, they decide to play hard to get. They eventually return to a corporate cubicle with a counter-offer for the show's contract person. They are set on holding out for better terms and more money. Humbly, moments later, they emerge without a cent more on the table. They then consider walking away or waiting longer. Surely the powers will eventually budge out of the desire not to lose an act that is drawing raves from the company. Sure.

That corporate meltdown never arrives. The twins surrender to a bleak reality: this show will go on with or without them, or at least that's the fear they are now nursing. "We had a long chat between ourselves, cause we was a bit depressed.... We realized that if we was willing to walk away from it, to do with our pride and things like that, then, we're gonna miss out on a massive opportunity and we realized that we wanted to be on stage, and the act that we're doing here. This is what we've always wanted doing. And then we went and signed the contract. We both decided that we couldn't really give it up."

There was a time in on a distant midway when performers felt the same way about the once-glamorous Ringling show, which never, with rare exceptions for proven stars, paid top dollar.

During a pre-final run through, Cirque's powerful and exacting owner decides that his newest darling is short by at least one big "circus act." He also rallies behind his directors, who believe that Gareth and Ashley are still short of the mark and therefore subject to sudden termination at any moment.

"Guy's verdict is delivered to the coaches. It's going to be a long winter. After judging their offerings, he left behind a simple message: Not enough."

To overcome not enough, the scouts again take to the phones. And they comb through cd's and tapes on file sent in by agents and performers. They are in search of a high-wire act that can fortify and power the second half. Failing to find one, they sign a noted Mexican juggler, Octavio Alegria, who can fill up a tent with pizzazz. Evidently, he is ushered quickly past the various phases of creation and analysis, right into the show.

Our Romanian singer is let go well before final dress. He will be replaced by a 26-year-old Canadian, Mathieu Lavoie. "I came here to be useful," the spurned Adrian Berinde tells Bravo, resigned. "But in the end it didn't matter. In fact, I don't think that anyone matters to them. What matters is the show."

At the airport, waiting to board a flight back to Warsaw, Berinda is greeted by Michael, a sympathetic friend who has come to see him off. The singer shares a skeptical view of what he was put through in Montreal. "The fact that I only met with my composer for half an hour during my hundred days at Cirque, that's not normal no matter what you say. Nothings anybody's fault. I think the Cirque must stay grounded, if it wants to continue to thrive."

On the eve of *Varekai*'s opening, director Dominic is hammering home his mantra to the cast: "There's three things that make the show happen: Emotion. Emotion. Emotion."

Their first paying audience is out there in the seats. *Varakei* proves to be by far the most exhilarating edition produced by Cirque since their *We Reinvent the Circus* electrified L.A. in 1987. Laliberte has pulled another one out of his seemingly bottomless hat of tricks, using a new director, fashioning a trio of exceptional new acts, putting more oomph and less angst into the music, including some of the best and classiest comedy turns ever seen in a Cirque show, and, for a drop-dead finale, pushing the Russians to create an almost unbelievable stunt from two Russian swings in simultaneous operation: A man from each is propelled into space at the same moment, passing the other in flight and landing on the opposite swing! *Bravo!*

Now, that's circus! That's old Barnum & Bailey! That's the stuff that sets our hearts pounding, that leaves us speechless in awe, that sends us home believers, and that makes us want to return.

Gareth and Ashley appear with the show in their character roles but not on the risley, which they have failed to conquer. And they will be let go at the close of the Montreal date. Ashley alone returns to seek an audition for the next Cirque creation — a flesh-tease for the Vegas mills.

"We need to see who you are," states a casting director to a large hall of hopefuls, each with a number on their backs. Ashley, number 13, walks about and dances a bit in a tank top. He will be accepted, again, into rehearsals for the next show, but he will not make it through to opening night for *Zumanity* at the MGM Grand.

Make no mistake, Guy Laliberte is the presiding genius behind a remarkably successful operation unrivaled in world circus history, unless you wish to bring in the old state-run Soviet Union empire. He is, as it turns out, his own best critic — so far. He has the money to make others do his bidding. And his word is absolute. And let's not overlook perhaps his greatest single asset: a genius for daring creativity. A genius to think outside of the box and go for broke.

To Cirque or not to Cirque? How to satisfy the rapidly changing expectations of circus-goers everywhere? Rare is the American show that does not reveal shades of the Montreal influence. They are "the elephant in the room," says Larry Pisoni with a sigh of resignation. They have, he states, "profoundly changed everybody."

Although Cirque du Soleil skips hundreds of smaller cities and towns, still its shows appear on Bravo, and its unique imagery is well known to the public at large. More and more people bring a certain Cirque attitude to the smaller shows that come to their smaller towns. Dale Longmire, who works on Walker Brothers, faces numerous nit-picking com-parisons from many of his customers. "They will say, 'Oh, well, we saw Cirque du Soleil.' And their expectations are much harder to meet. We are not a French Canadian import show of people on wires and no animals."

Pisoni feels that Cirque is a mixed blessing. "I never did care for the spectacle aspect of the circus." And Cirque, he believes, lays that aspect on too strong. Nor are its produc-tions friendly to kids, in his opinion. "They get lost. It's just too much stimulus. It goes back to the notion of spectacle."

The Ringling spectacle has changed, too. Obviously, Kenneth Feld wanted to stay in step as best he could, so he tailored a few of his acts in the Cirque mold—baby blue spot-lights, softer, more pensive music, balletic posturing in the opening and closing segments during intervals.

The Big Apple Circus had already started to shape its shows around a "theme" each season, so it escaped the onus of an outright imitator selling out to the latest trend.

Circus Oz, which tours the states every few years, was so subversively set in its theatre-heavy ways, that an imitation of Cirque, unless rooted in satire, would look needlessly gra-tuitous. In 1999, Oz turned away from skits about nuclear annihilation and took on simpler subjects for comedic effect. It spoofed old lawn bowlers and old-time circus artists who can't: a cannon act fizzles out at blast off. A trapeze flyer, too cowardly to fly, has to be pushed into the air by others like a frightened bird out of the nest. Barbie Burton, big-time star hilariously in need of constant attention from groveling fans, suddenly turns from clown to crack trampoline acrobat, jumping high and then sliding across a diving board for a sur-prise finish.

Circus Vargas (remember it?) was soon down to one ring, and in a tent that rarely enchanted, with too few acts worth paying to see. A mediocre sound system delivered a worn-out, seasons-old, tape recorded score. At the end of another endless tour through Southern California in 2003, the profitless show folded for good. (It reopened under new manage-ment in 2006, focusing largely on Southern California dates.)

From Hugo, Oklahoma, in 1998 came a totally new one-ring show, created on the backs of the multi-talented Chimal family from Mexico, Circus Chimera. The show's founder, James Judkins, had, ironically, come off the five-ring Carson and Barnes Circus, which he had managed for many years. Owner Dory Miller wanted to resume being his own day-to-day boss. "There were too many cooks," explains Judkins, "and it was time for me to move on."

It sure was, after he and Dory wrapped up the ensuing friction between them with a nasty fist fight, followed by the younger one's making a quick exit off the C&B lot.

Judkins, who started out in his youth as a ringmaster on the one-ring Circus Kirk, claims to have been inspired not by Cirque at all, but by a life-changing trip he took through Europe about the same time. "What struck me the most was the different atmosphere at most of the shows not in the U.S.A. They were high quality shows. Clean, bright, and gave the public a good show. Most of the U.S. shows, by comparison, were not high quality. They were just a series of acts without regard to lighting, sounds, comfort for the public. The public as a whole was being turned off by the circus industry."

Judkins dropped $1.5 million of his own money into Chimera. He handed $200,000 of it into the hands of one Douglas Lyon. We'll call that an act of blind faith. You'll remem-ber Lyon as the man who, twenty years before, showed Cliff Vargas a way out of the phone rooms into the light of a more honest operation, putting showmanship ahead of charity.

About two weeks before Chimera was slated to open, Judkins, waiting for spring dates he assumed Lyon would have booked and begun promoting, called up the office for an accounting. He received a return phone call from a staff underling, informing him that "nothing basically had been done."

Lyon's people were told that the man on the other end of the line was "an eccentric Oklahoma millionaire" and that they were not to talk to him.

Douglas Lyon did agree to fly out shortly before Chimera's opening date.

Judkins asked Lyon just what he had been up to.

"The most profound statement I could get out of him: 'It will get better.'"[2]

While Judkins was out in San Francisco with a tent going up and nobody at the ticket windows buying tickets, in another sphere, Guy Laliberte was dropping $185 million into a new Cirque show called *Ka* for the MGM Grand at Las Vegas.

Under the new Circus Chimera tent, an impressive first program was offered before rows and rows of empty seats day after bitter cold day. This was bargain basement Cirque du Soleil—without belabored attitudes or airs, and with a fog machine from K-Mart to spread a little cosmic Montreal mist. Cirque-like in its no-animals one-ring simplicity, in its artful costumes and posturing, in its non-traditional tape-recorded score. The show was full of fine things to enjoy, and it moved with crisp precision. I saw a couple of performances attended by maybe, what, twenty or so curiously entranced souls.

Gradually, Circus Chimera developed a loyal base of liberals who take smug relief in shunning traditional big tops. From a Web site, UC Berkeley Parents Network, a raft of maternal endorsements went up:

"It was a good value for the money ... and there were no animals, thus avoiding the ethical/animals rights issues that seem to come up with circuses."

"...sort of like Cirque du Soleil without the drama and the mystery."

"It's not a super-sensational circus, very homey and friendly but very good acts and very new."

"Ringling Bros. was awful and Chimera was great fun. We got 2 for 1 coupons at Longs."

"The music is taped and it is somewhat amazing that they stay on schedule with the music."

"Liked it better than the much higher priced Barnum and Bailey Circus. There were no animals — it's lively upbeat, multi-ethnic and just terrific. Well worth the highest priced tickets and well worth every one's respect. They're a new unpolished troupe but just great. Go enjoy!!!"[3]

But rarely did enough people come. Chimera's higher aims were marginalized by its tawdry context: an old fashioned carnival-type midway on the outside, too many time-consuming concession pitches during the performance. Nine years later and still struggling, Judkins closed the show on July 2, 2007, promising to return in 2008. Beyond the Bay Area, he may find that reinstating the animals will attract larger crowds.

No show has fallen farther in a desperate bid to equal if not outdo Cirque du Soleil than the modern-day New Pickle Circus. Ten years after Larry Pisoni was thrown out, and after the brief reign of the late Judy Finelli, followed by the fairly promising reign of choreographer Tandy Beal, in came Gypsy Snyder, daughter of Larry and Peggy. She arrived in association with another ex-Pickle, Shanna Carroll. The two staged an intense, theatre-heavy piece, *Circumstance*, in 2002. Locals loved it. Stress "locals."

Circumstance was described by its creators as a show about "the passionate bohemian ways of the circus performer, as seen through the eyes of a young woman, swept into the act, who learns that what seems ugly can be truly beautiful, and that life is too short not to face our fears and live our dreams."[4]

What a joy *Circumstance* was — for the first fifteen or twenty minutes. Then it turned relentlessly gloomy. One of its principal characters, a "prostitute" played by Olga Kosova, stalked the stage apron at intervals, casting a cynical stare upon everyone out in the audience. Had somebody out there run off without paying her? What a sad polluted reflection of the original Pickle Family Circus.

Snyder and Carroll's smug contrivance was not followed by another. Back to Quebec, they returned. Back to circus central, where the pair formed their own intriguing show, *Seven Fingers*. Its purpose, they stated, was to be "not a huge spectacle of fantasy and perfection." Rather, all seven members of the new company, who had all toured with the Montreal monster, were setting out to "demystify circus and to be very human."[5]

So, let's start in the kitchen. That's where audiences entered — through a refrigerator to reach a loft, where *Seven Fingers* was set. The performers appeared in their underwear, as if to be relaxing at home — or was this really a veiled brothel for voyeurs on a budget? Each spectator was welcomed and treated as a guest. The seven players acted out their various relationships and personal quirks through juggling, hand-balancing and aerial tricks. And true to the original Pickle Family backyard collectives of the '60s, they lived and practiced in a Montreal convent.

Yet to be seen on Bravo.

Returning to the Pickles four years later, Snyder and Carroll offered the deftly experimental *Traces*, a decidedly more appealing work suggesting yet another new form in which circus acts might flourish.

A raft of new circus-related troupes have each competed to reach a fussy and demanding public conditioned by Le Cirque to expect ground-breaking fare. Circus of Failure, a San Francisco–based troupe that quickly self-fulfilled on its title, featured during its brief heyday months a bearded lady without a beard, an aerialist who couldn't fly (how Oz-like), and so on, with a little free porno tossed in for seasoning. The four-piece "Killing My Lobster" orchestra supplied music. A caveman turned into an oversexed wife of a mattress. "Cheaper than a ticket to Cirque du Soleil," snapped the *San Francisco Examiner's* Anne Crump, "and 100 percent pretension-free!"[6]

From Paris came Le Cirque Archass, a self-described "post apalyptic" big top complete with simulated decapitations and burials, and — oh yes — a few harmless rapes thrown in on the side. All set in a city junkyard strewn with busted, non-sequined toilets, discarded cars and old tv sets. Gosh, these depraved Parisians might have made it big a hundred years ago on the Barnum & Bailey midway.

Which makes us wonder: is the old freak show screaming for a way back into highbrow respectability?

Still way ahead of them all, at the age of 44 in 2004 Guy Laliberte joined the billionaire's club. He is worth $1.5 billion. He shared some of his transparent secrets with *Business Week* online. The formula he devised for dominating the international scenes focused on "easily replaced performers." Spoken dialogue was eliminated in order to insure that diverse spectators could easily relate to the performance.

"Most important," stated Mr. Laliberte, out went the "expensive and controversial" animal acts. "I'd rather feed three acrobats than one elephant."

"He's the most fantastic audience you can have," said Lynn Howard, who manages Cirque's live-show division. "He has an incredible feel for how the public will react."[7]

Laliberte can also be callously insensitive to his employees. He fired an HIV-positive performer, Matthew Cusick, just as the gymnast was about to join the Las Vegas production of Mystere. After spending several months training for the role and passing medical exams with flying colors, Cusick was declared a safety hazard. His sudden ouster was answered by an angry public backlash in larger cities and by a lawsuit filed by Lambda Legal Defense and Education Fund to reinstate his act.

"I thought society had gotten beyond thinking that people with HIV can only do desk jobs and never come into contact with people," said Cusick.[8]

He had lived with HIV for ten years. His viral load was not detectable in two medical exams by a Cirque doctor. Even then, he disclosed his HIV status to Cirque before signing on.

Those words of Adrian Berinde at the airport—"I don't think that anyone matters to them"[9]—have haunting relevance here.

Cirque relented in the face of the Lambda lawsuit and agreed to rehire Cusick, but, shortly after rejoining an indifferent company, Cusick decided to leave rather than face more ill-will from his co-performers.

In 1997, during an Oakland date, Cirque was picketed by the International Alliance of Theatrical and Stage Employees for hiring non-union personnel at "starvation wages," reported to be $5.00 per hour.[10]

Cirque does not bring its spectators, as I've suggested, every last great act in the world, not by the dozens. And it likely never will. When the company needed another strong circus act for *Varekai*, mainly to address a lagging second act, juggler Picasso Jr. was contacted. Would he have submitted to the show's demanding directors? He speaks of working with his heart and smile, so he was a bit apprehensive, sharing with the Cirque agents a concern that his natural personality might get buried or repressed under the show's makeup and costume add-ons. But since he was already booked for Circus Knie, he did not pursue the offer seriously. The future is another matter for Picasso, who says that he is open to changes within reason. In fact, he does not rule out a Cirque contract, assuming it would not obligate him to a personality transplant. Another four or five years from now, he hints, and we might see him there.

How long will the public prefer Cirque's painted faces, its weirdly fantastic characters, and its bizarre sets? To be sure, these elements have helped bring back a lot of the otherworldly atmosphere which circuses once naturally brought to town—before Irvin Feld tore down the invisible fourth wall between patron and performer, invited everybody into the show, and gave away all the secrets. We want our circuses to be strange and exotic, like Floyd King once wrote, to be unpredictable and mysterious. We want to enter a world removed from our own. Cirque does this every time.

How long can it keep from looking old hat, too? So far, Guy Laliberte has managed to stay ahead of a fickle public with sufficient innovation and change, touring the universe of his wide-ranging imagination for ideas. And he has stayed far ahead of all his competitors out to grab a piece of his market.

There is only one other circus owner on the planet with the money and resources to mount a viable challenge: Kenneth Feld. The greatest tribute of all to the king of Montreal was paid by Mr. Feld in a calculated act designed to duplicate Cirque's outrageously insulting success. Millionaire Kenneth Feld set out to beat billionaire Guy Laliberte at his own game. And therein lay the tale of two showman as different as night and day. Mr. Feld! Your turn, please...

So let the immediate preparation for the imitation begin.

Enter Cirque du Ringling.

11

Ringling in Retreat

Circus fans, about to see a dream come true, anxiously awaited the first edition of Ringling Bros. and Barnum & Bailey *under canvas* in nearly fifty years. Maybe, at last, the Greatest Show on Earth would once again be just that.

The ballyhoo began on February 26, 1999, in the perfect place — Sarasota, Florida, where forty-three years earlier, the funeral trains of the last big top version of Ringling-Barnum had rolled into town. And now the tents were about to be resurrected. "For two hours, we want to throw a party for the audience," said 32-year-old Italian director Raffaele DeRitis, at the helm of the historic revival.[1]

Little could the fans have imagined what lay ahead for such a promising venture. The man who created it had all the money and power necessary to launch a full-scale golden-age renaissance. So much power and yet so little patience in sharing it with others. "They're not going to tell me how to run *my* circus!" he screamed one year after scrapping a cabbage patches spec idea during a production meeting. One of the show's "directors," Coleco, had pressed the boss for a little more creative control. According to ringmaster Antekeier, it "sent him over the deep end."[2]

The man's name is Kenneth Feld. And how ironic: for all of his money and muscle, the one resource he seems so short on is artistic resolve. Would this new under-canvas version of Ringling that he was about to unveil reveal a more courageous showman?

Following the death of his father Irvin, who stayed the John Ringling North format with flattering devotion — four production numbers spread through the program — Kenneth proceeded to shake things up a bit. At first, as we've already noted, he revealed strong producerly promise, coming in during the late eighties with some pretty exciting shows. They were paved with fancy pageantry, take-note new acts. Overall much of the old Ringling polish was there.

Feld was much more open to change. Why peddle a production format that North had pioneered nearly fifty years before? Why stay a stagnant course? Gradually, Kenneth Feld dealt a fresh hand stocked with old and new cards — his ideas and the ideas of others. He turned himself into a shrewd appropriator of what other circuses were doing in order to stay in step with the times. Call it the new Ringling smorgasbord. During a single performance, you could spot shades of different circuses in the rings and in the air. Sometimes it worked. Sometimes the result was a half-baked mishmash. Feld never fully developed a distinctive artistic vision of his own for the show. Neither had his dad.

Bits and pieces of the greatest show on earth. Stops and starts. That's how the younger Feld assembled it. He produced two atypically brilliant finale spectacles that stand nearly alone in their greatness: 1996's super-hyperactive "Airiana — the Human Arrow"; and, seven years later, another epic, arena-filling pageant with an operatic sweep — "Bailey's Comet." That same sizzling season of '03, one of the best editions of Big Bertha in years, the circus opened with "Ready or Not," a dashing procession of Asian acrobats spilling out from all the rings. There were highly amusing clown numbers and plenty of fetching new acts. The Globe of Death motorbike cage had six riders in motion at the same time. If the show veered off the track now and then, at least its excesses were in the right direction.

That edition was directed by William McKinley, who deserved high praise for, if nothing else, presiding over a finale of breathtaking proportions. In every way, from costume design to the intense chanted music and the announcing, Bailey's Comet was a powerhouse of old-fashioned big-top imagery. The payoff was not just a man on fire (the comet) being shot out of a cannon. No, the payoff was the entire outlandish build-up itself, made especially thrilling by the verbal gymnastics, Holy Roller style, of ringmaster Johnathan Lee Iverson turning himself nearly on fire with revivalist zeal.

On the downside, the expediently eclectic Kenneth Feld who runs Ringling can't seem to hold a single thematic thrust long enough to sustain the two halves of a performance. If only he had the steel to tell a director, "Okay, go with it from start to finish. Paint the entire show in comet colors. Flavor the entire score with your original comet refrains. Blow up the format and go for broke."

Half a greatest show on earth is what we usually get. Some years, Mr. Feld can lift our spirits sky high during the first half, sending us out on a buying blitz at the concession stands during intermission, then, back in our seats, let us way way down. And you'll sit there staring and wondering — what happened? Where did the show go? So cynically opportunistic is the man, perhaps he has it all figured out that, once the intermission concession haul has been made, audience buying power drops off dramatically, so why bother with the rest of the program?

No respecter of talent alone, Feld hired the Guerreros high wire troupe from Colombia to perform the extremely rare seven-high pyramid (the same stunt introduced back in the late '40s by the Wallendas, who were the only ones to do it for decades). Great move. Did Mr. Feld then pay dramatic homage to the Guerreros by spotting them were such a feat belonged — over center ring? No, he did not. Their rigging was erected over "ring 1." Of course, in Feld parlance, there is no "center ring," there is only "ring 2." And so, perhaps in the man's reductionist mind, it mattered not that one of the best circus thrills of all time was demonstrated down by the cheaper seats in an end ring.

Kenneth grew up in the shadows of his dad, a born huckster who departed from Johnny North in quality. Irvin would throw a show together on mixed elements and create a big three-ring splash, sometimes more cinematic than real. For a time after Irvin died, Kenneth did not forsake the formula, and he has rarely allowed himself many moments away from the desk of power. He became "known for being a cut-throat businessman who did not have the same, great love for the circus as his father,"[3] remembered Kristopher Antekeier in his book, *Ringmaster*. In fact, many fans and insiders believe the son to be much more ruthless than his circus-loving father. Two years before veteran clown Duane Thorpe could retire with full benefits (after working on the Ringling show for nearly 40 years), Feld called him into the office, and said "It's time for you to move on." Thorpe was devastated.[4]

To the press, Kenneth Feld shows the face of a regular guy just doing a job. Here he is, in his own words, being interviewed by Tyler Currie of the *Washington Post* in 2003. See how much passion you can detect between the lines:

> I don't have any specific skill. I can't do a trapeze act or things like that. The first job I had with the circus was finding talent.... I don't think a day after I started full time with the circus I ever thought about what I did as work. The good days, the bad days, whatever, it's coming to a place to play. The play is that you get up in the morning and none of us know what's going to happen. People see me in a suit and they say, "This is a business guy that runs it." The business came later. My heart and soul is always in the show.[5]

He was a lot more blunt with author Ernest Albrecht, in a manner that needs little in-between-the-lines guessing: "All I care about are the customers. When you cut through everything, the customers are the only thing that matter: They're the reason behind why I do everything I do. I cater to the customers. I do what I think will sell, and that keeps changing."[6]

He also pays daily attention to the bottom line, and that evidently keeps changing, too. Feld has followed a policy begun by his father of gradually reducing the number of performers on the roster. Increasingly, we saw more one-act displays. For a spell, we saw a show title that read, roughly, "Ringling Bros. and Barnum & Bailey Sears." In 1992, if you had happened to drop in, you would have witnessed probably the weakest-ever edition of Ringling in a three-ring format — so anemically understaffed that it did not carry even a single flying return act. The bare-bones '92 lineup was framed around the three good-looking young guys called N/Motion, "a hot new rock and roll group" who sang songs as they moved around the arena on a creaky mobile stage. Poor Jim Ragona, the ringmaster of record that year, was shunted to the sidelines and given only a few acts to announce. What sort of a vision was this? Had Feld and his directors taken the time to think through their concept, they might have found ways to weave their rock singers more effectively into the program. They might have asked themselves, why not give the under-utilized Jim Ragona a year off from ringmaster duty?

William Painter, the director of record for the lackluster 1992 show and for the superior edition the prior year, did not come off looking like a man in charge of anything. So what if Painter had directed Bob Hope and Andy Williams? After two seasons giving notes to elephants, tumblers and the obsessive hands-on Kenneth Feld, Painter joined a long line of ex-Feld directors. The father was loathe to grant anyone the title "director." The son has at least accepted the word into his vocabulary.

Corporately speaking, Ringling is in the very best of hands. There is a good chance that the Feld family will turn out to have achieved the best record for long-term operational stability. First and foremost, the Felds are wizards at marketing and spin. As we've already noted, they are masters at working the media and rewriting their own version of circus history into accepted fact (with more than a little help from writers who have worked for them in publicity and program magazine copy). And they are amazingly good at marketing and merchandising. Like father, to a degree like son.[7]

Image is much more important to the obsessively hands-on Kenneth Feld than matters of thematic unity or act selection. You may have seen the shocking exposé on CBS's *Sixty Minutes* about the devious measures taken by Feld to keep a freelance writer from authoring a book about his family and alleged animal abuse and the breaking of child labor laws at the circus. The writer, Jan Pottker, had done a short piece outing the late Irvin's bisexuality. Kenneth learned, through the clandestine services of Clair George, a former deputy directory of operations for the CIA and head of covert operations, that Pottker was at work on a book enlarging upon the article.

So Feld engaged 36-year-old Robert Eringer, a spy novelist, to befriend Ms. Pottker and offer to collaborate with her on a non-circus book, anything to detain her from the Feld exposé. This Mr. Eringer did, engaging the trust and collaboration of Pottker at a library meeting. Together, they penned a tome about the Mars candy family. Feld put out lots of money (up to millions, said some) for Eringer's surreptitious services and for secretly funding the publication of the book by National Press Books, of Bethesda, Maryland. A $25,000 advance sent to Ms. Pottker by the publisher had actually been funded by Feld. Incredibly, everything up to this point was unknown to the unsuspecting author. When she finally found out what had been going on, she learned from Charales Smith, a former CFA for the circus, that she had been under Ringling radar for eight years and that "Kenneth Feld wanted to ruin my life."

Before losing his job at the circus, long-time vice president Allen Bloom warned Mr. Feld that he considered the whole operation to be a bad idea, and that he did not approve of it. According to Bloom, Feld replied, "It doesn't matter."[8]

Back to the show itself, which is what should matter the most. Feld continued cutting back on the number of performers. There were fewer three-ring displays. And with less of everything, how does a calculating producer compensate? One way is with filler. Comb the audience for volunteers to take part in silly, time-consuming clown routines. Hire a David Larible, specialist in audience participation, give him 15 or 20 minutes in each half, and you've knocked off a good half-hour's worth of real acts you don't have to pay for.

Enter the "power clown," a term coined by the *Wall Street Journal's* Kelly Crow, casting a nasty glance at prima-buffoons like Larible who earn super big bucks for padding the program. Not since the days of Dan Rice could a jester hold circus owners hostage to their greedy demands and swaggering egos. Star clowns, of which there are precious few, have agents. They "often get a private dressing room and gourmet-food spreads while other clowns have to share hallway space for costume changes and ride the circus shuttle to grocery stores," crows Crow, who conveniently ignores an American history of market-driven rewards for outstanding achievement in all sectors.[9]

The "power clowns" get royalties, she reports. Some pull rank and display snide disrespect for fellow funsters, who make as little as $180.00 a week. Some insist that others prepare their props. And so on. In our book, the point is not about how much these select few make; after all, even the Ringling brothers rewarded their star performers in past years with higher salaries and special perks. Think Lillian Leitzel holding court in the backyard under her cushy private dressing room top.

No, the point is whether these arguably overpaid comedy relievers are being used by Kenneth Feld to camouflage his diminishing cast of real circus performers.

Feld went out and hired David Larible, and Larible, in Feld's opinion, proved to be a great audience pleaser. So much so, that Mr. Feld agreed to a contract extension granting Larible at least two 15-minutes spots in each half of the program. It is happening because the boss believes that audiences like to see one recurring clown throughout the entire show. What Mr. Feld does not talk about is the money he saves in being able to engage fewer jugglers and acrobats as a result of Larible's extended ring appearances.

Bello Nock, showcased on the other unit of Ringling, signed a contract for a $600,000 annual compensation. A gifted acrobat and thrill artist, Nock makes a better case for himself even if he, too, wears out the welcome mat. His numerous appearances throughout the performance consume a collective total of *forty* minutes.

Larible may have charmed the masses his first one or two seasons out. After that, he came off more like a tired annual ritual that one does not dare criticize — an overpaid ego consuming too much dead air and stopping the fading show in its tracks. Alas, he and Feld broke a contract and parted ways at the end of the 2005 tour. Larible told the *Wall Street Journal* that he was going out on his own. "I can't sit in my glory," he stated.[10] Considering the ill fate of numerous "stars" in past years who went out to seek better terms or form their own shows (that folded fast), Larible may be in for a long, laughless sit.

Feld had the circus field entirely to himself, and then came Cirque du Soleil to ruin it all. Even to Ringling's diehard fans, the show was looking more second rate than ever, randomly thrown together. Feld's calculated smorgasbord smacked of imitation. How could he ever duplicate Cirque du Soleil in huge arenas? He couldn't. So he thought up *Barnum's Kaleidoscape*. Whence the name? From a boyhood fondness of Feld's for kaleidoscopes.

The show's director, DeRitis, revealed that spectators could anticipate a story about "ordinary people who became performers in the ring before the ticket holders." Funny, wasn't that exactly how Cirque du Soleil's first show to hit the states unfolded? "And we want to encourage the audience to wonder about what happens behind the scenes, to include the characters in the show, their romances and hatreds."

Predicted the boss, "Tented entertainments will be a thing of the future." Referring to North's 1956 pronouncement declaring the big top a thing of the past, countered Feld, "Ringling's statement was valid for its time, but the tent now gives us the ability to practically deliver circus to the door of the people who ordinarily can't, or won't, come to arenas. We want to reach new suburban and exurban communities."[11]

The tents for Ringling's outdoor return were more fantastically imaginative than even those for Cirque. They looked as if Walt Disney Concert Hall architect Frank Gehry had designed them. Inside a reception tent, circus characters cavorted with incoming patrons to lend a super-friendly atmosphere. 87-year-old Antonini Traversi whipped up old tunes on a keyboard. Over yonder, 27-inch-tall Istua stood on his hands on the top of a counter top. Entertainers all around smiled and shook hands, signed autographs.

Popcorn and lemonade for sale? How about, instead, another cappuccino, or maybe a fajita or a designer salad en route to the little show in the larger top up ahead? Music rang through the air. A mood of happy, slightly kooky old-time entertainment prevailed.

Inside the biggest tent, you beheld the most gorgeous setting imaginable, complete with red carpeting, cushy reserved chairs upholstered in red velvet with gold trimming, and even, for the super rich, your own personal sofa. The program itself was warm and entertaining — and a little bit too passive to generate must-see word-of-mouth. With the show starring David Larible, whom we'd seen many times already on Ringling, Mr. Feld evidently believed he could get away with the slim roster of real acts.

Along with Larible's usual audience-participation shenanigans (and his imitation of Emmett Kelly's famed spotlight-sweeping routine), there were some agreeably fine turns in a classy mode: among them, mouth juggler Picasso Jr.; equestrienne Sylvia Zerbini putting a circle of beautiful horses through intricate maneuvers; on the low wire (read, *low wire*), a fellow walking it on stilts with a girl standing on his shoulders — neat stuff all except for a thick safety rope which seemed hardly necessary given the act's proximity to the ground.

At intervals during the program a woman who resembled either a hippie or a chic homeless lady wandered in and out, leading us to wonder if the director — or the boss directing the director — was trying to make a big Cirque-like statement?

Mr. Feld's bid for a slice of the adult yuppie market ended on a high note of acrobatic excitement. What, if anything, did this lovely Ringling return to a tent lack? Unfortunately, true to the Feld formula, there was little thematic focus to *Kaleidoscape*. In fact, it looked more like the Big Apple Circus than it did Cirque. Well, the producer had stolen away two Big Apple alumni in the form of a husband-and-wife team, bandmaster Rik Albani and composer Linda Hudes.

The show would earn raves from nearly every critic who reviewed it. *Circus Report* would declare it superior to Cirque du Soleil.

From the *Austin Chronicle*: "Heightens our joy in and appreciation of what circuses are — and helps give the often undervalued performers in it their due respect. It's as extraordinary for that as for delivering so much pleasure. And damn if it didn't make me feel like running away with the circus."[12]

"Barnum's Kaleidoscape has no bogus 'plot,' and no pretension. No new age soundtrack," observed Andrew Pan in the *Chicago Sun Times*. "Unlike the pseudo theatrics and special effects of Cirque, Kaleidoscape celebrates the brilliant legacy of the American and European circus — it's raucous, alive, human, personal, crazy and, at times, bizarre.... Feld and company have offered a refutation of the idea that there was ever anything wrong with the circus or circus people.... P.T. Barnum, who started it all in 1871, would be exceedingly proud."[13]

Feld's bright new toy fancied by the critics rolled onto Bryant Park in New York City on November 21, 2000, to compete for patronage with the Big Apple Circus at Lincoln Center. The day-and-dating maneuver struck many as a thieving challenge. Fear and loathing at Big Apple pushed one of its board members, Alan Slifka, to share a sense of competitive doom with the *New York Times*, fearing that his company could be "driven out of existence," and that, as he saw it, Kenneth Feld wanted "to cripple the Big Apple Circus." Hardest for Slifka to fathom, he said, was why the city of New York itself would, in effect, invite Ringling "to crush" Big Apple (by renting them public park space). To the same press, Feld predicted that *Kaleidoscape* would prove be a "major profit center" for his various concerns and that he hoped to bring it back "year after year."[14]

Remarked Paul Binder, none to thrilled, either, to see his sacred territory invaded by a circus with deep pockets and a well-known bent for coddling the press, "If Kenneth Feld decides he wants to come into our markets, there will be a competitive situation. Audiences will have to decide which one do I go to."[15]

After New York, Mr. Feld's venture into art suddenly crashed. Down went the tents. In a strange second chapter eerily reminiscent of the Ringling funeral train of 1956, back to Florida went *Barnum's Kaleidoscape*. The show had been out less than two years. It was getting great reviews and doing good business, so went the spotty reports. According to one, both Big Apple and *Kaleidoscape* played to large houses in New York during their overlapping dates there. Feld told the press that he was merely taking time off in order to frame a new edition of *Kaleidoscape* around the talents of his star, David Larible. He never did that.

What, then, went wrong?

Now, we are going deeper into the murky psyche of our show owner under the lamp. Like his dad, Feld is very successful promoting established properties — Ringling, Disney on Ice; and like his dad, an utter failure at ground-up innovation. To begin with, that clumsy title, so infuriatingly hard to spell. "I would have called it Ringling under a tent," says John Pugh. "I would have said the return of Ringling Bros. to the tent. It's a winner by itself."

Secondly, no matter what they called it, *Kaleidoscape* was incredibly impractical from an accounting standpoint. Insiders estimated that the show had cost $25 million and closed in the hole. This was really strange, because Mr. Feld is considered a genius at staying profitably above the bottom line. Bob Mitchell, who loved *Kaleidoscape*, has surmised like others that even had Feld's one-ring darling played to one packed house after another and sold out all of its designer dishes in the reception tent, it still couldn't have made money. The cost of hauling it in too many trucks over long distances between major cities was prohibitive.

Nor did the modest seating capacity help matters. Where, we ask, was the boss's business brain when he hatched this one, or did romance get the best of him? Compared to *Kaleidoscape*'s 1,800 chairs, Big Apple sat 1,980 on a typical lot, Cirque, 2,500. Feld's ticket prices were less pricey than Cirque's, too.

Now ladies and gentlemen, before we continue on, here's a real surprise! *Direct from Italy*, the director *himself*, Mr. Raffaele DeRitis, has offered — right here, right now — to share with you some of *his* firsthand insights on working for Kenneth Feld.

If you please, Mr. DiRitis...

"I found a sincerely passionate man with a real competence in what he was approaching. He had an incredible knowledge of European performers and of one-ring circuses in the last 30 years. He has a unique sense of foreseeing the smallest weak point very early, and a good knowledge of theatrical tools, from design to lighting or sound technology."

So, Mr. DiRitis, could you tell us how you felt about the end result that you directed called *Barnum's Kaleidoscape*?

"There is a very specific company culture that pushes you towards the feel of some polished live cartoon show. Even if they push the creative team to be as much visionary as possible, I didn't find them ready to start from some unusual theatrical vision."

And what might that vision have been, sir?

"For example, they always refused every kind of element turning to romantic, surreal or dark."

"Among other possibilities, I loved to do a circus with the decadent feel, to exploit the sense of past coming from P.T. Barnum's name."

Why didn't you?

"For a time, we worked on an old fashioned concept, trying to give it a new turn, then everything turned toward this strange luxury world, that I find anyway beautiful. I was not simply directing a show, but creating a full environmental concept. I think that the final result was something between what I had wished to do and what they always did. It was more predictable than surprising, but for a popular audience was somehow amazing."

Too safely commercial?

"But there were other big problems. Besides Mr. Feld, his vice president Tim Holst and the creative team, almost nobody in the company ever realized the sense and the complexity of what was going on. It was just too far away from their idea of show business."

Thank you, Italy!

Summing up here on the midway of fallen icons, Kenneth Feld's under-canvas experiment was simply not impressive or memorable enough to generate the word of mouth that might have driven droves of people out to the show, making it possible to raise ticket prices and enhance revenue. As wonderfully nice as *Kaleidoscape* circus was, it lacked a flamboyant edge — a theme, a compelling hook or gimmick, something to leave the customers breathless. When you go out singing the salad, that's not a good sign. Feld relied too questionably on David Larible to provide the hook. In fact, without this time-consuming clown around, the producer and director would have been forced to engage more acts and go deeper, and they then might have delivered the knock-out punch of a true tentbuster.

Maybe New Yorkers decided to stick with their own tried and true Big Apple Circus. Maybe Feld's survey consultants told him what he did not want to hear: it's going to be a long ugly haul to box office salvation.

In the end, though, we are back to the beginning: Unlike Guy Laliberte, Kenneth Feld lacks the will to strike a distinctive vision and hold it for the duration of a whole program. He doesn't do "art." Too messy. Too time-consuming. Too infuriatingly uncontrollable at times. Creatively impatient, Feld much prefers, it would appear, to rely on market and demographic downloads, and to incorporate the proven creativity of others into his own programs.

Back to his usual tricks, Feld continued to turn out his upbeat circus samplers, and they are less talented as time moves on. There are fewer acts, and fewer outstanding star turns. How can a show which presents some of the most accomplished artists in the world — for example, Sylvia Zerbini — moments later peddle a lifeless array of forgettable offerings? I'm talking the 134th edition, one of those half greatest shows on earth. The first part sparkled; the second part sputtered to a withering halt, like a carnival ride shut down for repairs.

We sit there in a black hole, wondering in the near darkness if they have stopped the thing to resume rehearsing it? Oh, that's it — David Larible, in no real hurry, is climbing the stairs through the seats, and a light is on him — *that's* the focus. He is taking his sweet time selecting more volunteers, bringing them down into the arena to work his shtick once more.

How much time has he knocked off? Another forgettable 15 minutes. The show's momentum is lost, the pacing, shot. We wait listlessly for something to happen.

The next year, 2005, brought a noisier, more hyperactive program. Now, Mr. Feld, in producing association with his daughter, Nichole, was clearly enamored of the UniverSoul Circus, a black-owned show that targets its intense energy to African American audiences. So why not a little bit of that for Ringling? Feld went out and hired two black announcers, nice enough guys, to share mike duties. Before the show began, we were exhorted to rise from our seats for a little arm waving workout. During the performance, one of the announcers answered questions related to the acts supposedly asked by members of the audience. The answers were more distracting than informative, especially as delivered through a loud and scratchy sound system. Clowns jumped up into the seats and into each other's laps in flirtatious romps, a rude distraction from the program in progress — or were we not supposed to be watching the actual performers down in the rings? Large rubber balls got tossed into the seats (same as what happens at UniverSoul), and we were challenged to catch them and toss them back. (Crash helmets are advised for front-row ticket holders.)

Did this Ringling edition have so little confidence in itself that it had to resort to so many audience-pandering side actions? The "music" was loud and long, and rather nondescript, not unlike the droning beats of a packed disco at midnight. Producers Kenneth Feld and Nichole Feld had produced what surely must rank as the most irritating edition ever of "the greatest show on earth."

Were there any good acts? Yes, quite a few, actually. There were the amusing Bello Nock turns; the Chinese through their hoops and up their poles; the high wire guy (even without his felled partner), dashingly unafraid up there like a true old-time circus daredevil. Trouble was, everything was over-pitched, like the theme song relentlessly reminding us that

"We are the circus!" Feld does not produce circus programs. He produces two-hour-long circus commercials.

How does Sylvia Zerbini feel about such a messy showcase?

Tactfully, she replies, that were she putting the show together, there are elements that she would not accept. She would make changes for certain. She would take a closer look at every aspect of the program. She would likely edit out mediocre acts and work on upgrading others to achieve, overall, a more polished performance.[16]

And then came another season, and our nation's once blazing circus hit a new low in showmanship when it shucked aside its three most enduring symbols of tradition and power. Welcome to the new *Ringless* Bros. and Barnum & Bailey. Half a circle at the front end of the performing area was decorated to look like half a ring. This was heralded as the revolutionary new break-out edition bearing a totally new Ringling-Barnum identity. It was quite different, alright. It was closer in spirit to a half-ring kiddie cartoon circus — and about as Disney as it could be. Maybe the shrewdly successful Mr. Feld was aiming for the moppet market, aiming to turn a new generation of children into tomorrow's circus fans. He surely was not aiming to please any adults. From the *Los Angeles Times*, typical of how some critics have reacted, came this: "The show is now so over produced, it makes the Oscar telecast seem like an Arctic monkey's gig.... The show comes off like an aging soft-shoe guy, dancing within an inch of his life as a rising ocean of flop sweat encroaches on his desperate grin, who thinks that because he got his ear pierced the kids will now think he's cool."

Built around a trivial story line about a multi-racial family of wannabe circus stars, the show was rigged to special effects and to video projections of the show in progress on giant screens. And for all its hyperactivity, strangely it lacked a strong detectable pulse. Among a catalog of sins, count this the *cheapest looking show on earth* ever to bear the Ringling name. The dark spare setting was about as glamorous as a tarmac. Ex–*American Idol* contestant Jennifer Fuentes, serving as one of too many announcers, came off on the big screen sounding like Tinkerbell. Other video distractions included talking elephants who favored hip hop jargon. Ironically, the show's highlight appeared in a video segment — against black and white film footage of the actual Ringling circus under canvas during the 1920s, they juxtapose the cartoon image of an elephant hanging by its trunk from a moving trapeze bar. Quite touching.

Kenneth Feld's daring deconstruction gives us pause to consider what a sacred thing the circus ring is. In it, many things happen that happen nowhere else. Even Shamsheeva's delightful performing cats and dogs suffered in this ringless setup where some of their best tricks got edited down — or out — or rearranged. The act made a far zestier impact the year before in a real circus ring with Big Apple. Among a few other engaging entries, a group of rambunctiously ambitious young Chinese acrobats on the rough-and-tumble side, the Yunnan Flyers, kicked up some genuine excitement with novel castoffs from a Russian swing into a four-person human chain anchored to a trapeze bar. The goal of each of three leapers, in succession, was to lock legs with the last until they are all linked to the lead flyer at the trap. Neat, nifty stuff harkening back in spirit to the older tent-show gusto when aerialists, untethered to safety lifelines, took real risks. When "daredevil" and "trick" were not dirty words. Too bad for all the extraneous nonsense that surrounded it.

Do Ringling audiences still expect a semblance of real circus? Evidently so, for Feld, who listens to his audience, must have heard them telling him, we want it wilder! He added a tiger act to the program before the first year of a two-year season was finished.

Beyond the new half-ring Ringling, beyond the blatantly misleading tv commercials advertising it that feature the big gripping traditional circus acts it does *not* contain, what next? On an even drearier note, how long can the Felds keep their controversial menagerie out on the road? Supersensitive to public preferences and market feedback, is it merely a matter of time before the Felds are persuaded by Madison Avenue to send out their elephants for good — and send in another power clown?

12

Reparations for Jumbo?

John Pugh is a man on the run, wanted for owning a circus that dares to present animal acts. Pugh is moving as fast as he can to stay ahead of his enemies who dominate city hall meetings, who threaten shopping mall owners and make ugly faces at circus fans. He is racing to keep one signed contract ahead of the Animal Liberation Sideshow—a gnarly band of activists bent on closing down every traditional circus in the world.

John Pugh's travails are so tense and trying, it's a wonder he hasn't thrown in the towel and joined the other side. Not that he hasn't been tempted. "I'm in the wrong business," he wryly confesses. "I should be in save-the-animals business. Instead of letting the animals support me, I should get people supporting me for getting rid of the animals."

And still, he takes it. He takes the abuse of PETA (People for the Ethical Treatment of Animals) in a thousand vexing ways. In his darkest hours, seeking out places to play and lots to play on, John Pugh must tread a political minefield of resistance at nearly every turn. We can imagine him believing that he is being chased through a bad dream. First to appear in the Animal Liberation Sideshow are the City Hall Stalkers. They are experts at making life miserable the year around for mayors and members of city councils. They will shout down anyone for supporting the right of an old fashioned circus to pitch its tents in their backyards.

Next to appear: the Chain Link Martyrs, masochists who lock themselves to fences and toss away the keys in order to stop the sinister passage of patrons onto arena parking lots. Not until the cops arrive with blow torches in hand to reopen the gates, can the public go watch pachyderms in frilly feathers herded around the hippodrome track by highschool drop-outs yelling insensitive-sounding orders under their breath.

Our next display, folks: the Bleeding Heart Academics. Heading up this collegial group who specialize in angry accusations is professor Warren Churchill, noted expert on animal abuse and open-mouth darling on cable TV, famous for such pronouncements as the one comparing the victims of 9/11 to Nazis. Here inside the Animal Liberation Sideshow, Professor Churchill will preach that known arsonists responsible for setting fire to animal research facilities have not gone far enough. Too timid! "The infliction of property damage upon entities engaged in the willful perpetration of omnicide constitutes the limit of legitimate response to the crimes at hand!"[1]

Among John Pugh's most outspoken critics are the Double Standard Divas. Today's top honor goes to celebrity show horse champion Stefanie Powers. She sent off a letter of ire to a town supervisor in Southampton, urging him to reject Pugh's request to bring circus day to the city. Why? Because his elephants are kept in line, so claimed Ms. Powers, by metal bull hooks. What Powers did not address was her own sport's known use of spurs in the painful training of show horse jumpers. And, furthermore, what Ms. Powers did not acknowledge were the abrasive barbed wire fences over which hapless horses, such as the one she rides, are forced to jump.[2] Strange lapse of a celebrity's over-worked memory?

John Pugh can probably recite by heart the lectures he has heard from our next platform icon: Lisa Wathne, a spokeswoman for PAWS — Preservation Animal Welfare Society — who evidently believes that for an animal to do anything taught to it by a human being (such as, we guess, a dog chasing after a newspaper) is an outfight offense against nature itself. Hear her out! "I have been in Africa three times, and I have yet to see an elephant standing on its head."[3]

Chasing after John Pugh and all of the terribly human people he employs are the morally superior Peeping Police Blotter Toms. They comb local felony reports for any and all evidence of wrong doing by circus people. They are driven to convert every alleged act of rape and robbery, incest and murder into the act of a circus criminal who must also abuse animals. Whenever Pugh checks the Circus Criminal Web site, he risks learning that he may be harboring not only animals under duress, but cocaine-addled roustabouts, popcorn venders on a tear, child-fondling funsters and garden variety deviants — unlike, of course, their many counterparts out in society at large.

Good news, folks! Here in the Animal Liberation Sideshow, there is comic relief for today's beleaguered circus man. There is *Kayla the What Is It?*, perverse possessor of the Superior Posteria. On it, the winner of a recent Valentine's Day auction was awarded the thrill of posting a personal log. Kayla the What Is It? is brought to us courtesy of PETA's top dog, Ingrid Newkirk and her "Complete Press Sluts." Now, who really is Kayla? She/he/it is "Kevin Worden," Transgendered Lettuce Lady who helps PETA raise funds to sponsor festivals of domestic terror against the accused subjugator of animals.[4]

Now move amusingly along, folks, to our next exhibit — over there in the far corner of the tent: a most shocking monument to the profession that John Pugh has fought so valiantly to keep alive: the Shackled Elephant. It's the work of the Subversive Sculpturist, rebuking Jumbo and his like, and it's on loan from Bridgeport, where it usually stands not far from the Barnum Museum and along the same street over which the Ringling elephants parade each year in public disgrace from the rail yards to the local arena.

Now, if Mr. Pugh should seek a weekend away from all this madness in some safer place like, say, sunny Spain, he runs a real risk of being trampled to death by the Horned Nudists. And who are they? They are the angry exhibitionists who jog down the narrow streets of Madrid to ridicule the annual stampede of bulls after thrill-seeking runners through the capital of matador machismo.[5]

Upon his return to the states, at least John Pugh won't be run over behind the "Adults Only" curtain in our Animal Liberation Sideshow. There, he need only shake his head in disbelief at the sordid spectacle of Max Standing Vigil over His Gory Pile of Dead Dogs Stuffed in Trash Bags! Dead at the hand of Newkirk's Hypocrites of Horror, they were discovered on a Virginia roadway near PETA's headquarters.

Pugh's worst nightmares are far from amusing. Always lurking out there with the intent to harass, badger and bankrupt are the Multi-Tasking Thieves. Today's exemplar of moral turpitude is Dawn Young, arrested for swiping CDs from Starbucks when not swiping mink-bearing animals off Midwest farms and releasing them back to the wilds. Worse yet are The Virtuous Vandals, who at any moment might set another old-fashioned menagerie ablaze.[6]

So there they are, folks — are you going to applaud or walk away in silence? Now, let's give John Pugh a well earned rest. And let's give his defenders a chance to respond. For one, the *Circus Report*'s late Billy Barton, commenting on the above-mentioned arsonists: "The real horror story is from England. Animal acts are no longer permitted in Metro London where Austin Bros. Circus was victimized when animal rights activists actually set fire to a horse tent and destroyed the horses, justifying their barbaric behavior with the remark that horses were better off dead than with the circus!"[7]

The fanatics who would rather see a horse in ashes than in sashes are beyond earthly reason. And that's why a number of beleaguered circus owners have asked me to tell you, folks, how sorry they are for not being able to include bike-riding bears and ball-balancing seals. And if you purchase a bag of our new low-cal, carb-light, trans-fat, salt-free peanuts, hoping to toss a few into a big grey trunk, you're in for a big letdown. You see, the elephants don't live here anymore.

The show owners are doing their best. They are a tactful lot. They can only shrug their shoulders, take another deep breath, try another town and hope for enough vacant lots with which to string together a season of dates. Some areas (think red states) are better than others (yes, think blue). "I play the New England corridor," explains John Pugh. "It's probably the toughest area for a tent show to play because there's so many regulations, codes. You think a guy going to put up a skyscraper somewhere goes through it. We go through the same thing three or four times a week. It's murder."

Pugh usually arrives for his few minutes before a city council or a permit board after the city hall stalkers have spent a year harassing the same people with phone calls, e-mails, faxes and threats, with angry speeches at council meetings and protest walks. "What happens," he continues, "is that the people that have owned the properties that we've been playing on are being harassed by the animals rights people." Or, "You've got somebody who is the CEO of some big corporation that's sitting in a white tower miles away. He gets two or three letters, maybe a dozen letters from animal rights people, and says, 'Oh, my god! I don't want to get into this. Why are they bugging me? How much are we getting out of renting to that circus, and they're only playing that mall for two days? ... Oh, jeez, I just don't want the hassle.'"

The dice, ladies and gentlemen, are loaded against the hard-working men and women who still strive to bring you the genuine circus experience as best they can. Says Norma Cristiani of Walker Brothers, "You get a committee, and there's got to be one person in every town that hates the animals in the circus, so they start raising hell, and when they do, then your committee doesn't want to book the show."

And even if the committee says yes, you still might face ugly opposition the day you arrive. From PAWS or PETA, take your choice, swallow your bitter pill. Here's what can happen: When Carson and Barnes played Ojai, California, members of the Cliff Vargas tent of the Circus Fans Association of America, showing up one afternoon to take in a performance, were nearly assaulted by nasty stares, angry shouted profanities and a barrage of hate banners from do-gooders crowding both sides of the street leading up to the circus. Perhaps the only thing worse than a radical harassing city hall is the one who doesn't get his way at city hall.[8]

"It's absolutely unbelievable what they're doing," adds another Walker Brothers staffer,

The menagerie offered education and exotica to children of all ages (courtesy of the John and Mable Ringling Museum of Art, Tibbals Digital Collection).

Dale Longmire. "Maybe people won't buy the tickets because maybe a member of PETA is on the chamber of commerce in a certain town and he'll say to all the members, 'You can't sell tickets to the circus because of the animals!'"

In the eyes of Newkirk's minions, it seems that there is nothing the circus could ever do to redeem itself from whatever it did in the past.

When is enough enough? The tide may be turning. Frankie L. Trull, president of the Foundation for Biomedical Research, in the summer of 2005 called for Ingrid Newkirk's immediate resignation after the discovery of the dead dogs, and after growing suspicions that PETA had been collecting and killing adoptable kittens and puppies for a long time. "It suggests a very dark and twisted secret agenda," asserted Ms. Trull. "Hard though it is to believe, I am aware that some radical animal liberation activists regard pet ownership as the moral equivalent of slavery and do not believe in pet adoption, spaying or neutering."

A few months before, along a Virginia roadway not far from PETA's office, a construction worker had discovered body parts from over a hundred dogs stuffed in bags. "If Ingrid Newkirk didn't know what was going on, it raises a serious question about her competence. Some reports say this may have been going on for months, even years. And if she knew about it, she should resign in disgrace, as a gesture to people who expected their PETA donations to help animals."[9]

"I rescue dogs from shelters and make them stars in show business," dog trainer Bob Moore told me. "They kill animals."

Here's what David Rawls, former owner of the Kelly-Miller Circus, has to say:

"PETA — just a good excuse to pilfer money from people who don't know what they really do. They raise about $17 million each year, and don't spend a dime to help or care for animals. HSUS is in the same category. The public over the last several years has begun to realize that PETA is not warm and cuddly but full of shady truths and acid tongues."

Paul Binder, too, believes that negative public perceptions may be turning a corner. "I think that it's finally getting through to the American public that PETA are extremists. I do believe they see that. There are some who will never see it. They are brought up in a culture that's separate from animals. And they can't imagine being around animals. They have this Dumbo mentality. If you're working with animals you're somehow being cruel to them. It is so far from the truth in most cases."

A lot of people in other walks of life are beginning to speak out. And some are starting to get mad as you-know-what. John Pugh, wherever you are, you may have some friends in the political sector at last: Here's Australia's minister Warren Truss, who says he's not going to take it anymore. Truss made a speech at the Victorian Rural Press Club in Melbourne, basing his remarks on information provided by the Center for Consumer Freedom. He called PETA "not an animal welfare group" at all. Heck, Mr. Truss, are you back there? How about coming out here on the platform and sharing your findings with our crowd! Okay? Here he is...

> PETA's leadership had compared animal farmers to serial killer and cannibal Jeffrey Dahmer, compared chickens to Holocaust survivors, and pronounced a shark attack on a little boy was "revenge" against humans.
>
> But even more concerning, it has been alleged in a U.S. Senate hearing by the same organization that PETA has provided aid and comfort to people associated with two groups considered domestic terrorists threats by the FBI — the Earth Liberation Front and the Animal Liberation Front.
>
> According to the FBI, the two groups have been responsible for more than 600 crimes since 1996, causing more than $43 million in damage. The ALF even brags on its website that the two groups committed "100 illegal direct actions" — like blowing up four-wheel drives, destroying the brakes on seafood delivery trucks, and planting firebombs in restaurants — in 2002 alone.[10]

Now, truth on the midway: We're not going to shy away from a checkered history, folks. There have been activists out there protesting animals acts for well over a century. In 1880, Henry Bergh, president of the American Society for the Prevention of Cruelty to Animals, complained about the horse Salamander having to jump through hoops of fire. After P.T. Barnum offered assurances that Salamander performed free of danger, Bergh dropped his campaign to have the act banished. In 1881, a fake story leaked to Denver newspapers alleging that Adam Forepaugh fed stray dogs and cats to circus tigers outraged local Humane Society officials for a time.

In days gone by, some animal abuse did exist under the tents, though not likely to the extent insinuated by today's crusaders. "I have often been asked if the training of animals does not quite generally involve considerable cruelty," wrote William Coup, reflecting on his own experiences as a show owner. "There is nothing essentially cruel in the method of training."

Coup acknowledged at least one painful exception in the example of how horses were handled. He had once witnessed methods "so cruel," he wrote, "that I told the trainer, if he could not invent a method which inflicted less torture, he might quit and we would have the horses sold."[11]

It has always been in the best interest of circus owners to protect rather than abuse their animals. Alf T. Ringling, a great lover of zoos, once talked up a dream of establishing an animal farm in Puerto Rico for the purpose of preserving endangered species. He worried most about the giraffe and the hippopotamus, the two creatures most likely in his view to vanish.[12]

Circuses did once subject animals — at least now and then — to injurious tasks with scarce compassion. Buckles Woodcock recalled the time in 1939 on the Big Show when the elephants were put to work pulling wagons off flat cars. This came about in the wake of the 1938 teamsters' strike, which hastened John Ringling North's resolve to eliminate 300 horses and 100 working men. Until he could purchase enough tractors to pull the wagons off the trains, he turned from horsepower to pachyderm power. It was not a pretty sight at the rail yards. Silver Madison told Woodcock that the elephants were "ill suited for such work, and they stumbled over cross ties and railroad tracks, especially at night."[13] A lot of time was required each day to treat the battered bulls for injuries inflicted by railroad spikes, broken bottles and other sharp objects.

That was yesterday. Circuses and their trainers have cleaned up their act almost beyond reproach. In fact, many circus animals today are better off than they would be in their native wilds or in an open field. Sylvia Zerbini ruefully compares her horses to their country counterparts. Sometimes while driving between towns, she comes upon the sorry sight of anemic-looking animals in pastures who appear to be withering away in the sunlight for lack of care and food.[14]

The late Tommy Hanneford had a charming reply: "We treat them just like you do a human. You get the best food, and of course they work, they do their act, and you know, some of them are like old performers. They love to do their act."

John Pugh wishes that he had health insurance equal to the policies that his own animals enjoy. "My God, I would be so lucky to get the health care that my elephants got. They fly these guys in for endoscope examinations ... of the elephants to see what their metabolism is, when they travel, and everything they said was that the elephants really did enjoy being around the circus."

Pugh remembers the day when some of his bulls, away with another show and with off time, were back. "They drove onto a circus lot last year, the very lot we were on, and the elephants could see out of the truck the circus and they were chirping and hollering like, 'Oh, my God! We're back home again!' It's really sad because of those few people, that thousands are not going to see it."

If a racehorse person, being interviewed on television about the legendary win of Sea Biscuit over War Admiral in the thirties, can say, "Sea Biscuit *wanted it more*," does not a circus owner have equal credibility in conversing on the mental state of his animals and on whether or not they actually enjoy performing for the public?

Circus people believe that a clear majority of Americans still prefer the animals. "A lot of people that come to the circus, if they don't see animals, they're mad," says Norma Cristiani.

"Oh, we're glad to see animals on the circus!" is a recurring message in the e-mails which Walker Brothers receives, according to Dale Longmire. He estimates that those favoring furry traditions are about 65 percent of his customers.

The same reality is advanced by Barbara Byrd of Carson and Barnes. There are circuses without animals on the road, she states, that are bombarded with requests by the public to reinstate them. Those shows get plenty of complaints, too, by disgruntled customers.[15]

Want to know something truly depressing? The jury is still out on this one. PETA may yet win the public relations battle unless enough circus fans rise up and make their voices heard at city hall, in on-line chat rooms, and in letters to editors; most of all, unless they patronize traditional circuses en masse. Unless they scream from sea to shining sea, "We're mad as hell, and we're not going to take it anymore!"

Some insiders will acknowledge constructive changes that have been implemented, partly made in response to the activists. "They made everybody clean up their act," concedes Longmire. "And so they should be proud, but they should leave these people alone and let them make a living." And let today's children enjoy the magical interactions between man and beast that flourish in a circus ring — as they can nowhere else. If a nationwide public backlash against the hypocrites of horror is to occur, its forces need to join ranks sooner rather than later, warns Longmire. "They better start doing it now if they're going to, or it may be too late."

In England, where the animal rights movement began over a century ago, Billy Smart's Circus did away with exotics in 1994, starting a modern-era trend towards the retention of horses and dogs. The presentation of these animals that are considered common pets by man seems less repulsive to PETA and to the public it sways. The Smart's Circus move was made to "bring the circus into the twentieth century."[16]

Newkirk's troupes aim their biggest guns at Ringling-Barnum, an easy, high-visibility target because of its appearances in the largest metropolitan areas where major news coverage is almost guaranteed. Says the less-harassed Barbara Byrd, whose Carson and Barnes usually sticks to smaller towns, when the pickets go after her they're not likely to snare attention from the mainstream media.

PETA filed a lawsuit against Ringling for illegal acts designed to thwart its activities and effectiveness. They accused Kenneth Feld of illegal surveillance of "individuals and entities such as PETA." Sound familiar? Newkirk claimed that Feld hired former CIA operative Clair George (yes, here he is again) to oversee spying and document theft. Under testimony, George admitted to having received paychecks from Ringling in compensation for acts of wiretapping and videotaping activities of PETA and other like-minded groups.[17]

Here's what sadly may happen to all circuses with animals if the new trend is not checked: After suffering years of PETA-funded harassment from all angles, John Pugh in 2004 retired every one of his elephants from the program. And a lot of troupers silently wept. These are tense times for the big trunks. Actually, easier times, for they are doing fewer tricks in the ring these days — everything to minimize the spectacle of excessively difficult-looking stunts. Notes Sylvia Zerbini, circuses can't risk being accused of hurting the animals, so audiences are witnessing a slate of simpler maneuvers. When, for example, the elephants appear, they may do a couple of waltz steps, lay downs and sit ups — just enough action to please an audience — the children in particular — without raising unpleasant suspicions.

Will we ever see another Opal, out of the Polack past, standing on just one foot at the top of a silver pedestal adorned with red stars? Not likely, answers Zerbini, fearing what the public might think.[18]

Next stop for the vanishing menagerie — Pittsburgh?

Getting a little too depressing out here? Yeah, most of the fun stuff is gone, and what a lonely wind it is without banners to blow, pennants to whip. You came out, we take it, to have yourself an old-fashioned holiday under the great American big top. You imagined acres of waving white canvas, exotic sights and sounds and smells. And you had to run into all this nastiness. Okay, you're asking, why stay around for more of the same? Let's go inside that small vinyl top over there all by itself. See it? At least it's off limits to the protesters who are making you feel — we know — like retrograde voyeurs on a medieval midway.

Let's ask the people who work with the animals to speak to you from their own everyday experiences. What a loss it would be if the circus one days leaves them all behind. You've been to the Animal Liberation Sideshow. Don't say you weren't warned.

13

Gunther in Black

In a strange way, throughout the 1990s one of the most interesting acts on the Ringling show never appeared in any of the rings. You'd have to look hard — beyond the immediate spotlights — to find it, so quickly might it pass by whenever they herded the elephants into the arena and around the hippodrome track. Through the spangled shadows raced a riveting, ghost-like figure in black overalls: none other Gunther Gebel Williams. He had never really retired, but was still out there doing one of many things he had been doing with circuses ever since his boyhood days back in Germany.

Gunther in black — he could never quite let go of a passion for animals that had ruled his entire life. Gunther in a chasing procession of bull handlers, at the edge of a ring quietly monitoring the flow of action. Gunther, ex–circus star, maybe still a circus star in his mind and to residual fans in the seats savvy enough to spot his ever-radiant aura.

During twenty-one seasons as Ringling's top headliner, he was up every morning shoveling dirt, inspecting hoofs, feeding tigers — so went the account spun by Gunther himself. "I've never ever expect something from somebody else what I can do, and whenever [I]use a broom or clean out cages, clean behind elephants, [I]don't do it to impress somebody. I do it for animals."[1]

One of the greatest circus animal trainers who ever lived could never really walk away from the big top. And he never did. He had only called it quits, he told the press, so that he could make a classy and graceful exit — before his luster vanished. "I don't want somebody to come up and say, 'Oh, I saw him ten years back and he did much more. It was much better.' I don't want this. You come better, you come older, and to be really good, you have to say good-bye."[2]

So, good-bye, Gunther.

Even if the exit was carefully scripted, the aging Mr. Williams departed on a high note. During his years presenting an impressive variety of exotic creatures, the many accidental bruises, cuts, sprains and fractures that Williams inherited in the line of duty required two dozen surgeries and five hundred stitches. He was said to have appeared before an estimated one hundred million spectators, more, they would claim, than any other performer in any field of live entertainment.

One critic described him "the Nureyev of the circus for balletic acts with ferocious animals." His employers dubbed him at one time or another "Lord of the Rings," "the Caesar of the Circus" and the "Peerless Potentate of Pachydermia!"

Here's what maybe distinguished the man more than anything else: elegance. Everything Gunther did looked so easy that no one could imagine him spending long grueling hours in training sessions on the road or during the off seasons. In the master's words: "You do something, was looking so easy, and never really recognized how much work is behind it, you had to do. Maybe I need longer in end, I like to do everything perfectly."[3]

Two major reasons kept Williams with the circus after retirement: He continued to tutor his son, Mark Gebel, who had taken over the acts; and the show made valuable use of Gunther's celebrated way with the animals as a public relations tool in its war against PETA. So he was given the title, Vice President of Animal Care.

A number of performers who had the good fortune to cross paths with Gunther share fond memories of a soft spoken giant of natural warmth, ready to reciprocate their affection and lend friendly encouragement and support. They also speak of a man who in self-imposed silence had to endure, day in and day out sometimes, the verbal abuse of the activists who disdained everything for which he stood.

Dale Longmire recalls the occasion when he and Ted Polk went down to Venice to visit Gunther, about two years before he died. During their get-together, the three were talking about how rough it was trying to stay in the business against the constant attacks of PETA, PAWS, ALF, ad nauseam.

Gunther shared the pain: "Daly [his nickname for Dale], you know, when I walk these animals from the train to the building, I have had people spit in my face. You know what it is like? You can't do anything about it."

His humane approach to animal training techniques was of no value to the fanatics with their posters, pamphlets, sneers and taunts. In fact, Williams had carried forward the modern-era tradition that omitted the whip, gun, chair and dramatics associated with the fighting demeanor of Clyde Beatty. These gentler methods actually drew from the famed Durovs of pre-Soviet Russia who pioneered the motivating concepts of positive reinforcement over fear of punishment. French trainer Alfred Court excelled in this school, and his acts were acclaimed by U.S. audiences when John Ringling North brought Court to America in 1940.

Robert Mitchell strongly believes that it was Gunther's example, more than the Durov tradition, which transformed circus animal training and presentation in the states. Almost every man who worked in a cage full of lions or tigers during the Gunther Gebel Williams era tried to look and carry on just like *him*.

Williams told *20/20*, "Most important thing in animal training starts with respect. Let him come a little closer.... I try to teach him directly from the beginning. 'I respect you. You be tiger, and I be Gunther.'"

The TV cameras of *20/20* caught the star backstage "chewing out" an elephant named Tody for breaking formation too early. Gunther faced her like an errant child: "Tody! When I say left, left is left!"[4]

Tody, we were told, got the message.

Gunther's most captivating moment during the performance was the quietest one of all. To the sound of his sharp voice commands carried across the rings, the elephants responded by executing their tricks. In his foreign tongue, Gunther seemed to be calling out — Now move! Now stop! Now sit! Now sit up! Now turn!

The elephant was his favorite animal, he said, complimenting its intelligence and sensitivity. One of his bulls, Nellie, had been with him for more than forty years. Now, tell that to the bleeding hearts out there on the picket lines who believe that the natural world is a better option.

Williams one season wore a live leopard around his shoulders like a stole. He once led around the track a "trained" giraffe, which bore no evidence of serious study beyond mastering an even gait for the parade. In his heyday, the GGW acts employed 30 people, 21 elephants, 22 horses, three camels, two llamas, three Shetland ponies and 12 Russian wolfhounds.

When Norma Cristiani was taken backstage by an old childhood friend, Charles Smith (then Ringling's trainmaster) to meet the Great One, the encounter left an indelible memory.

"This is my friend, Norma," said Charles to Gunther. Gunther took Norma's hand and kissed it.

Norma was so mesmerized standing face to face with an idol, she gushed, "Oh, well, I won't ever wash it! You're such a fabulous trainer!"

Williams could not talk long, begging off to check up on a sick tiger. "I have to go over to the cars tonight and stay with it," he explained.

After he was gone, Norma wondered if it was a polite excuse to cut the visit short. No, Norma, it wasn't, Smith reassured her. "Yeah, he'll stay there until that tiger either dies or gets better."[5]

Said daughter Tina Gebel to *20/20*, "If either one of us gets sick, 'Take an aspirin,' my dad always says. But if it's an animal, he'll wait to three, four, five in the morning till a vet comes."[6]

Sylvia Zerbini shared a warm rapport with Gunther, for they both worked horses. When Zerbini, who also did a single trap act, was appearing with her father's circus in Minneapolis, Williams dropped by to see the show, and after the performance he looked up Sylvia to say hello.

"He gave me the biggest hug, and he was just happy to see the horses, how well they worked and how happy they looked. And the only complaint he had was that my trapeze was too high. I'll never forget that."

"It's not necessary, Sylvia," said Gunther, "to work so high."

Replied Sylvia in her artistic defense, "But it is, Gunther. It makes people have a little more respect for me."

Gunther followed Sylvia backstage. "It just made me feel so good, cause he took the time, put his arm around me, walked me to the stables and just talking about the animals, and he loved the way I worked with the elephants with my father.

"It was just something that I always cherish."

Another trainer who drew inspiration in Gunther's company was Svetlana Shamsheeva, who came on the Ringling show from Russia in 1999. She presented house cats, canines and doves, and her techniques also drew upon the Durov tradition that Williams honored. Svetlana grew up in Lipetsk, where she spent many happy hours at the local zoo doing volunteer work. She developed a particular rapport with the Himalayan bears. She learned to perform with one in the zoo, and was spotted by the director of the Rostov Circus on stage, who hired her to work in his show. That led Soyuzgostsirk (the Soviet circus administration) to offer Svetlana a contract. She went on tour throughout Russia and often abroad, winning awards for her riotously amusing dog and cat routines.

During her two years with Ringling's red unit, Svetlana sometimes found herself between shows practicing in one ring while Gunther was working in another. The two grew to share an almost uncanny sense of how each other was able to communicate with their respective animals. To listen to Svetlana try to explain the intricacies of getting through to a cat or a dog is to feel a strange, almost mystical bond at the root of how the most successful trainers manage to gain the incredible cooperation of their charges. It is to feel in the abstract the miracle of friendly persuasion — a mode of rapport well beyond the rote handing out of kibbles to reward a trick correctly done. Getting to that end point is the real mystery to the neophyte.

Svetlana on Gunther: "When he practiced with some animals, I was in the public seats, very interesting to me. And he watches me like I see, and he show me — 'Look! Look at animals!' And see my reaction, and we talk, not English, not French, not Russian. We talk with him like own language. I understand each him move, and he understand each my move when I practice in his cage. He not stay hour or two hours. He stay 15 minutes and like that, very slow applause. Very quiet applause, like that show me and go."

Are you beginning to get a sense of the non-articulate exchanges between trainer and trainee? Okay, this may be easier for you dog owners out there to understand. Svetlana describes some of the things she will do to coax a cat or canine against its nature into some clever positions and movements.

"To push animals — 'Okay, I do it! I do it!' — but he never be happy. In the ring, you all the time can see this right away.... Any kind of animal like it when you start conversation with him.... Believe me, animals like this, like, understand a little bit more and if you need this move more. And this animal do it, and you tell him, 'Oh, you are so good!' He do it. 'You good!' You touch and you give him treats. Believe me, he like this like human. Same system."

That special bond to which our Svetlana alludes can become so complex that a subsequent trainer, trying to take over working the same animals, may be unable to get them to do the same routines long-perfected and performed. Svetlana tells the sad story of Russian liberty horse trainer Alexei Sokolov, who retired, hoping that his daughter would carry on the act.

"She can't take one trick from her father. Not talent."

Sokolov ended up outside the ring on a pension, his horses in disarray, a very unhappy man. He told Svetlana, "I'm die and my act is finished."

The average citizen among us up or down the block can teach a dog to perform a few simple functions. Stand still. Sit up. Go fetch the paper. Any of these taught actions, of course — if PETA is to be taken seriously — are just cause for the confiscation of all imprisoned pets in every household on the grounds that they are being forced against their natures to do things they otherwise would not do. (We will refrain from discussing acts of violence committed between totally free non-performing animals in the state of nature.) Indeed, even seeing-eye dogs, according to Newkirk's soldiers, should be rescued from the blind, liberated and returned to — well, did they say where?

Svetlana shares more trade secrets. I encourage you to reach between the words. There, in the mist, you might gain a fleeting sense of a trainer's emotional approach based on patience and body language — and maybe something spiritual, too.

"Need to teach dog and cat very good with each other. Take time. Second, need to teach dog not go four legs. Front legs in the ring, back legs on ring curb. Funny physical position for quickly move. For cats, it's difficult. This position for sit-down is like a jockey. How I do it? I needed hours and maybe years to explain this. Ten years, one assistant work with me, and I can't explain to these people right now, this point, this point, this point. Really inside you.

"You can't learn this," she says.

She prides herself on presenting high-breed pedigreed Persian cats. They pose a bigger challenge. "What is Persian? Big flossy cat. Never jump. Just sit down in beautiful position."

Regular non-exotic house cats don't stand a chance with this trainer. Why? They are too easy to teach. Says Svetlana, "Persian cats not ready to move. Just lay down."

Why hire those pretty do-nothings in the first place?

She relishes an Olympic challenge. And all for mere esthetics.

"Because it's beautiful, for Persia."

Her furry primas are kept, zoo-speak, in some tony touring quarters in the circus back-yard. They enjoy their own little front yard play and relaxation area which extends out from a 47-foot trailer under their own little "special tent." All in all, 12 cats, 12 dogs and 45 birds share the space, and they eat haute cuisine, courtesy of their master's generous allowances. "I buy food from my own money. Best food available in U.S."

The rewards for a good job done in the spotlights are one more perk for the pampered superpup or celebrity cat. "For each trick, like cheese. This dog like liver. Some dogs like pork, some corn."

The ways and moods of Gunther and Svetlana deepen our understanding of a rare unspoken dialogue we share with our four-legged friends on this enormously complex planet. Is the anti-circus iceberg starting to melt? Even animal rights activist Kiley-Worthington was moved to acknowledge what a profound role the circus can play in educating future generations to the efficacy of our relationship to animals. Ms. Kiley-Worthington? If you please...

"One of the startling things about circuses is the way the wildest creatures learn to understand a wide range of human words; and how it's keepers and trainers are responsive to the animal's own language.... I don't want a world in which there is total apartheid between animals and men.... I would like a true new circus in which animals communicate and display the astonishing capacities we are only just learning about."[7]

Paul Binder is nearly beside himself in disbelief over the PETA-driven campaign and its supporters to render the circus a menagerie-free zone. "This notion that animals and people are supposed to be kept separate is the most ridiculous thing I've ever heard. The entire country was an agrarian country made up of people who lived with animals all the time. And nowadays, if they don't know that they *can* or believe that they can, then we're lost. We're suddenly not participating with nature at all."

PETA came ominously close to scoring a major public relations victory when Mark Oliver Gebel was put on trial, December 2001, in the county of Santa Clara (California) for allegedly beating an elephant named Asia with a bull hook that left a scar and traces of blood. According to witnesses, they saw Gebel shouting at the elephants to move on before he struck Asia. The prosecution rested its case largely on a video frame secretly shot by animal activist Pat Cuviello. Christine Franco, supervising director of the Humane Society of Santa Clara Valley, claimed that she saw a "nickel sized red spot behind Asia's left front leg."[8]

The circus haters, taking advantage of the national attention, decried the use of circus animals, claiming that animals are chained for long hours at a time. And when the public has gone home, they are abused in secret.

Under closer courtroom inspection, the incriminating photo turned out to be not very reliable. The defense rebutted it with testimony of its own from an expert who swore that he could not detect signs of skin abrasion or blood. As Bob Mitchell puts it, the whole sorry affair was a legalized witch hunt. "Upon occasion I had done the exact same thing with elephants. There is no way that a red spot can be left."

A little ketchup, maybe, from an overly zealous city hall stalker or a virtuous vandal?

Gebel was acquitted after five days of testimony, and only two hours of jury deliberation. To toast the defense verdict, Kenneth Feld took out a full-page ad in the *New York Times*, "An Open Letter to Animal Rights Groups." In it, he accused his enemies of "creating politically motivated lawsuits, violent and sexually titillating ads, publicity stunts," all aimed, he claimed, at trashing "responsible circuses, aquariums and zoos."[9]

Feld moved ahead in fearless fashion, if anything, more determined than ever to flaunt his traveling zoo. He pushed humorous images of the animal stars in billboard and newspaper ads. "SIX TON DIVA," headlined one. Another screamed out, "I AM TIGER. HEAR ME ROAR." In yet another, a lion's mouth was wide open with wry jungle ferocity. The amusing text read, "FLUFFY? YES. CUDDLY? NOT SO MUCH."

Were the Feld flacks taunting PETA to bring on more of the same? Nobody could accuse this producer of striking his menagerie and heading up to Montreal for a Cirque-directed conversion to a three-ring ballet on wires without animals.

Questionable corporate conduct aside, this big show boss deserves credit for having done probably more than any other circus owner to educate the public on how circus animals can be ideally cared for, and on what a fine purpose circuses can serve by exposing children to these exotic creatures from all four corners of the shrinking globe.

Feld's pre-show outdoor livestock display area is a class act all in itself, complete with pull-out information cards on the history, behavior and lore of each specimen. Spectators observe the animals close up, where they live, how they are fed and cleaned. They can watch lazy lions lounging like spoiled zombies in a fairly spacious fenced-in compound, and they might wonder, is that all these brutes ever really wanted? They can feed peanuts, still, to the big bulls. Can reach out and touch a trunk.

The show distributes fliers and pamphlets explaining its position. One, titled "Caring for the animals at the greatest show on earth," stresses how the circus complies with laws, and expounds on the many activities in which Ringling is engaged from charitable donations to world wildlife funds and outreach programs. "For more than 120 years, Ringling Bros. and Barnum & Bailey Circus has been at the forefront of animal welfare. In fact, working with the United States Department of Agriculture, we help set the standards for animal care and maintenance."

To a newsman for a Dan Rather CBS-TV "Eye on America" segment, Kenneth Feld stated, "The first people who tell me that there should be no animals in the show will be the public when they don't show up."[10]

Sylvia Zerbini finds the whole situation highly depressing. She is not sure about the future. She believes that protests are in order when animals anywhere are being mistreated. At the same time, she speaks with persuasive respect for what her employer had done to ensure the best possible living and work conditions of its four-legged stars, and she believes it unfair and unfortunate that Ringling is taking most of the heat from animals rights groups. Kenneth Feld, according to Zerbini, spares no expenses for the animals. Whatever is needed — however many carrots, however many apples — they get, no questions asked. In fact, she states that they are actually treated better than the people.

And still, the anti-circus activists are never satisfied, and they seem to be winning, as Zerbini sees it. She believes they have brainwashed the public and may be causing it to turn away from the traditional program. Especially disheartening to her is the way a chain of PETA antagonists will throw inflammatory handouts in people's faces, accusing them of patronizing a business that exploits animals. She has lived through their negative impact on circus attendance.[11]

Likewise, Svetlana Shamsheeva can not say enough for the show's unstinting attention to the care and feeding of animals. For example, the Feld organization offered to fund a costly and very chancy operation for one of Svetlana's dogs, plagued with an intestinal blockage. Its life was saved. Having performed in many rings far and wide, when it comes to animal welfare, Svetlana, profusely grateful, calls Ringling "the best circus in the world."

Gunther Gebel Williams died of cancer at the age of 66, only four months before Mark Gebel's trial in 2001. At least the father was spared the anguish of having to watch his own son and protégé unjustly accused of animal abuse in a California courtroom. On top of Gunther's grave in Venice, Florida, a chronically angry animal-rights do gooder, Rachelle Thorne, decked out in a red leotard, black shoes and black cape, danced like the devil to celebrate the animal trainer's passing. Thorne was soon arrested on a number of municipal infractions including obstruction by disguise — a first for the Memorial Park Cemetery, a private property which had never needed police intervention until that eerie episode.[12]

Poor Gunther. Or lucky Gunther? Had he lived a lot longer and had his vision not weakened so, causing him to have to wear unflattering glasses (not the mark of a glamorous sawdust hero, and perhaps the real reason why he had retired so early), would he today be presenting, by whispered voice commands alone, a ring full of flossy Persian house cats?

14

There Go the Shriners

The same dark season when John Ringling North struck down the Ringling tents for good, the indoor Shrine field began to unravel. That year, the grand marshal of the California temples ousted Polack Brothers over a long-festering feud about magazine ad revenue sharing and other nasty money matters that can reduce grown men to playground bullies. Louis Stern, who with his late partner Irving J. Polack had raised Shrine circus standards nationwide to a new level of artistic supremacy, was banished from Shrinedom in the Golden State. And the temples were thereafter prohibited from publicly advertising their show dates. Now, they could only sell tickets to their members.

Stern, who had rightfully billed his product as "a sparkling jewel among circuses of the world," was out on the street in his biggest market—"the mother lode," as Robert Mitchell puts it. Without the Shiners, Polack Brothers proceeded down a slow unflattering slide into meandering mediocrity. As the years went by, Mitchell believes that Stern, who retired at the end of the 1976 tour, either lost the will for excellence or lost the wherewithal to compete against a newer generation of indoor producers bent on snatching up as many of his dates as they could. The younger, more aggressive producers (most of them ex-performers) cut corners and outbid each other mercilessly in their quest to wrap their seasons up in Shrine security blankets. The programs they brought in at a lower cost to the sponsors were naturally inferior to what Polack had delivered in its prime. Nor did the Shrine temples help their cause any by pitting one producer against the other in a game of diminishing returns. Didn't somebody say you get what you pay for?

Today, rummaging through the remains, you'll find plenty of half-baked indoor shows. Typically, they offer haphazard entertainment scuffed up on the edges with pony rides, bungee bounces, photo ops and peanut pitches. They are usually assembled on the quick and cheap to satisfy a local sponsor or entertain a crowd hustled in through the mass distribution of free kids' tickets. Ever been to one?

In 1981, Tommy Hanneford, producing for the Shriners down in New Orleans, presented a roster of acts and parades that we would call barely above adequate. By then, you see, the John Ringling North format which Hanneford, like most of the others, followed (four production numbers spread throughout the program) had run its course and then some. The frugal Hanneford trappings were more like token attributes to approximate the Ringling style. There were enough good acts, yes, to satisfy, period. During the same sinking era, perhaps the most generous of all Shrine producers was ex–wire walker Hubert Castle. He usually came through in a big way, once joking, "My acts make more than I do annually."

Soon enough, Castle would be gone from the road. Hanneford still powered on, probably producing the largest number of annual Shrine dates. And there were other retired performers such as wild animal trainer Tarzan Zerbini, gradually taking over for the departing Hubert Castle. They all fought for Shrine contracts, and, together, their competitive fury amounted to a fair assault on circus art. Even Hanneford himself, who once rode horses in the center ring following in the legendary footsteps of his famous uncle Poodles, now resorted to carnie concessions. He was so good at merchandising, the *Circus Report* one season hailed him as the producer who had sold the most pony rides during a single date. Now was *that* something to celebrate?

The Shriners once gave America some of its best circus experiences, thanks, at least, to Stern and Polack in their early years; thanks also to Orrin Davenport, who commandeered a yearly string of winter stops laden with Ringling's top stars, set to the music of the big top maestro himself, Merle Evans. In fact, so prominent were the Davenport programs that Art Concello, managing for Ringling, faced nagging complaints from his ticket holders: "I already saw that act last winter at the Shrine Circus!" Thus, for a brief bitter period covered by the trades, an effort of John North's to prohibit, by implied threat of termination, his headline attractions from going out on the off-season with the Shriners and Davenport backfired into a public relations nightmare.

In the modern era, the erosion of Shrine circus respectability is partly a byproduct of dwindling membership rosters. Fewer and fewer of the temples are even producing any more. In their heyday, almost every one of the country's 190 Shrine clubs sponsored an annual circus. Now, the number is about half that, and it continues to drop.

The changing cultural and political landscape is another reason why you are less likely to see a Shrine circus in your home town. The animal rights activists along with a more demanding public conditioned by Cirque showmanship have caused more and more temples to shy away from all the work it takes to haggle out a contract with a promoter, secure an arena, set up a ticket-sales campaign and then sell its members and the general public on the idea of patronizing a show.

Worst of all, PETA makes life as publicly embarrassing as possible for any Shrine temple that dares to condone animal stars. In fact, *if* PETA-posted claims on its Web site of alleged criminal conduct on the part of certain Shriners are to be taken seriously, then a number of potentates and their colleagues come off looking like a brigade of greedy, pleasure seeking operators. They are cited by PETA's peeping police blotter toms for chasing after fast bucks and for doing things that men have been known to do on the off hours such as tossing huge tips at lap dancers. Kid stuff, that? Okay, then how about the alleged embezzlement of large sums of money for their own personal cookie jars not marked "Children's hospital fund"?[1]

The Shiners are also known, not so gratefully within the community of big tops, for pitting the producers against each other in the vicious biding wars I've already mentioned. It's the producer who offers to supply the acts, the ringmaster and — since we are speaking in the abysmally music-deficient present tense — a cd player. Also, it's the producer who gets to bring in the carnival games. The sharing of profits for these extras can be factored into negotiations, and this can make things ugly.

"A sparkling jewel among circuses of the world"? Not so anymore.

Beware of the show cluttered with pony rides, bungee bounces, and too many hula-hoop acts in the performance. Not the sign of artistic prosperity.

According to South Carolina–based Sherwood Kaiser, who serves as president of the American Shrine Circus Association, many promoters take advantage of the temples.

How's that?

He explains that when certain producers (whom he declines to name) bring in a bad show, audiences are turned off, and attendance drops sharply the following year.

Circus producers and their industry sympathizers see it a little differently outside of South Carolina. They point out that the temples are largely to blame for threadbare programs against which they rail. The Shriners force the bids down so low, that the promoter who agrees to the chintzy terms can ill-afford to bring in a first-rate roster on a Shrine-string budget. Sometimes, you won't even get a semi-respectable second-tier slate of acts. The Shriners end up with egg on their faces. The customers walk away mildly disgusted, less willing to tolerate mediocrity in the name of charity. And the promoters are cursed for being—well, promoters.

Let's bring out veteran Norma Cristiani, whose sawdust travails give her a big picture view. Norma?

"For a long time, everybody was fighting for a contract from the Shrine, and they were undercutting each other all the time. And it finally got to the point where the show suffered. They could offer only so much. Naturally, the first thing they do is cut the show down."

Another big ticket item that pits temple against producer are the lucrative concessions. In other words, who gets to pop the corn and sell it for a fortune? And how do the potentates behave on this issue, Norma?

"Their own worst enemies. First of all, they took over the concessions. That's where the circus owners make the most money, not always in tickets."

Time to ask a defining question here: Just who bears the big top burden in this finger-pointing tiff? Since the Shriners are the ones who control the kitty, they wield the most leverage. So as we see it, the Shriners must bear the burden of proof. They are the actual circus producers. It is they who hire and use the promoters as talent agents to secure and present the acts. And, as circus producers, the Shriners aren't doing a very good job lately—if artistic impression means anything.

Bob Mitchell unspins it for us. (This is not for the children.) He refers to the temples and the circus promoters, respectively, as "pimps and whores." Is there a more stinging insult to be paid to the at-each-other's-throats collaborators of your typical modern-day Shrine circus?

A number of better seasons back, Tommy Hanneford, on his way to Detroit with what many considered one of the finest shows he'd ever arranged, did not realize that his good work would have no bearing on a contract for the following season. Unbeknownst to Tommy, the next year's date had already been nailed down by a rival producer. Most thought that Tommy's competition had passed a nice wad of greenbacks under a table before inking a secret agreement.

The Shriners may claim to be only the Shriners and the victims of unscrupulous circus lords on the run. Don't believe a word. Once again, it is the Shriners—and not the Tommy Hannefords or the Tarzan Zerbinis who grovel for their business—who control the purse strings, who decide when and where circus day will occur. They decide who will furnish the acts and the "music." In fact, it's theoretically possible for a temple to demand a live band if it wishes to front something other than piped-in '80s disco. And temples can, and have, held out for this type of act or that type, or for less of this and more of the other.

It's a depressing tango of sinking outcomes, and it adds little to our American circus world, already under siege from PETA's anger and Cirque's dominance. The mediocre shows that are cobbled together to satisfy the terms of a contract — or a throng of comped-in moppets and their parents — do little in this artistically elevated age to advance the sagging image of U.S. circus fare. Saddest of all is to see the Shriners descended ingloriously to the level of carnie merchants on a par with Canada's Dick Garden.

It was Mr. Garden, some of you may recall, who brought us, years back, the infamous Toby Tyler Circus under canvas. It came complete with portable seats that collapsed during a New York date, injuring many and leading to legislation in the state of New York outlawing such shoddy accommodations.[2] It is the same Mr. Garden who now, working the free kids ticket angle to the hilt, can pull into San Francisco's Cow Palace during a Saturday matinee more people than will sometimes turn out to see Ringling. The same Garden who clutters the arena with carnival attractions and then, for a program, fills it with acts boringly devoid of merit. And if that is not reason enough to consider an early exit, there is the loudly amplified recorded music, causing some of us to flee this circus from hell in the name of eardrum preservation. Back to the desperate thirties, such inferior producers take us. Back to the tawdry conditions that Louis Stern and Irving Polack said no to when they resolved to travel a higher road, beginning the journey in Sacramento, California, for the Ben Ali Shrine Temple.

In that same city exactly 70 years later, the same temple puts out the sort of rambling hit or miss programs you are likely to see around a ring or three in these threadbare times. Only now, the messy festivities are staged under a make-do tent rather than indoors. Why? Either because that's how Cirque du Soleil does it, or the local arena wants too much money.

In 2005, Ben Ali made known a bold decision to forgo all animal acts. Said the temple's recorder, Jim Culver, they were open to trying out a more modern approach on their audience base. Others within the organization hinted at pressures from PETA as being the actual motivator for this policy turnabout. Culver admitted that attendance had been declining for Shrine circuses in general. And he stressed his own temple's desire to try a different format. The no-animals trend throughout a growing number of shows did play an influence, he conceded.[3]

The Sacramento Shriners put their circus under canvas — that is, most of it. The rigging for a flying trapeze act was placed outdoors, and on a mildly rain day, the flyers did not fly either before or after the under-canvas portion of the program. The rigging evidently could not be hung in the tent, in which three small rings overlapped each other at the edges in order to fit the restricted space. Also in there, worse still, were precariously flimsy structures of portable bleacher seats with narrow foot rests. Wet from raindrops, they did not invite customer confidence. The memory of those failed Toby Tyler seats came eerily to mind. Customer alert: The producer's name is Jordan International; bring your own chair in the event you can't land a first row seat and do not have the mountain-climbing gear to scale the "grandstands."

During the extended pre-show, a gaggle of Shrine clowns did their homemade gags and raised a few lazy laughs; a local group of 20 young female gymnasts from a private school clad in matching outfits gave a demonstration of repetitive acrobatics. It went on and on and on, causing a non-local to wonder if the school itself was a sponsor exacting a payoff. During the humdrum exercise, a man went around the house peddling three-dollar tickets for children wishing to have their photo taken with "Spiderman" during the intermission. There were pony rides in one of the rings, a bungee bounce in another.

Finally, the marching Shriners entered, as usual, and the actual program commenced.

Yet, as is the case with many such second-rate companies, there were a few redeeming moments, headed surely by the showmanly juggling of Justino. Working with a face-attached mike, Justino talks to the audience while he keeps balls and clubs impressively airborne, dashing at hurricane speed from one side of the tent to the other. Almost as impressive are the three Alvarado Sisters, executing a terrific three-person statue act. Alex, a solo clown from eastern Europe, is one very funny fellow, especially when he avoids audience volunteers (or shills) and refrains from imitating David Larible. The Hartzells, too, working with a complex cross-exchange bow and arrow relay system (after a labored workup), deliver a knockout climactic trick.

This "no-animal" circus, unfortunately, consists mostly of not one or two, but three hula-hoop performers; of an apprentice juggler nowhere near ready for even this so-so program; of yet another motorcycle-up-the-inclined-wire turn; and more of those awfully nice, eager-to-amuse clowns who also happen to be the sponsors. Surely the program's biggest surprise is an act so rousingly rambunctious, so full of old tent-show oomph that once lit up our pre-PC rings, that it sends the entire audience sailing off into a whirl of shared delight: *Moore's Amazing Mongrels.* Up and down slides, through barrels, over barrels, bouncing on hind legs, dancing, jumping ropes, standing tall with front paws extended, running around the ring, balancing on wires — a wonderful mess of star mutts barking and leaping over each other and kicking up a doggy cavalcade of amusing mischief. All of them found and rescued from animal shelters.

The earthiness of Moore's act reminds us of what the modern era has lost. It reminds us of how the great American big top used to put audience and animals into glorious contact with each other. Of how much richer the show was in its embracement of the "human condition," which, after all, is related to the "animal condition." For both, do they not, share the same planet? And both have interacted from time immemorial in many remarkable ways.

Wait a moment: did they not tell us beforehand that the show would have no animals in it? When pressed to explain the surprising change of heart, Jim Culver clarified that what he actually meant by "no animals" were no *exotic* animals. The thinking seems to be that if it's an animal that lots of people relate to in their everyday lives (unlike bears or tigers), it's okay.

On their way out, patrons were handed circus survey cards and invited to critique the performance. Ben Ali's 2005 edition was termed a big patron pleaser, in the words of the temple's Garry Darrell, who tallied the results of the survey. However, between sixty to seventy percent of the respondents, according to Darrell, expressed a wish to see the wild animal acts return. But they also said that not having the animals would not dissuade them from returning the next year.

Perhaps the Shriners in Sacramento are now deferring to political correctness, Darrell grants, disclosing that the temple is not at this time inclined to bring back exotic animals in future lineups. Besides, Darrell stresses, they got a great response without the jungle stars.[4]

Perhaps these carnieized shows are what a growing segment of the Shrine customer base actually desires — a ride aboard a live animal; a photo of your little darling with a clown or a comic book hero; long, drawn out intermissions allowing ample time for mother nature and more junk food; a few really good acts to make all the concessions and rides seem worthwhile at reasonably affordable prices; and all of it rendered in a party atmosphere.

And yet. And yet. Fewer and fewer people, they tell us, are showing up to Shrine circus parties. And fewer and fewer temples are even bothering to put them on these days. In both Oakland and San Francisco, where the old Polack show played eleven-day engagements to good houses each year through the booming fifties, there are no such events any more. Instead, what you might find in those venues, if anything, are the paltry offerings of an indoor promoter preceded by the saturation of free kids' tickets, and with virtually no advance publicity. So, unless you have a child who comes home with a coupon, you might never even know that a circus came to the local civic auditorium at all.

"Here come the elephants!" cried the ringmaster at the Oakland auditorium, minus the arena-filling crowds that once patronized the Polack show when it played there. In marched a clown leading a midget "pachyderm," actually a little mutt dressed up to resemble one.

And here come the Russians!

What a far cry from the American circus tours of the famed Moscow Circus back in the sixties. Today in the states, immigrating Soviet jugglers, acrobats and aerialists are on their own, freelancing their skills to American promoters like Cornell "Tuffy" Nicholas, son of Count, who operates what he calls the Moscow State Circus. While most of the artists on his roster do, indeed, hail from Mother Russia, there are others, like Ricardo's "Strata Cycle," that do not. Missing, too, are the lavish orchestra, the bareback-riding ballerinas and the dancing bears we thrilled to when the Moscow Circus from the old Soviet Union toured America in the sixties. In their place? More bungee jumps, photo ops and concession pitches before, during and after the regular program.

Nowadays, the Americanized Russians are out there on the indoor midway, too, selling coloring books, lifting children on and off ponies, applying clown makeup. Being cool about it all in an adaptable, American kind of way. And, in-between, chatting on cell phones to whomever. Tis a pity that we get them in such an unflattering showcase.

After the fall of the Soviet Union in around 1989, a steady influx of Soviet circus stars has given new life to American big tops. Many of them are grateful for the work, because the generous, life-long securities they enjoyed under the old Soviet system are no longer to be had. "Circus in Russia, not so great now," says teeterboard titan Andrey Kovgar, who should know. "Not at all like it was in Soviet Union."

Many of the sixty-plus arenas built to house permanent year-round circus troupes under the old USSR have been converted to casinos or flea markets or night clubs. In the golden age of Soyuzgostsirk (circuses of the Soviet Union), an artist, whether she worked or not, counted on full pay year-round and a generous pension after only 20 years in spangles.

What can the same artist rely on over there these days? "Just a couple of days a week."

The Russian clown Vallery rues the depressing turn of events. He points out that today in Moscow, you need a lot of "inside connections" in order to stay even semi-employed. Without those contacts, unless you are willing to deliver pizza on the side you are better off taking your talents elsewhere. And the U.S. is one of the biggest elsewheres on earth, even if its shows are currently in a state of expedient disarray.

"The circus I remember, it's never going to happen again, I think. That circus, when the music starts, lights off, it was just incredible."

In Valery's words, only "some people who have money and some positions, they could

A gift of political history: Top Russian acts once confined to the Soviet Union, such as the Doveicko troupe seen here, circa 1979, now appear frequently in U.S. circuses (author collection).

survive there, but talented people like me, I just do my work, whatever. If you like it, take me. But I'm not going to bend over, so let me go."

Svetlana Shamsheeva has endured the discomforts and hassles of trouping, Yankee style, compared to far cushier times in her native land. Here, she is forced to travel more frequently to play dozens of cities during a typical season. "In Russia, you worked one month minimum. Here, two days, three days sometimes."

She once counted on regular paychecks back home, no matter what. Now, when she works for the reorganized Russian Circus organization, Rozco (which receives some funding from the government — Putin is believed to be quite sympathetic), Svetlana is on her own every day she is not performing. "If you don't work, no pay."

Nor will they welcome her back, like they used to, with open arms and an open company checkbook. If Svetlana dares to return with more animals than she left with, she risks being told, "You know, we now cut any kind of dog act for less animals because we don't have money for feeding animals in Rozco, and we cut for each act."

At the sight of an expanded kennel, they will lay down a depressing message: "And you bring three more dogs? No, you can't!"

In America, yes, you can; that is if you can land a contract to cover the cost for the additional pet food and backyard accommodations necessary to pass muster with the USDA. Even then, you too might have to do a little "cherry pie" (pre-show concession stuff, etc.) to pay for the extra expenses.

Take a kind glance beyond the carnival that precedes the Moscow State Circus, as promoted and produced by Nicholas, and you might be glad that your kid got hold of a ticket and talked you into taking him. Sure, you had to pay $22.00 for your own seat. That's still a fair bargain these days. And once the real program gets underway — late, as always, due to you know what — there are those highly inventive Russians who, when in top form, can make you forget that you wandered into just another concession pit.

At precisely sixteen minutes after the show was advertised to start, it starts. Or does it? No, the finely attired ringmaster is making a pitch for coloring books.

"Look inside the cover for a free ride during intermission!"

After a drawn-out sale to extract more pre-show revenue, the performance finally begins. Down an inclined cable slides a woman hanging by an iron jaw. Clowns toss large balls back and forth between themselves and the audience. Five girls work hula-hoops in a flashy manner. A clown and a small dog (the one who poses as the elephant upon entering) are fast and funny. One lone contortionist, sporting terrifically unusual moves, somehow manages to make her act more interesting than what two or three contortionists usually accomplish together. Clowns pile up onto each other in zany acrobatic pyramids. One of them does a wacky quasi-strip.

A few humdrum offerings follow — an audience dance competition; a motorbike rider up a steeply inclined wire. And then comes a half-hour intermission. Patrons pour out onto the track, which has once again been turned into a mini midway, for more of the same.

The second half begins with a cleanly pleasing four-women aerial ballet. After this, comes a most clever novelty: toy clown robots cavort and dance, bounce across a trampoline and walk a rolling globe. "They" turn out to be just "him," a solo joey shedding a two-clown costume. And he proceeds to work a rousing trampoline-springboard routine.

The show reaches a heart-pounding conclusion with complex ensemble jump roping. These Russians bring off an astonishing array of maneuvers. One jumps on his hands, another on his back. The only thing they don't do through the whirling ropes shall remain tactfully undescribed. Three of them wind up stacked atop each other in a spectacular jumping formation, and they don't miss a beat. Ladies and gentlemen, *that's* the best jump rope number I've ever seen.

The audiences is nearly on its feet in delight. What a rousing climax to a grab bag of a show — so fly-by-nightish, in fact, that it does not sell a program magazine and is unable, when contacted, to provide the names of its own performers. How ironic for an outfit whose

Web site touts their celebrated origin. Still, in some ways the Florida-based version of the Moscow State Circus proved to be much more pleasingly to the point than what the Shriners up in Sacramento offered earlier the same spring.

Total performance time: 1 hour, 28 minutes (exactly what is promised on the show's Web site). Total time selling concessions and rides from the moment the performance was scheduled to start: 50 minutes. If a single child with two parents attended, the total cost, excluding all the extra rides and concessions, would come to $44.00. See why Mr. Nicholas does not need a sponsor?

How to catch this show or others like it that shun costly advertising in favor of the free kids' ticket angle? If you don't have children of a certain age, your best bet might be to buy yourself a cheap house trailer and park it on or near your local civic auditorium. Oh, yes, live in it, too. That way, when a stream of mobile homes roll onto the parking lot next to the arena and you notice colorful objects being unloaded, you'll know the Russians have arrived.

For myself, it's hard not to recall a superior season before bungee bounces and hula-hoops, when top flight circus artists from Europe thrived in great shows that took out splashy newspaper ads to herald their arrival. When a real live band was there to underscore and pace the excitement. When artistic pride filled the air. When Polack Brothers Shrine Circus was, truly, "a sparkling jewel among circuses of the world."

15

And the Band Did Not Play On

Just a thousand more fanfares — only a thousand, Maestro, if you please!

Time to talk about music, or the diminishing lack thereof. You may have heard that long ago in a distant galaxy, circus parades filled up Main Street to capture the attention of prospective customers. Massive uniformed bands atop gilded wagons of red and gold blasted forth through cities large and small, thrilling the ears of onlookers with marches, waltzes, polkas and more marches. A steam calliope on its own added a more melodious shrill to the grand processional advertisement. Altogether, the hearty music makers whetted the public's appetite to hear — we repeat, *hear* — more of the same. So out to the big top went entranced spectators following after the boom boom boom and the blast blast blast of excitement and glamour on the move.

Out they went, to a grassy green lot where white canvas billowed in the wind, where flags waved a welcome to circus-goers, where a calliope sweetened the air and barkers shouted, "This way to the big show!"

Out they went to see Robbins Brothers or Sells-Floto, John Robinson or Barnum & Bailey, not just to watch daredevils flirting with death in perilous midair dives or crashing blindfolded through paper hoops over cantering horses. Out they went to hear the circus band play.

The band was always there. Ten men or thirty. Brassy and loud. Sometimes off tune or naggingly out of sync. Yet always a vital force of fiery brass and shimmering piccolo, pushing the official program of displays rhythmically forward. Tumblers were drummed down the track. Circling ponies, serenaded with waltzes. Crashing cymbals and blaring trumpets marked the dramatic high points. And on the midway around the sideshows, African American musicians spiced up the atmosphere with minstrel and ragtime tempos.

During the long-ago "golden age" beginning in the 1880s, it has been recorded by master observers that a band would employ as many as thirty or more "windjammers" (in the parlance of musicians). These robust practitioners put out more brassy blasts, more tuba honks and piccolo chirps in a single day than most musicians today produce in a week. Those were the days before union-organizer James C. Petrillo came on the scene with a vengeance. Petrillo would love to have billed per toot, blast or drum roll, so insistent was he on generous compensation. By badgering the musicians to go on strike and hold out for more money, he turned them into one of the highest paid groups on a reformed circus lot.

Before Mr. Petrillo put an end to expedient wages, music rang richly and freely through big tops coast to coast. Just as they were starting to rival Barnum & Bailey, the Ringling brothers hired famed Italian coronet soloist Signor A. Liberatti, to compose for and direct thirty men in uniform. The expansionist-minded Liberate one season threw in 20 more players to beef up pre-show concerts. Yes, fifty altogether. Early arrivals enjoyed at least an extra half-hour of music and, then, a good two hours more once the show got underway. And once it did, the thirty Ringling regulars tore through a tempo-rich roller coaster of jigs and gallops, marches and fox trots and tangos, cascading from cue to cue. And not once, wrote Earl Chapin May, "missing an impressive chord or crash, never growing weary of well-doing during four hectic hours each circus day."[1]

If some of the acts did not live up to customer expectations, the jaded circus-goer could still sit back and listen to a rambunctiously varied concert under waving canvas peaks.

Music was so critical to circus day that James A. Bailey built a forty-horse bandwagon, the Two Hemispheres, for the 1903 tour. The epic, moving showpiece cost him $4,400. A monster tableau on wheels flanked by lions and bears, each of its sides bore carved continents and the coats of arms of many nations. The red driver's seat was supported by gold-leafed eagles, the rear, by life-sized wooden elephants. Behind and above a team of forty horses rode the grand military band led by professor Carl Clair. Thousands crowded the streets of America to behold an irresistible combustion of music invading the morning air. This complicated and time-consuming free daily ritual constituted possibly the most expensive advertising campaign ever undertaken in show business.

The great tradition of circus music began its last epochal ride in the spring of 1919 at Madison Square Garden, when a young Merle Evans, who would occupy the conductor's post for fifty seasons (never *once* calling in sick), first led the Ringling windjammers. His coronet and overall direction, favoring oomph to the max, so excited a jubilant John Ringling that the circus king, shortly after the first show, told the new bandleader, "Young man, you nearly blew me out of my box!"

Now, to be more than spinmasters about this, let's get real about what the revered Merle Evans did and did not achieve during his legendary career. There are many opinions concerning the quality of his music that range from very good to very unimpressed. In fact, measured in terms of quality alone, the sound he directed was all over the lot. This had much to do with the actual talents of the musicians he was able to recruit and keep. A circus music man had to endure all sorts of distractions and ordeals — mud and rain, bumpy railroad rides in cramped quarters, oven-like heat under canvas on summer afternoons, freezing nights under canvas through spring and fall. So the variable Evans sound gave you the circus from A to Z, from mud to magnificence depending on many factors working together or at odds on a given day — the temperature inside the tent, the mood of the men on the bandstand, unexpected delays during the performance, and the Maestro's own state of engagement.

Listening to old tapes of Merle Evans conducting (and this generally applies to other tent show bands of the time as well), some of the variable music symbolizes the rough and tumble world of the big tops. You can almost hear echoes of windstorms and roaring tigers back of the tent. You'll see acrobats spinning and prop hands rushing about, weeds around the ring curbs, aerialists flying high, muddy potholes on the midway. It's all there from the grit to the glory. It was never smooth sailing on the Ringling bandstand.

From sloppy to forceful, in tune or out, somehow Evans evoked in hurly burly fashion the sounds of the living big top. Was he so sensitive to everything around him that a

Bandmaster for all seasons — Merle Evans, the "Toscanini of the big tops" (courtesy of the John and Mable Ringling Museum of Art, Tibbals Digital Collection).

perfectly rendered score would somehow betray the messier realities of circus life? A crash of cymbals and a bolero of escalating drum rolls — and there comes a line of acrobats flip flopping across sawdust. A slackening off of the tempo into ragged indifference, and where are we now? A glitch in the program? A fatigue in the ranks? Then a sudden rush of harmonious musicianship through a beguiling beguine, and the sound is back in surging focus.

Evans played pop tunes of the day, and he threw in the classics now and then for rest-ful counterpoint. Pep and pizzazz. Rueful or reaching. He laced them all together with elab-orate fanfares piled one upon another. In 1931, he spirited his men in red through *170* cue changes.

The sound that Evans and other conductors like him brought to the big tops was a rough collage of sunshine and shadow, of astonishing artistry and rowdy buffoonery, of madness and magic and spangled imperfection. Under a tent, you never got studio-quality music through and through, although sometimes, you got more: While lovely Gina Lipowska danced in the center of circling horses, the band sank into the lyrical "Stranger in Paradise." While a five-act display of aerialists took to the upper reaches of the tent, Evans scored their exploits with an unforgettable string of tunes modern and old —"Way Down Dixie," "Mr. Sandman," "Hoop De Do," "Swanee," "Say Hallelujah!" and "Who." The season was 1955, the last one led by Evans under canvas. Listening to a tape of the band diving into a speeded up "Mr. Sandman," you can almost hear cables squeaking against pulleys lifting the artists aloft. And from that urgent refrain forward, Evans and his men ride the music with smooth crackling gusto.

Remarkably, although he favored uptempo most of the way, the maestro was unafraid to cast quiet attention onto an act he deemed worthy of such. He seemed to know that, without contrast, the score would become stale and redundant. When hand balancer Alfred Burton appeared late in the 1955 performance (working atop a tall ladder, building his ele-vation on a series of blocks tossed to him from his father on the ground), Evans slowed down the band into a restful rendition of Karl King's "A Night in June." He seemed to be telling the audience, "Relax, folks, sit back and savor the subtler shades of this equilibris-tic feat."

Actually, the slow decline of live music around a ring had begun thirteen years earlier when Petrillo's musician's union struck the Ringling show during its spring opening in New York City. John Ringling North refused their demands. The men walked. This marked an early warning bell for what was to come. North was young and cavalier and smarting over a union trying to tell the paternalistic Ringling firm how to compensate its employees. He told Mr. Petrillo in effect where he could go. The musicians went there too.

And how did the show go on without them? North went up town, purchased a record player, rounded up a slew of 78s at local music stores and scored the program the new elec-tronic way. Even the elephants, that season cast in the George Balanchine–choreographed "Ballet of the Elephants," managed to stay reasonably on pointe. North and company tracked down a record that sounded very similar to the circus polka which Igor Stravinsky had com-posed for the bash. The big bulls in their water-proof tutus did not notice the difference. Prodded by the tap of bull hooks against their skin, they danced emphatically on. Well, they were not yet unionized — or represented by the Animal Liberation Sideshow.

Mr. North was only making do the Sparks Circus way. You will remember that, back in 1931, Sparks did not go out with a band but opted to play phonograph records through a primitive sound system. According to suspiciously affirmative reports in *Billboard* (a weekly trade journal that rarely criticized circuses), audiences either could not tell the difference or actually preferred the modern method, for it gave them a score produced by the playing of records that were made by forty to sixty studio musicians under ideal recording conditions. The swinging ladder routine that season on the Sparks show was "well timed and cued by mechanical loud speakers," reported *Billboard's* man on the scene. "It seems strange at first to hear music emanating from somewhere, with traditional bandsmen invisible, but as sequence progresses, one gets accustomed to the 'canned' idea."[2]

The first circus not to include live musicians did not return to the road the following season or any season thereafter.

Boasted Johnny North to the press eleven years later, the striking musicians were not hurting business at all and the show might not even carry them in future seasons![3] Was he ahead of his time in 1942? The next year, when North got kicked out of management and replaced by his cousin, Robert Ringling, Petrillo's demands were finally and fully met. The musicians returned to the tent.

We could argue that North was flat wrong. Here on the midway of circus wisdom, the sight and sound of a real circus band is too powerful a force to dismiss in haste. You let those music makers go at your own risk, Mr. Sparks. And when you haul in your Circuit City substitutes, no matter how sophisticated, you rob the show of the very element that has made it so excitingly irresistible: it is live. At each and every performance, what we see is happening in real time. In the flesh. The wire walker up there will have to prove himself once again, or else. So, too, the trampolinist or the equestrian. We are witnesses to a spectacle that is not born of illusion. We know that anything can happen at any unexpected turn—a flyer falling out of rhythm, a juggler blowing a constellation of clubs. Or they could all land their tricks, every one of them, producing a stream of dazzling achievement moment by moment.

So, too, the force of the band. Both forms of expression, music and motion, are merged in rare harmony. The overall effect can thrill in ways unobtainable through electronic collaboration. You need to have all the positions occupied by living, breathing souls in the here and now. Try to imagine watching a circus unfold in total silence. How long would you hang around?

"A circus is the other half of a human equation which we cannot separate from the souls born with us," wrote Earl Chapin May. Comparing live to canned music, Mr. May argued, "It is not and will not, until life is no longer, duplicate or approach those raptures and rhapsodies radiating from a bandstand filled with genuine Windjammers."[4]

When the band is there, one group of living artists are working with another group. Each feeds off the other in ways virtually impossible to achieve when the music is pre-recorded and piped in. A good band can make each act more continually interesting. It does this with the appropriate cue changes, with drums rolls and fanfares to bring on the performers, highlight their best tricks, and send them off in glory. Shifting tempos and tones serve to accentuate the different parts of a routine. Effectively rendered, they are the hallmark of a top director contributing to the ever-changing, ever-advancing stream of big top action.

All circus programs to begin with are what? A miscellaneous collection of acts under contract to perform their routines in a program yet to be laid out. How do you bind them together to create the impression of a single aesthetic force? Costumes are nice to look at. Lights provide more visual candy, too. Still, without music, the costumes remain as silent as the artists inside them, and the lighting effects can only illuminate actions that seem strangely lifeless until the band strikes up, the ringmaster blows his whistle, and the parade spills out onto the track.

Turn the music off? Tell me what you see.

I see a failed enterprise making do on the cheap. An enterprise that sold its soul for more profit, or out of desperation to stay on the road another chancy season.

The circus is the most real of all entertainments. It can ill-afford to shortchange one of its most vital features. Who else waved a maestro's sure baton in modern times? Boom Boom Browning, who had beat a drum for Merle Evans, beat up a breezy, more timely sound under the Clyde Beatty tent in 1961 working with about only ten musicians. Henry Keyes, who conducted for Polack Brothers among many shows, was one of the best. So was Clement Tocca, about as good a circus music man for the modern era as they made. Tocca played for the Shrine circuses generously produced by Hubert Castle. At the Portland date in 1981, Tocca delivered a score that held its own against top-drawer circus acts booked by Mr. Castle for the beautiful three-ring spread.

Another bandleader of high repute was Jack Cervone. He fronted a terrific group for the high-flying Dobritch International Circus in 1968 at Los Angeles. That same musically memorable year, Sid Kellner's short lived, phone-room infamous James Brothers Circus, which had gone out under its first tent, made a lively splash turning out a dandy roster of good acts, paced with punch and zing by Tom Fewless leading only seven talented men.

When Cliff Vargas became serious about turning himself into a tanbark titan, he fumbled through a number of understaffed bands (one centered around an accordionist) until landing dead center in the realm of modern-day jazz. Steve Carroll, in 1981 when Circus Vargas was starting to take off, came in with jazz-intense charts. Trouble was, some of the acts looked totally ignored by Carroll's non-stop enthusiasm for cool cool cool. This was not circus scoring as much as a sidebar jam session full of hot stuff, but now and then oblivious to the action down below.

A few Vargas bandleaders later, and we got the gifted James Miller. He revealed as much passion for jazz as did Carroll, but he knew when to share it and when the show needed something else. With Miller on the bandstand, Circus Vargas rose to its highest level of showmanship. During the peak years in the mid-eighties (and thanks to modern amplification, reducing drastically the number of musicians needed to produce large sounds), Miller crafted a forceful, straight ahead score born of contemporary rhythms. And he did it working with as few as six other guys in uniform. His contribution to the show in 1985 followed the eclectic Merle Evans approach. Musically, Miller moved back and forth between upbeat show tunes, old familiar circus gallops, and, with increasing focus and frequency into the second half of the program, excellent jazz arrangements. Some of his music called to mind a Buddy Rich big band gig, it was that up to the moment and that sharply delivered. Altogether, Miller's musical input gave the show the sort of dramatic variety in pacing and tone that makes for great circus. The Vargas sound was so compelling, it would even influence how Ringling set its own programs to music.

And how sadly short lived it was. Mr. Vargas began recording the entire score and playing it back to audiences once the show finished its early spring dates on prime Los Angeles locations. And then, only a season or three after that, the band no longer played at all. Circus fans, naturally crestfallen, nonetheless talked up how remarkably good the taped music sounded, and it did, to be fair. Yes, for a recording, it did. A live drummer for a time hung around to add drum rolls at key points. But the music did not have quite the same impact as when it was played live. As when we could see the musicians up there over the performers' entrance, working in the present tense, fanfaring and crescendoing away act by act by act. There is no evidence whatsoever that Mr. Vargas gave his operation a box-office boost by abandoning the live music which had marked his fleeting heyday years. If the fans told him how clever he was in reproducing it through modern technology, he was not well flattered. Within another "canned" season, we were listening to a now-familiar score. And a dream of classic excitement was already slipping away.

Cliff Vargas proved to a lot of show owners, each facing their own economic down-turns, that you could supply the music without the musicians and stay in business longer than Sparks did after it switched to phonograph records. And so, following the Vargas example, other shows began downsizing their bands, or outsourcing to electronics. This risky trend is not recommended for producers who yearn for long careers on today's polyester trails.

You the customer can now step up to a red wagon, purchase a center ring seat and count on never seeing a single musician. You can look forward to a more artificial experience. No circus has suffered so in the quality and appeal of its program as has Carson and Barnes. Maybe it has something to do with a missing bandstand? Here is a show still stocked with plenty of animals (and not just gratefully energetic dogs rescued from pounds); a show still with three active rings; still with a big old-fashioned tent; still setting up in a new town every day. A circus so wonderfully old hat that it cries out for the band it no longer has. Cries out!

Dory Miller, who with his wife Isla opened their first tent show in 1937, loved the down-to-earth nature of the business. He loved the nomadic, new-town-every-day existence. And he kept his old-time five-ring show going to his last day.

He considered himself to be the luckiest man who ever lived because of his passion for circus, so claims his daughter, Barbara, who, with her husband, Gary, continues to keep Carson and Barnes on the road against daunting odds. Dory's entire life rotated around his one abiding love. Even when the family went out on a vacation, usually they traveled to see another circus.

Hands-on Dory never tired of waking up each day to a new lot. And in each new crowd that showed up on the midway, he took heart. Whether the tents went up on green grass or over mud and slush, he enjoyed it all. And he enjoyed watching the show whether there were two hundred or two thousand souls in the seats.[5]

Here's what Dory told me long ago: "No one is disappointed in the a.m. Horses ... camels ... zebras. Truck after truck ... weirdoes and characters around. It can only happen at a circus. We all have so much ham in us whether we know it or not. The circus is a home — a different world. Circus people are dedicated regardless of the conditions."

Carson and Barnes usually put out a more than decent sound. Some years, the sound was top-drawer from first fanfare to last blast. For example, on the Del Rio lot in 1974, Jim Gibson was there on the bandstand, he and only four other players. Surprisingly, they registered a clean, proficient sound, good enough to help make circus day in Del Rio one to remember. Move ahead by four seasons when Perry Johnson, now leading Dory's music makers with a group of ten — count 'em, ten — favored a wonderful old-fashioned style. The whole program zipped and galloped and flew ahead at a sparkling gait, thanks in large part to the band.

Young Wally Eastwood, a tremendous kid juggler of hurricane-paced executions, lit up the mud-splattered tent. Equestrienne Luciana Loyal rode with her usual passionate flair. The long mount was thrown by seventeen nimble pachyderms under the sure control of Donald Carr and John Carroll. There was a charming aerial ballet, "A Touch of Hollywood," and a festive spec, "The Reign of Caesar." A youngster barely in his teens, billed as "Martino," executed a perfect headstand on a swinging trapeze. The Rodogels and the Morales flew upwards off springboards through twisting formations, landing on perfectly formed pyramids. Missing from the program that day were two of the three flying trapeze troupes and a solo high-wire act, out due to a tornado two days before in Johnson. Still, there was plenty to watch and hear. Johnson's men kept the hurly-burly stream of action in rousing form, and the entire thing clocked in at an efficient one hour and thirty-five minutes. Brevity is a virtue under the tents.

By the time that Carson and Barnes got to Half Moon Bay in Northern California thirteen years later, the same story could not be told. Now, yes, even Mr. Miller had settled ignobly (final taps, please) on a taped music substitute. Doing it the Vargas way was one thing and maybe an acceptable alternative to no band at all. Doing it the Dory Miller way was not, period. The man, it seems, was electronically tone deaf.

The pre-recorded C&B *original* "score" proved to be an embarrassing excuse for music, truly an insult to the ear of anyone brought up on Western culture. So bad, in fact, that it sounded more like a budget soundtrack produced on somebody's home computer. The show sold out one of its most valuable assets when it gave up the band. Actually, the Millers would have done their audiences a favor by at least doing it the old John Strong way with a phonograph player and records of familiar tunes. As it was, the hapless program lacked the sure-fire push of a good live band that can makes things seem whole and connected, paced and complete.

Through the tone-dead nineties Carson and Barnes trouped, along with a growing number of other circuses no longer committed to carrying many if any musicians. A pity. And today, thank you Sparks and thank you, Mr. Vargas, we have arrived — the sale of earplugs on the midway should make somebody a small fortune — in CD hell.

There are some modest exceptions that veer clear of the all-night discotheque: Give Jim Judkins a modest hand for having wisely invested in the creation of an original score, taped for his Circus Chimera when he took it out in 1998. In its inaugural tour, at least Chimera's music sounded distinctly Cirque-like (as opposed to generic whatever). Not so, most other CD-dependent shows. Today's producers show little regard for the musical content of the performance. Even the late Irvin Feld fought a nasty battle with the musician's union to cut the Ringling band down to around 14 men. Now, what's left of them is fairly hidden from view at the end of the arena in a caged enclosure. And the music they make, now and then noteworthy, yet bears no distinctive style of its own beyond pushing out a strong, modern-sounding beat.

On the CD front elsewhere, the acts usually show up with their own pre-recorded music, and typically the promoter or show owner will acquiesce, glad to be free of having to score the action. As a result, circus programs in these tuneless times sound more like those top 40 disco stations on remote programming which adhere to a single style with droning repetition. We are no longer at the circus. We're at a bar on the Castro or a strip club in Atlanta.

During the Shrine Circus in Sacramento, produced by Jordan International, the CDs mostly shot out Vegas or MTV, except when Moore's mongrels came on; then, we heard old Broadway. What a quaint relief, however temporary, to the reigning banalities of all the rest. And even if the music was not all that bad, the brain-dead delivery system and the random order in which the CDs were played fostered the impression of something patched together on the fly. There is little unity here, certainly not of the sort that a James Miller could provide were he totally in charge, with real musicians working inside the tent. Jordan International has no score. It has no band. And by handing over the music to the acts themselves, Jordan International sounds and therefore also looks more disjointed than it need be — as if a juke box randomly programmed by customers were playing away in the background.

The Moscow State Circus, on balance, sets its best Russian acts to some very good music.

Keeping music excitingly alive in the present: the Big Apple Circus band. *Top row, left to right:* **Kaoru Ishibashi, Sam Wiley, Jr., Neal Persiani, Jason Brown, Bob Suttmann.** *Front row, left to right:* **Kristine Norter, Director Rob Slowik, Johnny Hodges (courtesy of Bertrand Guay/Big Apple Circus).**

At Oakland, the sound system was atypically fine for such an operation. The New Cole Circus, now pitching its tents for the next chapter, has gradually phased out the band, too. It was one of the things in which owner John Pugh took pride before deciding that he could no longer afford to take pride. Now on New Cole, one guy sits above the performers' entrance, where once a whole band gathered. He works a CD player and adds touches of live instrumentation from a keyboard. The guy's name is Leigh Ketchum, the lone survivor of the older bolder circus, previously known as Clyde Beatty–Cole Brothers.

There was a marvelous moment on New Cole, 2005 edition, when Ketchum played "On a Wonderful Day Like Today" at the top of the second half of the program. And what a wonderful day it was during the brief rendition. Maybe he was playing over or along with a pre-recorded CD. But playing he was, and suddenly a light was turned back on, and all at once there was a living breathing soul on the bandstand, a one-person infusion of the unmistakable spark that once, multiplied many times over, enlivened circus shows like no electronic gadgetry ever could or ever will.

So, what about it, Barbara Byrd: will we ever again hear the real thing under *your* tent?

On the run, she admits that the band was one of the few things she hated giving up. If she could *afford* the musicians, she insists, she would love to have a band again. But she won't settle for a watered down combo like an organ and trumpet. At least seven or eight pieces, and for that, warns Barbara Byrd, the economics are prohibitive.[6]

Well, there you have it — or don't have it anymore. Another once-great tradition on American circus lots that is vanishing, vanishing, vanishing before our eyes and ears.

Not quite. There's yet another tent show about to make an appearance on our disappearing midway. It's a surprise charmer called the Big Apple Circus, and it comes with live musicians. Now tuning up; you won't want to miss it. Yes! Yes! There's more ahead, and only a few features away!

So now, while we're waiting, what say we bring out Merle Evans and his famous concert circus band for just one more encore? Maestro, if you please, would you favor the crowd with a rousing reprieve of your music for "the little aerial" as you call it, starting off with "Way Down Dixie in New Orleans," rolling upward after the aerialists through your zippy "Mister Sandman," then into "Hoop De Do" and "Swanne," "Sing Hallelujah!" and "Who?" Please let the people hear that gloriously tattered world of wonders on parade — like a wind of ghostly windjammers from a thousand circus days past whistling through canvas peaks on blaring brass, chirping piccolo and crashing cymbals — cheering the great circus stars on...

16

Minus Clyde Beatty

Once upon a circus, the show slipped into town at dawn. A train of silver and red or yellow and blue screeched and rattled and jolted onto a rusty siding next to the old ice house as early morning darkness gave way to fresh daylight. Then it lurched to a shuddering halt. Men and boys stood by, all eyes on the unfolding ritual. Soon, brightly painted wagons were being pulled across flatcars from one to the next until they reached the runs, down which they rolled, each rumbling onto the pavement below with a thud. Horses and tractors pulled them off to begin the long slow haul to a vacant field a mile or so away.

At 6:58 a.m., while local resident Gene Darnell, owner of the Circus Café, looked on along with a gaggle of other early-rising circus fans from as far away as Forestville, Pee Wee poked his trunk through an opening in a stock car, ready to join his cohorts on their walk to the grounds. Two minutes later, Bill, an elephant handler, asked a towner standing by, "Is this Santa Rosa?"[1]

Down at the fairgrounds, more boys stood around shivering in the promising darkness, gazing up Bennett Avenue for a glimpse of the first wagon to arrive — for something bearing the words "Clyde Beatty Circus."

We had been waiting weeks for this day to come. Newspaper ads promised "Clyde Beatty in Person!" Large letters spelled out "BRILLIANTLY NEW SUPER SPECTACLES ... A GIGANTIC RAILROAD SHOW—NEW STAR STUDDED EDITION ... SCORES OF INCREDIBLE IMPORTATIONS ... THE RETURN OF THE SAFARI!" Most of all, the fearless wild animal trainer himself would this day be making an appearance in our own town. Would this be one of those days we read about in the newspapers when the daring subjugator of jungle beasts might have to fight off their unexpected fury?

At last, action on Bennett Avenue. Barely visible a block or so away, poking through the mist, were four long slender white poles extending in front of a wagon coming our way. Circus day was here!

The wagon turned at the corner on the east edge of the fairgrounds and rolled onto a vacant field of grass and weed across the street. One after another in slow steady succession, more wagons and trucks followed. Then came a parade of elephants. And within an hour or so, as the squinting sun widened its glow, huge rolls of canvas were being dropped onto the field. Kids were signing on — yours truly, one of them — to help with the setup for a free ticket to the show. We climbed into roofless wagons filled with hastily loaded bars and

Crowds once gathered at dawn to watch circus trains unload (courtesy of the John and Mable Ringling Museum of Art, Tibbals Digital Collection).

frames that would make up the portable seating. We were instructed to lift the heavy pieces up and over the edge of the wagon, then let them fall freely to the earth below. Quickly, the steel sections were grabbed by others and dragged across the dirt to various locations; over these sections the canvas for the big top would soon be spread.

We were a part of a nomadic community, helping to unpack its mysterious properties and spread them over common ground — over a place where, on other days, boys rode their bikes through weeds or batted balls and ran around make-do bases. Sections of dingy white canvas were now being laid out over the skeleton seat frames like parts of a puzzle. And circus men were showing us how to lace them all together. The steady clanking of stakes being driven deep into the soil gave the whole thing a wonderful music. A personable young man in a white short-sleeved shirt who supervised the canvas gangs shared some insider information with the boys. "We never wait to put up the tent. Even if we arrive in a city a day early, I say, up it goes. You can never count on the weather, so it's always best to get the canvas in the air and guyed out as soon as possible."

Everything that circus people said sounded fascinating. They had secrets. They knew how it all worked. Their strange and glamorous world would be here for one day only, then gone. In less than twenty-four hours, gone. That made them and their ways even more interesting. It felt almost as if, before the first show in Santa Rosa was close to beginning, they were already in their minds moving on to the next town. Arriving and leaving at the same time. All around them, you could almost hear a gigantic circus clock ticking impatiently away.

Back in those great one-day circus days when you rose at the crack of dawn to take the whole thing in, you got to watch the guts of it all take shape before your eyes. What could they hide? They needed your help. They had too much to worry about to be bothered by niceties. This was about as real as entertainment could get: a familiar hometown field upon which the tents rose; the sharp smells of exotic creatures from far-off lands; the entrance of weird-looking characters onto the grounds — sideshow curiosities? The gruff-voiced men who moved the wagons and drove the stakes. And the dazzling daredevils in their bright shiny tights who flew through the big top while a brass band played. All of life was there that day, from the seedy to the sublime and back again. The circus had everything.

Norma Cristiani, when for a season she was out booking dates for Carson and Barnes, at one presentational pitch to a prospective sponsor was confronted by an older gentlemen, his arm raised.

"Could I ask you a question, ma'am?"

"Yes, sir," replied the circus agent, eager to sign the sponsor.

"Do you have any of those hootchie kootchie dancers?"

Replied Norma, intent on shooting down any concerns about old-fashioned impropriety, "Oh, no. We don't have that anymore."

To which the visibly disappointed questioner remarked, "Well, I don't know why. That's where I got my sex education!"[2]

The world of the old American circus encompassed a whole lot of reality, folks — from a hootchie kootchie sideshow containing girlie revues, gambling and other assorted adult diversions, to the Olympian acrobats in the main tent twisting and twirling through space under a star-studded canvas sky. It was one heck of an operation that employed the most diverse work force you'd find anywhere. Single trap star La Norma, who flew over the center ring, also appeared, per contract, like virtually all the other performers, as a costumed character in the elaborate production parades. "There was not one minute for you to sit down and get bored." She loved the camaraderie: "We were all nationalities, we were from all over the world, and still we felt like we were all together."

All classes and conditions, colors and creeds. A universe of languages between them. And, together, they packed into one glamorous day a veritable cross-section of life's many moods, challenges, and wonders. Step right up before the big show begins! We're going to bring out one of the most amazing things you'll ever see! Right here, and it's free!

By noon, Santa Rosa sunlight was in full bloom. The Clyde Beatty tents were up and stretched out, swaying in a gentle breeze, their flags and pennants galloping gaily.

Inside a small menagerie top, a modest sampling of four-legged creatures stood passively on display behind rope barriers. Inside the big top, men were still pounding stakes into the ground, attaching cables from here to there, pulling more stuff out of boxes. It looked like they hadn't got everything up quite on time. In fact, that afternoon the *Santa Rosa Press Democrat* reported that the show's arrival down at the ice house had been delayed by an hour on account of the circus train's being shuttled onto a spur track at the Bellevue Avenue crossing to make way for the south-bound "Eureka Flyer."[3]

I purchased my own copy of the official circus program magazine. It was printed in bright red, black and yellow. On the cover, the snarling face of a vicious tiger with a menacing red tongue nearly leapt off the page. To his side, there was a picture in black and white

Behind the bravado, a young Clyde Beatty co-authored *The Big Cage* (Circus World Museum, Baraboo, Wisconsin).

of Clyde Beatty, dressed in a white hunter's outfit and thick leather gloves. He held a chair between his hands, a whip in one and a gun in the other. A handsome smile on his face revealed pure fearless confidence.

"Clyde Beatty cordially welcomes you to his 1952 edition of the Clyde Beatty Circus and his gigantic railroad show!" rang the ringmaster. "And now ... the show is on!"

Con Colleano combined a flair for dancing with rare acrobatics on the low wire (Circus World Museum, Baraboo, Wisconsin).

First to appear before the large crowd filling up most of the seats were the Voises and the Franks over the end rings, doing fast and funny maneuvers on aerial bars. Then came a bunch of clowns down the track, each one showing off some goofy costume or amusing contraption. Next, while Zeakolen Walsh appeared in the center ring cage with "the jungle's most deadly enemies" — a tiger and elephant — in the side rings, Joan Lewis and Milonga Cline presented ponies and pachyderms together, drilling them through nicely paced maneuvers.

Mr. Beatty's show had plenty of ponies on the bill — ponies who pranced on their own in patterned circles; ponies who appeared with horses and elephants and dogs.

And it had lots of neat human acts from Brazil, from Spain and Denmark, and from France. The George Hanneford Family with Kay Frances kicked up the sawdust with bare-back riding. Two men from Sweden, the Ericksons, did a hard-to-believe head-to-head stand separated by three rubber balls! From the golden age of the twenties came the still flamboyant Con Colleano on the low wire, in a solo display titled "A Bit of Old Madrid." Right here in Santa Rosa, here he was — the first performer ever to execute the extremely tricky *forward* somersault. Colleano took the center ring, bolero style, with the fierce passion of a victorious toreador dancing for his life. Moving rhythmically back and forth, he held the audience spellbound with his movements. Now he faced his greatest trick, that legendary forward spin that you might never see attempted unless you saw the great Colleano. Now still and tense on the silver strand he stood, testing his balance, testing the tension, pushing down slightly and bobbing a little to the left, a little to the right. Pausing and thinking the whole thing out in his mind before he did it. Testing some more. Growing suddenly still. Settling his mind, and finally throwing himself upward. Around he went, landing perfectly on his feet! The crowd cheered.

Display four was headlined "Special Barbette Production." One girl over each ring did the loop-the-loop on a single trapeze that turned 360-degree revolutions. This was one of the ensemble numbers devised by the famed director of circus spectacles, whom Mr. Beatty had hired that year to bring additional glamour to his program. The magazine played up Barbette's importance, telling us how he had come to the United States at the start of World War II from Europe after captivating circus crowds abroad with a most unusual single trapeze routine.

Earlier that spring when Barbette showed up at the Clyde Beatty winter quarters in Deming, New Mexico, to prepare the program, he scavenged through old costumes in search of materials for rescue and reuse. He found none. When Mr. Beatty happened to notice his new director tossing the old out into the garbage, he gasped.

"Oh, but Barbette," sighed the boss. "Shouldn't we save them for a rainy day?"

Snapped Barbette, "It will never rain *that* hard, Mr. Beatty."[4]

The women assigned to perform in Barbette's productions were called "the Beattyettes." Their work took the show off the grass and weed into the air. Their most spectacular effect had them whirling by their teeth from a carousel rigging, each with large butterfly wings attached to her arms. In another turn, the Beattyettes swung from swinging ladders and Spanish webs.

Barbette brought touches of ballet to the big top, not unlike other visionary souls before him who had sought to exploit circus art by making more elaborate use of its aerial apparatus. To spin his art in the world that traveled by night, sometimes through mud and rain and cold, Barbette had to endure what no Nijinsky ever would put up with. Endure he did, tolerating the physical hardships, the bum lots and the depressing inconsistencies of circus trouping with a rare sense of humor.

After the loop-the-loop girls, the joeys returned to stir up more amusing mischief on the ground. Then the ringmaster's whistle blew: "Presenting performers and animals from all parts of the world — *Return of the Safari!*"

The big spec circled the track. Our mayor-turned-guest-circus-celebrity, Alex McCluskey, rode atop the elephant "Big Sid." The drama was building, for we knew — everyone in that tent knew — that the next act to appear would be the star himself. Santa

Beatty in action fostered the dramatic imagery of dangerous interactions between man and beast (Circus World Museum, Baraboo, Wisconsin).

Rosa was about to face a hazardous encounter between man and beast. Would the darker forces of nature tear the script up and do the unthinkable? What might happen today?

A great fanfare from the band, and then, "Attention, please! Will the vendors kindly refrain from selling and please retire from the seats! Thank you. Now, ladies and gentlemen, boys and girls, owing to the dangerous nature of the next act which we are about to present, we ask that you please do not move upon the track or in front of the big steel arena. Calling your attention now to the large arena. We take pride in presenting to you the largest group of jungle-bred trained wild animals ever presented in one arena! Royal Bengal tigers, trained and now presented by a man who has starred in movies, on tv, and now on the radio. And here he is in person, the world's greatest wild animal trainer — the one and only *Clyde Beatty*!"[5]

Clad in safari gear, our hero dashed courageously into the tent, took a brief and serious bow, slipped into a small intermediary safety cage, shut the door behind him, then let himself into the big arena. Now, at last, the man whose daring exploits we had read so much about was face to face with the unknown. Would the tigers obey his commands or break rank and cause trouble? Beatty's cracking whip pierced the air. Gun shots went off. You got the scariest feeling that anything could happen in there. The band pounded out crescendo after crescendo, then charged into the slower, quieter beat of Ravel's haunting *Boléro*. It felt as if you were inside the cage with Clyde Beatty, glued to his every move. Waiting and watching and waiting. The tigers jumped from one pedestal to another. Would one of them lurch off course and attack another, or go after the trainer himself? Respect and obedience. Man and brute in a fierce tango of wills, the one ordering the other to sit up and lay down, to jump through hoops and over bars, to roll over and move this way, then that way, and then back onto the pedestal over there.

No matter what was happening inside the big cage, Clyde Beatty made it feel like the most important thing in the world. Would he get out alive? Would he keep his animals moving on cue, himself out of danger? It went by so fast. Now the trainer was sending his charges out of the ring through tunnel-like chutes of steel that ran across the track and out the tent into the backyard. The band was playing a furious march. Cymbals were crashing. The crowd was applauding. We were free once again from the horrors that lurk below the surface of not just the circus, but of a more dangerous world that exists beyond big tops and gaudy parades.

The steel arena was now being flung apart into sections and dropped to the ground to make way for the next acts. In the outer rings, the Al Hanel troupe and the Joannides Duo performed stunts on casting bars and slack wires.

Clyde Beatty — before there were no more Clyde Beattys — symbolized the raw masculine nature of the circus world. A world that pitched tough realities to the public. Beatty's act taught us that beyond and below the dancing bravado of a Con Colleano or the silly antics of a buffoon, life can be savagely competitive, a cruel proposition of conquer or be conquered. The circus once embraced it all.

At night, the performance looked even better, for the lighting effects, not noticeable in the afternoon when the sun escaped through the white canvas, made Barbette's butterfly ladies more angelic to behold as they spread their pink wings on high and whirled in flaring circles. But the tent was colder inside, and the hard wood planks at the far ends, where a kid with a free work pass was sent to sit, felt harder in the chilly night air.

During the show, as one act ended you could watch the roustabouts removing its gear from the tent, and you could feel in a lonely deserted way that they were already packing up the circus to move it as quickly as they could back to the rails down by the ice house on Sebastopol Avenue where empty flat cars waited to be loaded. Waited to be moved out onto the mainline and pulled down the tracks to tomorrow's town. By the time the "thrilling flying Voises" and the "famous flying Harolds" flew and the grand finale filled the track, the tent was nearly empty of its magical artifacts.

Circus day had come and gone — from the darkness of a late May dawn to the deepening of the next night. And the Clyde Beatty Gigantic Railroad Show would never return to Santa Rosa. The next day, on our bicycles, we rode out to the fairgrounds to study the impressions in the dirt left by yesterday's rings. There, faintly visible, were three circles fading away. There, too, were peanut shells and ticket stubs, the remains of a dream world forever on the move, arriving and leaving almost at the same time.

Within four years, the Clyde Beatty show was bankrupt. Mr. Beatty, they will tell you, was never much of an owner, though it had always been his dream to run his own show. Maybe he was too nice a fellow. He continued to do his act with the circus after it was reorganized and went out under the management of ex-Ringling tent show executives Frank McClosky and Walter Kernan. Beatty worked in the ring nearly to his death, of cancer, at the age of 62 in 1965. Dave Hoover, a Beatty cage hand who took over the act, could not duplicate the drama.

Society was tiring of the circus's more demonic side, of whips and guns and chairs.

Tiring of daredevils risking lives on free-swinging bars and high-wire walks. Of freaks on the midway who actually enjoyed being paid to be gawked at. Of hard splintery planks in chilly unheated tents. Society no longer quite dug the rough-and-tumble panorama that once invaded a town at dawn.

Fast forward by fifty-three seasons — from Santa Rosa, California, to Willow Grove, Pennsylvania. To a circus which once bore the name Clyde Beatty. To a grassy green lot buried back of a sterile complex of modern shopping malls in a Philadelphia suburb. To a faceless midway ominously vacant of people not long before a circus is scheduled to begin. There are, this day, no sideshow banner lines. Instead, on the side of a truck are the words "SEE SPIDER MAN LIVE IN PERSON! SUPERHEROES OF THE CIRCUS."

Inside a six-pole vinyl tent, the performance area is designated by ring curbs having been reconfigured to form, strangely, a rectangular area. The seats are all folding chairs of the kind we see in school cafeterias. During the sadly lackluster program that follows, not one horse or elephant, not one tiger or lion appears. Nor does a band play. Welcome to New Cole Circus minus Clyde Beatty. On display are all the artistic compromises which owner John Pugh believes he had to make in order to stay out on the road and out of the nasty radar of the animal-rights groups. After years of facing their wrath at city hall and finding fewer places willing to host his enterprise, Pugh retired the elephants and tigers.

Circus day never looked quote so uneventful as it did here in Willow Grove.

Pugh started out in English hall shows. After coming to the states, intent on trouping for a couple of seasons on the Clyde Beatty Circus, he was talked into staying on. From acrobat to manager he advanced. In 1981, he bought a half interest in the show. Now he is its sole owner, and he is one of the nicest guys in the business. Maybe too nice. He loves standing outside the front door after the crowd is letting out and overhearing people say things like, "I liked this show better than Ringling!"

And here he is in the year 2005, still trying to entertain an increasingly picky public with a scaled-down program designed to keep PETA safely at bay. "You don't enter a Rolls Royce in a demolition derby."

Besides, maintains the now abolitionist-minded Mr. Pugh, having just broken the animal habit, his marketing department has been nagging him for a long time to come up with something really novel that would tease fresh interest from city editors and television news directors. "You can say, 'Well, we've got a great teeterboard act,' but, 'You had a teeterboard act last year.' 'But this is a new one!'"

So, in addition to shunning big exotics from the lineup, John Pugh secured the rights (not nearly as exclusive as he thought) from Marvel Comics to incorporate the figures of Spider-Man and the Hulk into the 2005 program. (We also saw Spider-Man on Jordan International and the Moscow State Circus). Twelve days into the season, Pugh was high on the public response. "The reaction we have on the show this year is tremendous.... We just played Myrtle Beach yesterday, and we rocked 'em there. The people just loved the show. Almost three-quarter of an hour late last night to get the people in."

On the Willow Grove lot a few months later, New Cole is not exactly rocking the thousand or so souls who turn out to fill up about one-third of the folding chairs. Had Harold Ronk attended, he might have ruefully wondered, where did it all go? No band. No animals other than some house cats. Not even a *single ring*! Yes, where did it go?

It went the way of the last century. The name Clyde Beatty attached to this strange makeover would look fairly meaningless given Pugh's exercise in self-annihilation. Still, a name is a name and Clyde Beatty stood for high drama under the big top. So, then, using the same reductive reasoning, why not the New Ringling Circus? Why not Cirque du Apple?

Inside Mr. Pugh's new ringless tent as it appears in Willow Grove, what he offers the customer is a shadow of past glories. Give him the benefit of a new emerging vision. He threw together a number of well-meaning novelty acts in keeping with the "theatre type circus" which he is high on these days. Pugh says he now favors more of a variety show that will provide "a pretty nice place for all the kids to go," like a Disney theme park experience. This, though, is Disney according to John Pugh and his not-too-resourceful director-stager of the moment, ex-aerialist Elvin Bale. What they have cooked up is a rather bland substitute for what they previously produced using real elephants and real rings and, not too long ago, real musicians. The two men may need to engage a first-rate theatrical director or somebody from Cirque if they intend to convert over to the variety show format under canvas and still draw crowds. Otherwise, their own Pittsburgh may not be far up the road.

Not all is lost here. As with almost any circus, Pugh and Bale put out a few star turns to appease if not fully impress the modest Willow Grove crowd. We're thinking the crack Yan Dong Chinese Acrobatic Troupe, who offer a terrifically fast hat juggling exchange and who, in another winning turn, scamper up and down the slim Chinese poles, between which they nearly fly. Cool stylish showmanship sets them apart.

New Cole Brothers pushes the excitement level up a notch or two during the second half of the program because of the Asian acrobats just mentioned, and because of a young Pinto Neves, all of 15 years old, who throws a perfect triple on the return trapeze. The house cats of Maya Panfilova charm and amuse. And Pugh hits more pay dirt with a very funny Georgian clown, whose best bit is the theft of a woman's purse and his escape with it up a rope to the top of the tent. From there, he removes and waves for all to see the embarrassing contents, and then tosses them down onto the victim. Boffo buffoonery.

Too many of the novelties, however, like George Munteanu's slow and overly choreographed Human Slinky and Dancing Octopus, are too similar to each other and just not good enough. Spider-Man? He comes sliding down a wire to the cheers of the moppets. And the Hulk makes a couple of amusing entrances to subdue an antagonist. For a price, the kids can have their photos taken with the comic book heroes during intermission. They can also, for $5.00 apiece, take a ride on a non-performing pony. No animals, Mr. Pugh?

Something was missing there in a big way, and the older you were, the more likely were you to notice and feel it. No circus out there on the road seems to have suffered more the slings of contemporary politics and culture than John Pugh's sadly emasculated New Cole Circus of 2005. (Some of the elephants returned to the show the following year; customer discontent could not be ignored.) What was *not* there in Willow Grove that *was* there in Santa Rosa many seasons ago? The arrival of a circus train at dawn was not there. The setup in the a.m. and the teardown at night was not there. The sideshow was not there. Nor were the horses or the elephants, the lions or tigers. Gone was the band. Gone, too, were a dozen funny faces circling the track in wacky snappy walkarounds. (I say it's high time we return the words "clown walkaround" to high honor.) Not there were the noisy barkers. And not there were three fading circles left behind on a dusty fairgrounds field the next day for young boys to search out and reminisce over, dreaming back on the wonders that had passed through town. Not even a *single ring*! Gone almost in total was the circus we remember from our youth.

When children can see it first hand, says Barbara Byrd — when they are close enough to pet the animals, to feed the elephants and smell the earthy atmosphere of a tent show, then they're getting a totally different experience from sitting at home in front a television set half the day.[6]

It's life. It's what the circus from Beatty to Barbette once brought us.

They used to come in at dawn.

17

This Way to the Ballet

Turning away from brass and boom, the band hushed to a whispering melody as lonely and beautiful as a first love forever lost. Morton Gould's haunting "Pavan" invaded the air, and into a circus ring rolled a small make-believe stage, pushed on by an auguste clown. He parted the curtain, revealing three life-sized puppets — a ballerina, a sad Pagliacci and a happy harlequin. The two male figures, both in love with the ballerina, erupted into a jealous argument, bringing the object of their desire magically to life. Off the stage she danced, cavorting through a whirl of action as a procession of larger-than-life clowns with enormous Mardi Gras heads sauntered gaily on and circled her. The wonders multiplied when the merry auguste brought forth a magician in white face to conjure up miraculous feats of prestidigitation. Around him sprang a flower garden of colorful blossoms and yards and yards of festive garlands. The large-headed clowns took hold of them in daisy-chain fashion and followed each other happily off.

Now, you're thinking, I suppose, Cirque du Soleil? Something from Moscow? One of the new theatre-circus troupes out of Montreal? Well, take a closer look at the cover of the program magazine on which a couple of these figures are depicted — the lovely ballerina in golden brown toe shoes with a yellow crown fixture in her hair, the Mardi Gras clown behind her against a baby blue background, his outstretched arms clasping hers as she balances smilingly on one toe. Notice the words: *Shrine Circus produced by Polack Bros.* The year, *1953.*

Surprised? How could something so artful have come out of a time when American circuses pitched more powerful images to the public? Time to tear down some stereotypes, pre–Cirque.

"Carnival in Spangleland," the name of the enchanting work, was devised for Polack Brothers that visionary season by none other than Barbette. Yes, he's back already. We couldn't let Barbette go away so quickly. He deserves an encore. Such a fascinating figure. So creative around props and riggings. So admired and adored by almost everybody who crossed his eccentric path. Barbette. The stories about this legend abound.

Born, believe it or not, "Vander Clyde Broadway," he grew up — another believe it or not — in, of all places, Round Rock, Texas. Following stints as a member of the Alfretta Sisters, with whom he performed in drag, two years later the 21-year-old was touring the Orpheum circuit on his own, billed simply as "Barbette." He made it to the Palace on

169

Production director Barbette reviews costume designs for Cole Brothers Circus, 1949 (Circus World Museum, Baraboo, Wisconsin).

Broadway, and within a month, he was setting sail for Europe. Across the sea, he turned himself into a minor sensation, flying from a single trapeze posing as a woman, first over London, and then Paris, where he was wildly embraced. The French loved the surprise conclusion to Barbette's routine, when he tossed aside a wig to reveal his true gender. A subtle sense of humor garnished the act.

Barbette made his headquarters in the city of love. He would acquire some 25 trunks full of costumes, props and scenic effects. He loved the artifacts of circus and illusion, oh did he ever. He headlined for the biggest music halls and circuses throughout Europe, and he toured, too, across Australia and the Middle East. He played a roll in the Scallera film *La Tosca* and in Jean Cocteau's *Blood of a Poet*. Grounded by an illness resulting from an aerial injury suffered in 1939, Barbette turned in his costumes for a director's beret.

"The entrepreneur of enchantment" he was called by press agents for his work on Billy Rose's movie *Seven Lively Arts,* on the stage musical *Jumbo,* and around the rings of America's most prestigious circuses, indoor and out.[1]

Billy McCabe tells of the time when Barbette, while directing aerial effects on the Big Show in the late forties, found himself not well served by his "fame" up in Boston. At the Garden there, they were assigned restroom stalls for trunk placements and costume changes.

Snapped the entrepreneur, "After all these years in show business and among producers of the world, I finally ended up dressing in a shit house."

The fantastic Barbette excelled in the multi-faceted sphere of circus where elephants once paraded, even "danced" alongside ladies on pointe. Where, too, the grittier realities back of the big top offered hilarious, sometimes violent, contrast to the awe-inspiring displays inside. Either you had sawdust in your blood and you put up with all of the humbling hardships and insults, or you packed your trunk and escaped the humiliating slights for a stable nine-to-five job away from the spangled nuthouse.

Barbette's imagination inspired a rich repertoire of group numbers, most of them designed for lift-off over sawdust. He moved from one circus to another — from Ringling to Cole to Beatty to Polack. It was on Polack, though, where he seems to have made his most stunning contributions. Around a single ring, aerial spectacles have a greater impact on the audience. That Louis Stern would allow the 1953 program to include, among the six production numbers for it created and directed by Barbette, a five-person pantomime bearing little circus at all, speaks miles for Barbette and for Mr. Stern. You will recall that Louis Stern developed a sense of higher showmanship in the sinking thirties.

That memorable '53 Polack outing was a one-ring gem, richly stocked with first-class circus acts, each and every one an asset, from Alberto Zoppe's bareback riders with the comical Cucciola, to Klauser's Bears and Sonny Moore's hyper-happy roustabout dogs. From Australia came the Seven Ashtons, masters of Risley. Sending two men into the air at the same time, they executed "over and under" somersaults. Delicately precise Lola Dobritch, from Bulgaria, danced ballet over the low wire and also traversed it on a unicycle. The Schaller Brothers, Phoenix natives, combined gymnasts and high comedy on the trampoline. From China, the Jim Wong Troupe, for whom Barbette fashioned a special introduction complete with Chinese serpentina, scored with superb acrobatics and contortion. German chemist-turned-equestrian Albert Ostermaier rode dashingly aboard his dressage horse, Genius. Three Girls from Hollywood — a trio of elephants directed by Pink Madison — hailed from Siam via MGM's *Tarzan* films. Sonny Moore came from Grass Valley, California, the Zoppes from Italy, the Klausers from Austria and Germany. The Ward-Bell flyers were Americans through and through.

From Czechoslovakia, the Terrific Triskas supplied tense thrills on the high wire. At the top of their perilous three-person pyramid across the steel strand from a unicycle stood the fearless 5-year-old Karel. Have we forgotten anyone? Oh, only one of the greatest of them all: single trapeze diva La Norma from Denmark, who swung fast and wide in true single-trap fashion, drawing gasps and cheers at every breathtaking dive.

Barbette opened the show with a good-natured spoof of the old-time midway, "This Way to the Sideshow." He sent out cast members fancifully attired as familiar figures in a typical freak-show lineup, with a kindly emphasis on the non-kinky. "Beauty on the Wing," display four, brought back the human butterflies which we had seen the year before on the Clyde Beatty Circus. "Toreadorian Travesty," another satire, spoofed a "mirth-motivated bullfight." "Paris in the Clouds" sent the aerialovlies up the webs to the music of cancan.

Best and last of all, spotted between the Zoppe riding troupe and the flying-return finale, came "Carnival in Spangleland." The program described it as "a refreshing new concept of clowning in America. In it are merged pantomime, music and dance." The ballerina was played by Florida native Marilyn Hightower, fresh from seven years of ballet credits abroad. 40-year-veteran Chester Sherman essayed the merry auguste; his brother, Joe, the

"The Bird Cage Girls," conceived and directed by Barette for Polack Brothers, 1956 (Circus World Museum, Baraboo, Wisconsin).

Pagliacci; Ronnie Lewis Jared, the happy harlequin; and Denmark's "king clown" Joe Siems, the magician.

As the carnival faded from view, having charmed us in unexpectedly quiet ways, the nine Ward-Bell flyers were scaling rope ladders to reach their platforms and swings. Soon they were flinging themselves through somersaults and pirouettes, flying into and out of each other's arms. They were actually three separate troupes working side by side up there, and they brought the program to a heart-pounding climax when they threw three simultaneous mid-air exchanges. A perfect end to a perfectly balanced program.

Bravo, Barbette. Bravo, Louis Stern! The year 1953 probably marked the finest edition of Polack Brothers Circus which fans would ever witness, thanks to the open-minded producer and his extraordinary director, two visionaries unafraid to grace the cover of a circus magazine with images of ballet and fantasy. Unafraid to slow the show down for dreamy counterpoint. Unafraid to reach beyond the predictable. "Carnival in Spangleland" came and went with soft, surreal charm. Take another bow, Barbette! The world would soon enough catch up to your dreams and turn them into the circus itself.

Good or bad? Circus and ballet (both physical expressions) are so confusingly similar, yet so very different. And when the two forms are merged into an incestuous embrace, for one to live, the other must die. Sorry, Montreal. You can't have both in equal measure. The one waters down and blends the individual artist into the group; the other — guess which? — relies on the individual. The one is illusional; the other, real.

One must die. Truth on the midway, that I promised you. So, right here, before we go any further, we're going to bring back our visiting scholar from England, Helen Stoddart. She can give you a more academic take on the issue. Ms. Stoddart? If you please...

"Circus is, above all, a vehicle for the demonstration of taunting danger and this remains its most telling and defining feature. Physical risk-taking has always been at its heart; the recognition that to explore the limitations of the human body is to walk a line between triumphant exhilaration and, on the other side of this limit, pain, injury or death. The body is the circus is utterly self-reliant: it is preserved by skill and strength only; never by faith, fate or magic.... Friedrich Nietzsche turns to the circus to find a figure — the tight-rope walker — to allegorize man's precarious journey of development as a crossing over an 'abyss' during which he must face down limitations and exceed his potential."[2]

Ballet is dance, first and foremost. Circus is acrobatic, foremost and forever. So, if you want more choreography, be prepared to settle for less athleticism. You may think the Cirque-ballet crowd are giving you more to look at. In fact, they are giving you less to look at. What they are giving you, with safety lines and all those distracting special effects, is something more cinematic than real. True circus, first and last, is *real*.

John Ringling North, in his early producing days and full of his emerging showmanship, cooked up a clever publicity stunt by hiring Igor Stravinsky to compose special music and Russian dancer George Balanchine to handle the heavy footwork for a "Ballet of the Elephants." In its 1942 premiere at Madison Square Garden, it was a hoot, even a wow to some who glimpsed the roaring "corpse de ballet" before certain pachyderms off pointe lost heart and blew too many steps in their vinyl-reinforced tutus. This was *Circus*.

True ballet over sawdust? Bring on the Russians. Long before Johnny North's bull ballet, the Soviets were teaching masculine tumblers how to tumble more femininely. Following the nasty revolution of 1917, they took circus so seriously that they set out to exorcize it of hair-raising daredevils and sideshow gooks (such as the fellow who drove nails through his tongue). They sent jugglers and wire walkers to ballet school. They hired stage directors to help reframe standard circus acts around "themes." They recruited composers to create special music. And they mandated the use of mechanics throughout the performance. No more the unpleasant thought that an artist might accidentally fall to an ugly injury or death. The purpose of these changes in the ring was to honor "socialist realism," the Soviet catchword for a Godless society joined together in state-regulated, state-enforced harmony.

At the same time safely short of artistic suicide, the Soviets kept the animals on the bill. But now, the bears would be taught a fancier grade of footwork. Now, a tiger or lion would lay down next to an elephant in peaceful rapport — comrades resting after a long day's work in the fields. And now, the band also played wistful refrains. Gradually, the performer's mode of presentation from start to finish came to be valued almost as much as the tricks she offered. Do it with the grace of a true ballerina.

Strange how certain non-Soviet performers — like Francis Brunn, like La Norma or Pinito Del Oro, Gunther Gebel Williams or the Ayak Brothers — managed to mature in superior ways without matriculating through a circus academy. Increasingly, however, many of the students to graduate from the schools of Moscow or Montreal, Paris or London, began to bear the cautious markings of ballet.

Why? They spend too many fruitless hours trying to persuade the public that a theme is more important than a trick. That a circus is not a circus if it is only a circus. Ballet tells a story (if you can figure it out) in abstract movement. So, why not the circus? And therein lies the danger of infatuation. When young circus artists fall prey to the dance world, they are easily brainwashed into believing that, unless their routines convey stories or at least profound ideas, they have failed. To be merely an act is old hat.

Cirque du Soleil's blithering allusions to story telling, uttered in syntax that could mean almost anything, point to a new form of entertainment which might be called Circus Allusional. There are, indeed, a number of "circuses" out there which allude to be something other than circuses, yet without really making good on the claim. Like Cirque, they are a little bit of this, a little bit of that—so you decide. "With the performers of Cirque du Soleil," reads one of Franco Dragone's lyrical flights, "it is important to be on the lookout for any theatrical moments and to seize these on the spot. It is impossible to impose a scenario on a reality—a reality generates its own."[3]

Guy Laliberte and his faithful flock are unduly possessed of a need to identify their every movement with sweeping cosmic themes, be they "cyberspace, market globalization" or "the modernization and acceleration of communications that mean more than ever... the earth will go on turning, so what can we expect this new world order to bring?"[4] Well, for starters, how about a few really good new bareback riding acts not seen in ages?

Usually, the rhetorical flourishes oozing out of Quebec have only dumbfounded the average ticket holder here on earth. And they have driven a number of leading professional drama critics into guffawing disbelief. How, some ask, can a "circus" be this pretentious?

It can and it will as long as there are a sufficient number of real circus acts on the show to trump the verbal hallucinations. Cirque's quest for new forms advances a similar dream argued by cutting-edge eggheads in the old Soviet Union. Victor Kalesh, for one, spoke of a "hypothetical" program composed of many elements, not unlike what I am calling Circus Allusional: "In the 20th century, the people connected with the theatre dreamed of synthetical shows — a synthesis of combing the arts." "Only circus provides a possibility to see one whole thing consisting of several acts- elements. Not like theatre."[5]

The yearning to combine stage and circus has never worked, and likely never will. The noted English author Antony Hippisley Coxe called such experiments "bastard entertainment."[6] For that alone he deserves the platform. Mr. Coxe?...

"There can be no illusion, for there are eyes all around to prove that there is no deception. The performers actually do what they appear to do. Their feats of dexterity and balance and strength must never be confused with the make believe world of the actor ... for while an actor says he will 'play his part,' the circus artists tells you he will 'work his act.'"[7]

A circus combo — circus, theatre and dance — must give way to one of the three if any is to live. The others must settle for shadow status. Otherwise, what you have is a traffic jam to nowhere. And what will accompany it are cascades of lofty prose of the sort you'll find in Cirque du Soleil program magazines and press releases. For example, writes vice president of "creation," Giles Ste-Croix, "A rich variety of contrasts and confrontations of all kinds animate the characters and the plot. The audience can see the meanness and the generosity that co-exist in each artist, or see the feminine side of a muscular man. Just like a kaleidoscope, the show stimulates the imagination, providing juxtapositions out of which everyone can make up his or her own story."[8]

From Guy Caron: "The lions of the West are giving new life to the dragons of the East, changing our pace and life and balance of forces. As the pendulum swings back, we are discovering the cyclical rhythms of the Earth's forces and elements. In this perpetual movement of life and time, the Dralions come face to face with the eternal renewal of life's paradox."[9]

For those not quite on point who could use a Cirque-to-earth translator, the very earth-bound Bob Mitchell has this to say: "Let's face it. No one and I do mean no one can be more pretentious than Le Cirque. They do have it down to a science."

Cirque du Soleil for Dummies? Short of that, you and I may have to go to a Cirque makeup class in order to fully understand all of the hidden meanings embedded in their programs that we've been missing, from cyberspace and microprocessors to "life's paradox." We've asked a few circus owners on planet earth to tell us what they think. First, the Big Apple's Michael Christensen:

> I have a very clear opinion of Cirque, and I'm never disappointed when I sit down to watch one of their shows because I never expect anything other than who they are, and who they are is very very clear. Every time I sit down to watch a Cirque du Soleil show, I can expect to be boggled by the visual imagery, by the staging, by the technical wonders that they have because of the resources they have. I can expect to be taken to another world, and I can expect not to be particularly interested in the personalities of the artists, or to be move or touched. And so I'm never disappointed. They come through on those factors. If I want to be moved or feel that artists have made direct contact with me, I don't go to Cirque.

Now, from Larry Pisoni:

"It's got some great spectacle, and it's got music and the circus acts are the best you'll see anywhere. I just don't think ... I think there could be more there.... It's not a show for children, that's for sure.... They got lost. It's just too much stimulus."

John Pugh?

"Cirque has been a phenomenal show.... It's not entertainment for kids. It's a theatre production."

Animal trainer Svetlana Shamsheeva believes that Cirque does not fully honor the solo act. "Not a real circus," she says. "It's been circus and theatre and sports acrobatics.... You can't see the whole act.... In Soleil, just part of your act. Just a few of your tricks."

Those reactions are rather charitable compared to what some of the paid reviewers have had to say. Here is the *Guardian's* Lyn Gardner, commenting on Saltimbanco:

"The acts are fantastic," she wrote. "No, the lack of this evening comes not from too little skill, but too much window-dressing. It is undeniably a spectacle; it has the soft rock music, dry ice, sparkling lights and people floating around as if they were part of a commedia del arte troupe or popping off to a masked Venetian ball. It is unnecessarily distracting — just when you are admiring the Chinese pole act your eye is drawn instead to people gyrating behind them in rainbow-hued Lycra. It gives the impression that the circus skills are incidental, and that what is really on offer is a cross between an extravagant rock stadium concert and one of those showy in-house corporate entertainments that were fashionable in the money-making 1980s. If that tickles your fancy, fine, but you are buying top of the range eye candy, nothing more."[10]

From the Web site Slate Bryan Curtis observed:

"A great deal of Cirque-magic comes from its unapologetic Frenchness. Or, if you prefer, it's Quebecosity. By this, I mean that Cirque du Soleil shows make absolutely no sense at all. I studied the plot of Varakei for a solid hour before attending the performance. But, by the end of the second act, I was blubbering the same nonsense as the Goat-Man."[11]

Say what you will, Cirque's daunting cosmicity has the world talking.

When Cirque's founding artistic director, Guy Caron, returned following a ten-year absence to stage another show, what he theorized into stark existence was the numbingly downbeat, theatre-heavy *Dralion*. This one took Cirque to the abyss of a dark night in a post-apocalyptic world, making Circus Oz, in comparison, look like *Leave It to Beaver*. Among *Dralion*'s more alluring assets for the thinking eye, there were the bug-like figures which, stuck to the back side of a large glass-like backdrop, resembled an invasion of insects up against your living room window waiting to break through and finish off your supper — or you. Or, wait a minute. Were those tenacled grey blobs supposed to represent construction workers in drag hoping to land work in a big out-there Cirque ballet? Or were they the "Dralions" alluded to by the director, coming "face to face with the eternal renewal of life's paradox," only to find a sea of glazed eyes glaring back at them from the other side?

Around the interior edges of the tent, reminiscent of what struggling circuses once did to produce extra revenue, in high-tech neon letters glowed the names of corporate sponsors. Yes, sponsors. As if this outfit, already filthy rich, needed a couple billion more for special effects experiments on the moon. Maybe they needed it to pay for all the sidebar characters down there near the ring, posturing and pausing, and casting superior glances to a cosmos only they understood. Now and then, a few sizzling acts cut through the maze to render everything else academic.

Today's young Cirque-infatuated disciples are being lead up another dead-end street which we'll call Circus Ballet. They risk losing all touch with the roots of circus. They are turning their backs on the "trick." Stated California-born Shanna Carroll, who started out with the Pickle Family and ended up on Cirque's *Saltimbanco* working a finely choreographed single-trap number, "It's considered passé if you can recognize classical trapeze positions."[12]

The traditional big tricks on a flying trapeze out of date? A human pyramid crossing the high wire, "passé" for today's crowds?

A compelling example in recent seasons of the power of the classical position was turned by a four-man high on the high wire, performed by the masterful Gabonese troupe from Gabon, Africa, on UniverSoul Circus in 2005. The troupe moved slowly, cautiously, placing each footstep with tense precision while a slowed-down jazz riff as soft and shimmering as a quiet waterfall gave perfect music to a great classical maneuver. It reminded us of the raw, beautiful power that is eternally and exclusively circus. A power as real as the quiet courage of mountain climbers scaling upward. As real as life itself.

If this elitist attitude about shunning classical positions were applied across the lot, it would dismiss any number of revered tricks that underpin the history of circus art — same as the building blocks honored in ballet, theatre, the cinema and sports. It is a vain reach for acceptance outside the popular tent that favors the esoteric over the epic, a reach which loses itself in excessively detailed choreography. And it is a foolish disdain at that, reducing the trick to a dirty word.

Fog machines and special effects, posturing and pausing will come and go. The real benchmarks of circus art are the number of revolutions turned in flight, the number of clubs sent into orbit, the manner in which a pair of aerialists perilously interact. Without them, you are left with a *Corteo* or a New Pickle Circus. So on to the super abstract we go.

The gifted German wheel performer turned director Chris Lashua, who created *Birdhouse* for the New Pickle Circus, drew his inspiration, he told me, from the Mexican muralist Diego Rivera. He conceived a surreal factory setting where circus performers dressed as workers go through their daily labors, around and over ingeniously devised props. "I didn't

A scene from the stage work "Birdhouse," created by Chris Lashua, seen here in his German Wheel, for San Francisco's New Pickle Circus, 2004 (photograph by Larry Rosenberg, courtesy of Chris Lashua/Birdhouse Factory).

want to go into the fantasy world that is commonly seen nowadays. I wanted to do it in this real place."

Lashua constructed a clever work of inventive stagecraft, alright. "I wanted to take these acts that were circus acts and put them in a place that wasn't a circus environment."

The noteworthy result, when presented by the New Pickle Circus on the stage of the San Francisco Palace of Fine Arts theatre in 2004, appeared to impress a local audience consisting largely of friends and kin of the cast, and of students, along with their parents, of the San Francisco School of Circus, which operates the Pickle show.

By intermission, a little boy sitting in front of me blurted out to his mom, "I'm bored!" The mother disagreed.

Too much art can smother the most promising idea. Chris Lashua had crafted something so perfectly wrought—like one of those intricate mechanisms in a glass case at a mechanical charm museum—that it came out a brilliant frozen amalgam. What was it supposed to be other than a charming little curiosity? Obviously, not circus alone. Not ballet, either. So we were left to consider what a good theatre piece it might be if only it had a real story to tell. Situations are not stories. Stories to tell need full-blown characters engaged in escalating conflicts that come to a head. You can't tell a story half way. You can't hint at something like Cirque has tried to do, inviting each of its befuddled spectators to "make up his or her own story." We call that a yawning dereliction of duty.

So, then, we are left with ballet, as Lashua paints a half-touching animation in circus action of workers clocking in, plodding through another day of rote tasks and casual filtrations, and then clocking out. In the rich unsparing hands of Le Cirque, it's easier to imagine *Birdhouse* being turned into something far more spectacular and possibly varied enough, both dramatically and comedically, to keep a lad from complaining, "I'm bored!"

Slowly, ballet will strangle any circus that draws too close and embraces too much—that does not keep its Carnivals in Spangleland in check between horse riders and trapeze flyers. At least Cirque Eloize, another highly respected troupe from Montreal central, takes its allusionally charming wares to the stage where such things (like Circus Oz) rightfully belong. We are in a theatre, and therefore more apt to pay attention to the theatre in Eloize.

Rain, the latest production from Eloize, is about a circus show in rehearsal, so asserts its director, Daniele Pasca. He wanted to bring to life the snapshots of favored childhood memories. What he gave us, with little scenery, looked like a charming troupe of rejects on a bus and truck tour. *Rain* is more ballet than anything, modest in force and consequence. In spirit, it is like a perfect afternoon at play with circus-talented friends in the key of teasing and flirting, of showing off and dreaming—and trying. The mid-level circus skills on display lean a little too often and too heavily towards contortion and aerial choreography minus the big swings. They start to repeat themselves. A juggler drops too many items. A pole vaulting act is executed not on a pole but on a rather charitably wide plank. And, with few exceptions, so on down the line.

The laid-back *Rain* stage party ends up in a sea of water through which the characters splash about in joyful innocence. This fulfills the director's desire to relive his own boyhood during such wet days. How entertaining? In cities like San Francisco, where progressively-minded theatergoers pride themselves on being up-to-the-minute hip, and where local critics find it more politically correct to embrace a Cirque Eloize over a Barnum & Bailey, adoring audiences toss cheers at the most common circus tricks. This restfully poetic enterprise has a way of draining the blood out of an act, of darkening the pulse with its occasional mournful reveries.

Cirque Eloize founder and director Daniele Finzi Pasca made such a name for himself in New World big tops that Cirque du Soleil reached out and granted him generous freedom to bring his vision of theatre-circus under their tent. The still-born result, full of fascinating ideas floating about in lovely disarray, is called *Corteo*. And it stands as a stunning disappointment following its thrilling Cirque predecessor, the intrepidly balanced, red hot *Varakei*. *Corteo* is a special effects stage show, really, high on time-consuming creativity and meticulous character interactions, some of which nearly make sense, short on brevity, content and punch. If you like eye candy, this may be your ideal rest stop. Bring a pillow.

The tent itself is separated in two parts, with a curtain extending across the middle of the ring, bridged by permanent barriers on each side. Before and after the show and during intermission when the curtain is drawn, the audience on one side can't see their neighbors on the other. And on flat sections at the edges of the curtain, the names of more corporate sponsors are flashed.

Corteo drips with atmosphere and eccentric characters coming and going. Overhead at intervals, ladies in angelic white dresses float back and forth from aerial tracks. A crusty old ringmaster in red wanders in and out. Is he a symbol for a show that can't figure out what it is? Magical objects appear like invading artifacts from other worlds. Don't expect either a strong story or gripping circus acts to compel your attendance. Expect, instead, to lose yourself in another man's wandering imagination. Alice in Quebecland? Something like that, perhaps. What we get are house acts, created, it appears, on the cheap to simulate the real thing. Most of them — like an ersatz multiple casting number performed from three cradles — fall short of memorable finishes. Never has Cirque du Soleil felt quite so boring. And never, at all the Cirque shows I've seen, did I spot so many empty seats — up to thirty percent of the house.

Their obvious disdain for tradition comes through with a crowning insult to the high wire act. Up there for no discernible reason at all, a lone woman, tautly attached to a thick rope serving as a mechanic, fusses back and forth across the wire, making a complete mockery of what the routine should stand for. The embarrassing irony of it all seems to have eluded the directors. Or did they purposely set out to ridicule and demolish one of the most dramatic moments in a real circus by rendering it so antiseptically safe?

What to make of *Corteo*? An off year in Montreal? The ultimate fantasy come true for Guy Laliberte? Utter blind allegiance to a celebrated director out of touch? What to make of it all when the program's most genuinely affecting moment is supplied by a ringmaster being hounded to make a return and whistling up a tender melody? Or when the program nearly comes to a stop during a strange little time-consuming Romeo and Juliet skit enacted by two diminutive souls on a portable Shakespearean stage?

If Mr. Laliberte can promote *Corteo* into a winner, he may have turned a critical corner, moving that much closer to a synthetical creation bearing a bold new identity. He may then have achieved what the Russians dreamed of doing. Or he may end up with more empty seats. *Corteo*'s yawningly embryonic reach may leave you with a newfound respect for the artistic brevity of the Three Stooges.

What ballet refuses into its world are many things that thrive over sawdust. To begin with, the daring aerialists whose skill keeps them in the air. Lesser talents use mechanics that enable them to work free of risk. And yet, even then, some of them allude to danger whenever reporters come calling. *Los Angeles Times* film critic Kenneth Turan interviewed Shanna Carroll and went away with a sense of traditional risk-taking in her act — an impression she

Real risk: coin of the authentic circus. Free-standing single trapeze sensation Pinito Del Oro, circa 1954 (courtesy of the John and Mable Ringling Museum of Art, Tibbals Digital Collection).

evidently did not counter but played along with. Even then, Turan wrote about a couple of falls she took, mentioning "a rigging system of safety lines" that absorbed both and spared her from injuries.[13]

Such dishonesty is an affront to the aerialists who take genuine risks, sparing themselves every time they go aloft, not just by skill, but by *artful agility* that is aesthetically satisfying. Repeat: *aesthetically satisfying.*

Real risk is the coin of authentic circus. And without risk, our big tops are being emasculated one by one. Dale Longmire, like many insiders, acknowledges all the "phenomenal tricks" that are possible when the performer is secured to a mechanic. And still he is unimpressed. So is Sylvia Zerbini, of the pre–Soviet, pre–Circus Ballet school. She grants that some of the performers who work with mechanics are interesting to watch — to a degree. They may do pretty things. The may execute artfully. But the danger is missing, and that is the element, maintains Zerbini, that gives the act real-life drama. The element that compels an audience. [14]

There was a day, believe it or not, when no performer on American sawdust would dare be seen wearing a mechanic. And that reality kept some circus owners in a perpetual state of dread. Fearing the loss of valuable assets, John Ringling was "so anxious for the safety of his performers," wrote Fred Bradna, "that he would chew a cigar to bits during a dangerous routine." [15] Today, circus producers rally to the defense of the employed lifelines. After all, if a star flyer falls, that could mean the end of a season's star attraction. It might also have something to do with liability insurance and worker's compensation, unpleasant things that owners might not like talking about.

They have a place in the circus, argues Carson and Barnes's Barbara Byrd. She justifies their use by the drive of today's more ambitious aerialists to push the envelope further. Byrd does not relish the idea of a performer being killed or maimed or permanently injured, so she has no objections to safety wires that are used discretely for artistic ends and that do not appear to be helping the performer accomplish the trick. [16]

Which is almost exactly what another apologetic producer, Paul Binder, asserts. Concerning those who snicker at the sight of safety lines, says Binder, "The so-called purists who say that are missing the point... the risk factor is still there even if you have all the safety.... I don't know any responsible circus director who is not concerned with the safety of the artist."

Remarkably (are you listening, Mr. and Mrs. circus owner?), few aerialists have ever fallen to their deaths. Many of those who did were the victims not of their own negligence but of rigging malfunctions. Lillian Leitzel fell to mortality in Copenhagen when one of her rings crystallized. Elvin Bale's cannon was ill-adjusted, causing him to overshoot the net and hit the ground. It left him paralyzed from the waist down. Rose Gold performed her act thousands of times, once from the Eiffel Tower 600 feet above the ground, before a flash bulb went off at the Civic Auditorium in San Francisco during a Polack Brothers performance in 1956, distracting Gold's critical concentration and sending her to the cement floor. She suffered arm, leg and pelvic injuries, yet recovered and resumed performing. Gerard Soules, who turned one of the most gripping single trap acts ever, became so spooked after two near-falls that he walked away and switched to presenting trained poodles. Bad move. Soules died cut up in savage pieces at the hands of a fired assistant whom he had picked up (through a sexual attraction) on a Las Vegas street. If only the management where Soules presented his poodles had not insisted on background checking the iffy man. If only Soules had not retired from the higher, safer altitudes of aerial work.

Paul Binder has a growing segment of society or city hall on his side. When a troupe of Moscow State Circus stars performed in Britain, they were forced to take hilarious precautions: Due to new European Union safety regulations causing insurance companies to limit perilous pursuits, the aerialists flew wearing hard hats. [17]

Meanwhile, we the people who pay money to sit at the circus are more and more stuck with a split focus: one eye on the "trick," the other on the "mechanic." Is that wire pulled too tightly? Is it helping the performer do the trick? Now, we are having to judge the routine on two accounts. We can never be quite sure, not when we are forced to watch "gassed up" flyers, in the words of Norma Cristiani. It almost makes you want to videotape everything for later scrutiny in replay. At the ballet, of course, this doesn't matter at all.

The use of safety nets or pads on the ground make fine enough sense. They allow the artist to prove her absolute skill. Into them, if she falls, there can be no doubt that she erred. Conversely, her feats well flown can be perfectly appreciated without reservations. With a lifeline, nobody can ever know for certain, can they? And lifelines encourage second- and third-rate wannabes to take to the air before they are ready, others to cram their programs with sloppy, ill-rehearsed tricks in a desperate bid to outdo each other. It all adds up to amateur night over sawdust.

Russian teeterboard king Andrey Kovgar, who now employs a mechanic for just a single trick, respects the idea of their absence. "When I see a very daring performer without mechanics, I feel that this particular person is real circus brave actor, so it's a real circus man."

In Russia these days, reports Kovgar, the use of lifelines is now up to the individual performer. Kovgar himself is "trying not to use it at all."

What else does ballet refuse into its world? It shuns the outdoor elements. It, of course, does not include animals, nor will it tolerate a succession of stars into a single program — too much a distraction from its faceless ensembles. Like the theatre and cinema, ballet does not offer reality but a theatricalized image of it. And on these terms, the circus is relegated to a supporting role.

Even the art of horse riding in the hands of our nouveau visionaries from Quebec has been refined down to something terribly fey. Their latest effort to conquer, subdue and reinvent the old horse act is called *Cavalia*. Created by one of Cirque's numerous co-founders, Norman Latourelle, *Cavalia* takes place in a huge theatre-like structure made of metal and canvas, in front of raked seats. To get there, if you are willing to shell out at least $31.85 ($167.85 for the full-throttle VIP treatment), you climb a series of metal steps through the imposing understructure of the seats. It looks and feels like a grounded space station.

The formal stage set, which extends from the far left to the far right of the rectangular shaped tent, resembles some far-off classical place, be it Ethiopia or the Sahara desert. As the show begins, slowly across the stage wander pilgrims. Acrobats appear, stopping along the way to engage in simple tricks. Then come the horses, in slower motion, too. As in the moody *Corteo*, nobody here is in any sort of a hurry. Everything was obviously designed to reach a more cerebral class of big-city dilettante.

Even PETA seems to have been silenced by this one.

Oh, yes, the animals. They are beautiful, indeed, and they appear to have taken up ballet, too. If only they had more exciting things to do. In total, the horse acts (if we might be so crude) could be dispensed with in about half an hour. Familiar dressage routines are repeated throughout a very long slog that will last well over two hours. Will it ever end, we begin wondering long before it ever does. And not before a horse rider or two or three caresses the neck of their animal partners, to make it clear, we assume, just how tenderly taken care of these regal specimens are. Just to offset the slightest suspicions that backstage, a horse might be treated like a horse.

Were they to run the program in half the time, of course they wouldn't be able to sell as many of their jet-set concessions. Since there is no free drinking water on the grounds, you'll need $3.00 for the bottled version. A program magazine — no, make that a "portfolio" in *Cavalia* speak — can be yours for a twenty dollar bill. Pardon me, World, but it's hard not to feel in the clutches of a high-tech fleecing operation and to recall the wisdom of P.T. Barnum's crack about the endless supply of suckers out there who can be sold almost anything if the ballyhoo jumps.

In Berkeley, California, they jumped for *Cavalia* like mad. Yes, P.T.

Here's a reality check: horse shows never have done well on return visits. Before *Cavalia*, there was another one, *Cheval*, put together by Cirque's Giles Ste-Croix, working on his own during a break away from Cirque. *Cheval* opened in Montreal in May 2001, but did not last beyond a tepid season.

So there you have it. That's what things are turning into at the circus ballet. And are any of you wondering with a sigh (ready to watch De Mille's *The Greatest Show on Earth* once again), how long the Cirque era will last? Here's a good place for us to stop and take a big-picture look at big top epochs down through time.

First off, the Yankees imported the Phillip Astley show, presenting very similar programs in permanent amphitheaters. Epoch number one.

Next, when the portable tent was invented in the United States in 1825, out over the backboards of American went a new kind of circus on red wagons — rougher and more free-wheeling — into and through the mud from town to town. Circuses could now go wherever there were people in small communities because they had their own canvas amphitheater in which to present the program. Epoch number two.

The third epoch — the three-ring heyday — began with the addition of a second ring under the Coup, Costello and Barnum top in 1873. John Ringling North ushered in epoch number four in 1938 by elevating the big show into a color-coordinated spectacle of rare beauty and style, interlocking the acts he imported from abroad with lavish production numbers. Altogether, the changes North introduced supplied greater variety, surprise, and a welcome semblance of artistic unity.

I'd say the North era officially ended with the arrival of Cirque du Soleil in Los Angeles, in 1987. So, 1793 to 1987 — that's a total of 194 years, or nearly five decades on average per epoch. Does this mean that Cirque, only twenty years old, has yet another thirty seasons of world-wide domination? It is not with glee that I raise the prospect.

Cirque or circus? To those of you in the younger ranks who harbor dreams of a career under some sort of a tent, here's my advice: Learn how to caress a horse's neck with loving devotion; how to wear a hard hat while flying through the air with the safest of ease; and how to pretend to be in mortal danger when the press comes around probing the perils of aerial work in today's virtual big top.

Sure, and *that* way to the ballet!

18

Bumpin' Back with a Voice

Now, ladies and gentlemen — we don't want to send you away all dreary and down-hearted, feeling like you've just attended a funeral. Not all is a lost cause on the midway. New acts, new shows come springing forth every lucky once in a while. You never know what next might roll onto the lot. Somebody somewhere could reshuffle all the lost pieces back together into an exciting new form and start up a whole new epoch. Somebody like the next, say, William Coup or John North, or Guy Laliberte.

Wait till next season. Hold onto your faith, and keep your pews! Here comes a promising example of how the circus can shuck aside the ballet and be a circus again. Here comes a troupe bursting with rhythm, sizzle, sass and shout. Yo! Yo! Yo! hollers the ringmaster. Duba do zomp go the acrobats, dancing out into the audience under strobe lights to a funky get-down beat. This company's jumpin to gospel and jazz, blues and Motown modern. Hey, look: The world's first black lion trainer! And over there — on stilts and in ritual garments, the Shamans of West Africa. You want elephants, too? Okay, enter Hannibal's army scaling the Alps.

Welcome to hip hop under the big top. To Cedric Ricky Walker's UniverSoul Circus, the first black owned show in a century. It's busting 'em up in big city urban places under a born again tent, routed to reach the hearts, souls and pocketbooks of Mr. and Mrs. It's-a-Black-Thang America.

Norma Cristiani is a convert: "I'll tell you a show I'm really impressed with. It's strictly circus and it's wonderful. I was so impressed with the message they're getting across to everybody. Not just black people, but everybody. From the minute you walk in, there's activity, because circus is illusion. I think you have to build that illusion with it ... excitement. And I felt that way as soon as I walked in there. They had the music going, everybody was happy. And they had plenty of ushers. And the show started and it was just — it never stopped! And it was good from start to finish."

Okay, now that Ms. Cristiani has you lined up for tickets, let's start with a little background on the pastor-in-chief of this happening new circus.

In his Baltimore boyhood, Ricky Walker loved going to see Ringling Bros. and Barnum & Bailey. He dreamed of one day running off with it, picturing himself (no illusions here) as a prop hand, as recalled by his pr guy, Hank Ernest. Walker thought that was as far as he could go, for he had never seen a single black person in the parade.[1]

Instead, Walker turned to working with pop singers. He fronted the first rap tour, Fresh Feet. And those tours gave him an education in how a producer joins artist to audience. Restless to prove himself on larger scales, Walker turned to working the advance for the "chitlin' musicals," black-themed plays with gospel-intense choruses that satirized personal issues on the minds of African Americans. Scenes of infidelity, wife-swapping and bar-hopping never failed to draw the biggest crowds. *Mama Don't* was the title of one musical; *A Good Man Is Hard to Find*, another. Drugs, crime and dysfunctional families were addressed in melodramatic fashion.

When Walker noticed young kids showing up at the chitlins, he spotted a potentially larger family audience out there hungering for entertainment they could call their own. He wondered, What else might families pay money to see? He brainstormed with Atlanta entertainer and DJ Calvin "Casual Cal" DuPre. A variety show? Animal acts? Hip hop musicals?

Why not a circus, suggested DuPre. The word instantly revived Walker's childhood dream born at Ringling Bros. If he could not be that fearless traveler crossing a silver strand high over center ring, then why not be the man's boss? Thus was birthed, in 1994, "The Universal Big Top Circus" (later renamed UniverSoul). They pitched their tent in some pretty bad burgs, smack dab in the guts of nitty gritty black America. In Chicago, they played crime-laced Washington Park. No problem. "Because," as Walker told the *Los Angeles Times*, "the community was so proud that someone was finally presenting an event that was the quality they deserved, that if you fooled around with the circus and did something wrong, you were labeled a community bad boy."[2]

During one engagement in the hard-to-please Windy City, UniverSoul drew 90,000 patrons, causing them to extend the run. Sorry, L.A. Yeah, we're still coming your way, but we'll be there a week or so late.

Walker is high on selling to the entire black family, such as it is, torn asunder in many cities where a majority of kids are raised by a single parent and rarely see a father around the house. Nonetheless, Walker has messages to impart to the younger generations about civic duty and personal responsibility, about pride and progress and self-control and abstinence before marriage. UniverSoul comes stocked with its own moralizing commercials.

As the show's public relations man, Hank Ernest, tells it, they are recasting the circus in the urban setting. He claims what they are doing has never been done before, and what they are doing has parallels to how African American musicians, through jazz, established a new art form.

The old form, maintains Ernest, was a ringmaster in top hat shouting familiar salutations to ladies and — well, you know the rest. The new announcer jazzes it up a little, and you won't see him in traditional red.

They feel like they've revived the circus.[3]

Walker and DuPre's version of soul over sawdust was soon rewarded with huge turnouts under a 2,500-seat tent. Inside, the black kid from Baltimore evidently stays as true as he can to his original mission, for his wares are obviously aimed at the overwhelming number of African Americans who easily dominate the crowd. All you have to do is take a look at the show itself. The music is a lot louder. Stress louder. The acrobats are funkier, the whole high-energy thing, more like a street fair than a unified performance. They present the best acts they can find and afford. Walker's early emphasis on African-American talent lead him up a very short dead-end street. He was so determined to stock the ring with his own kind that he claimed to have "rediscovered" South Africa's single-trap sensations, the Ayak Brothers, who had been performing "exclusively" through Europe until 1993.[4] Not quite. Another circus revivalist, Cliff Vargas, brought the astonishing Ayaks over to the states in the mid-eighties.

UniverSoul Circus featured a contortionist named Nayakata from Valencia, Spain. They signed the King Charles Troupe of comedy unicycle basketball players who had appeared with Ringling for a 20-year run. And the boss got to live his childhood Clyde Beatty fantasy vicariously by talking a cousin, Baltimore laborer Ted McCray, into assuming the role of Daniel in the lion's den. Family ties, as we've seen, nurture many acts, hot or not so. McCray has not been heard from since.

To provide the humor, UniverSoul picked up two Ringling Clown College graduates named Otis Gary and Irving White, along with Danise Payne from London, touted to be the first African-American funny face ever to appear in a British circus.

Ricky Walker spends a month or two each fall scouting the world beyond Harlem — itself, a strangely unfertile place — for new attractions. Africa produces far better acts. So, of course, does China, Spain and Russia, among the countries Walker visits, playing the role of John Ringling North on a shoestring. One of the stateside acts which got a lot of press coverage with UniverSoul were the thirteen members of Drumline, known as the "Senate" in their hometown of Atlanta. They joined the show after appearing in the movie *Drumline*. And what a huge boon to the bumpin' box office they were. "When the guys come in and start playing, the crowd goes crazy." said the group's leader, Demetrius Hubert. Down through the aisles, boomingly they entered, raising the tent with snares and cymbals. Into the ring they marched, breaking formation and dancing to 50 Cent's hit, "In Da Club."

"So maybe kids who wouldn't think a circus is cool will give this one a try," stated Hubert. Referencing happy days of his own at the Ringling show in Atlanta, he said, "I want to give kids today that kind of memory."[5]

Building an all-black performance proved impossible. The best that Walker could do was to describe his stars, who hailed from many countries, as being "all of them, all sons and daughters of Africa." The fact is, the bumpin' jumpin' show will probably never be as black as it would like to be. Why? Taking a thumbnail view of recent history, very few African Americans have shown much desire to undergo the rigorous training and life-long dedication necessary to make it big under any big top. There are but a few fleeting exceptions, and even they are modest at best. About the time, back in the sixties, when Ringling-Barnum hired its first black showgirl, Priscilla Williams, to work in spec and aerial ballet, Sid Kellner's James Brothers put the smoothly efficient, mid-level Flying Souls up in the spotlights. John Strong featured with pride a cradle act performed by the biracial team of Sugar and Spice. Let's cut to a comparative reality: Far and away one of the greatest aerial acts ever seen in this country, the Ayak Brothers (who happened to be dark-skinned), did not come from this country. Point made?

The King Charles Troupe, who did, offered frenetic free-form comedy in catch-as-you-can doses, "playing" basketball on unicycles. The novelty of their semi-orchestrated commotion back and forth between the hoops, good for a season or two, wore thin through overexposure on Ringling. What about blacks on horses, or with clubs? Off springboards or in the air? If they can excel elsewhere, from baseball lots to ballet stages and at the Olympics, why not around a ring? So far, the most engaging U.S.-born black circus entertainers tend to be hip-hop gymnasts. Why are they still missing from the parade?

Ventures Hank Ernest, not with much conviction and with little trace of race-based paranoia, UniverSoul evolved into a situation where the performers don't have to be black.[6]

In his first years running Big Apple, Paul Binder managed to teach and assemble some young acrobats out of Harlem. A few of them ended up with other shows, one with Cirque. Ultimately, Binder had to face the fact that the United States lacks the circus schools capable of cultivating native-born talent into bona fide performers who can hold their own against the constant invasion of first-rate stars from foreign shores. In fact, any ambitious young black — or any colored — American would be better off traveling to places like Africa, where new circus schools are proving themselves. I told you about the excellent Gabonese high-wire troupe from Central Africa. Wherever they trained, it was not in this country.

Binder himself agrees that even the schools in Africa are probably doing a better job than any of their would-be counterparts in the lazy U.S. of A. He mentions training centers in Kenya and Cairo. "Some acts come out of there, but very few. UniverSoul is grabbing whatever they can.... It's hard to compete with them. They are very successful."

Like most producers, Binder is open to the inclusion of top-flight artists of all colors and

Bringing a funky new beat and voice to the circus: UniverSoul's original ringmaster, Calvin "Casual Cal" DuPre (photograph courtesy of Arvonna Boyd).

creeds. "Not many black artists out there. I wish they'd come knocking on our door. We're interested."

Time to take a walk through a shabby, ill-lit concession top into UniverSoul's more imposing main text. See those neat banks of lights attached to each of the four poles? They will be elevatored up and down during the program to illuminate the action in a variety of ways. Look even higher — pretty impressive, huh, that dense maze of overhead lighting?

Here comes the new "mistress of ceremonies," Mabeline. And what a loud-mouthed contrast she is to the more sedately controlled Casual Cal, no longer here. Mabeline is a down and doin' lady; there is no other way to describe her raucous personality. Heck, she's grandma on parole from the 'hood. She screeches and carries on, her legs spread brawlingly apart. "When I say big top, you say 'Circus!'"

Okay.

At intervals during the program, Mabeline shouts, "Big top?"

And we shout back, "Circus!"

Not all of the acts are announced by Mabeline. Some are introduced by the pre-recorded announcements of a smooth male voice, and what a relief.

Neither is the music live anymore. Walker retired the band — or it fled after Casual Cal, who left UniverSoul to start his own show. In its place, a taped score delivered through ear-crashingly loud speakers sounds usually relevant. And like most taped music, what you get is a juke box soundtrack. Consumer alert: The speakers near the ringside seats could be bad for your eardrums.

We've saved the best for *first*. Sit back, stuff your ears if you must, brace yourself for a rough and tumble high-energy ride. Circus acts of note? Yes, about half a dozen in Univer-Soul's 2005 grab bag. At the top of the heap are the remarkable Shanghai Swingers, who execute stunningly complex flying trapeze maneuvers from multiple riggings. We've never seen anything like this from China. The Shanghai Swingers drop and leap and fly somersaults, one person sailing upward while another falls, the whole whiz of bodies passing each other in constant motion. Best of all, not a single item is missed. Utter perfection in the air. Monte Carlo gold all the way.

I've already talked up the Gabonese troupe, who respect high-wire traditions with quiet competence. There's another take-note black act composed of two dudes, acrobat Lucky from Johannesburg, hip-hopper Country from New Orleans. They've got it all, funky fun to acrobatics and soul spinning. In their first number, they are two travelers with suitcases, working a fast-paced routine across and around a table. In their second — in which they take us, in the words of Mabeline, "down to the dirty south, down to dirty New Orleans" — Country and Lucky are musical hip-hopists who could stop a stream of pedestrians anywhere dead in its tracks. Now, here's one for the books: Country throws himself into a perfect *sliding* head stand across the floor! Yes, he's on his head, at the same time *sliding* across the floor, perfectly upright. I've never seen *that* before. Have you?

Another thrill occurs when two guys are walking the wheel of death. One of them jumps unusually high each time the wheel reaches the highest point in another revolution. Old trick, sure. New, more daring delivery, oh, yes. And it's all done without mechanics.

And the least for last: Some Cossack riders are only pleasant to watch. The elephants, highly underworked these days for reasons already reported, show how to succeed in showbiz without really trying anymore. A four-star contortionist is about as good as the best; trouble is, there are so many good four-star contortionists out there, dime a dozen, as to make them all look like cookie cutter versions of each other. Another borderline entry is the program's deceptively Cirque-like opening; a lovely black ballerina postures and points while a lone violinist accompanies her. Then come the compelling Country and Lucky, followed by a festive Caribbean Flava of stilt walkers and "limabams" dancing in colorful costumes.

The clowns are at least characters as opposed to painted-on faces. One of them wanders into the audience and proposes to a woman, and is eventually reigned in by Mabeline. A sad/funny bit considering that, on the Friday morning when we attended, most of the women in the audience had kids but no husbands.

Still determined, after ten years on the road, to badger his customers onto a higher moral plane, this time around Mr. Walker stages a walkthrough panorama of black history. Familiar figures enter the ring for brief biographical announcements. And from this moment on, a number of obviously disinterested ticket holders are getting up from their seats and making a hasty exit. How sad that most of them are the young single women with children in tow. Mabeline is making an appeal for an end to "black on black crime, babies having babies." Oddly, the message seems aimed at the wrong crowd. Those who need to hear it either came to the party too late, or didn't come at all.

Unless you like super loud music, in-your-face announcements and extra long pauses that drag things down, this is a show that takes some work to get through. Since when did a circus have to be so stressful? For all of its authentic assets, what this sledgehammer-intense rumble is short on is better pacing and a little artistic discretion to go along with it. The show would also do its patrons a favor by selling a program magazine — or at least a one-page handout listing the names of the acts and the performers. The lack of such is more often associated with bare-bones carnie-circus operations that survive on the mass distribution of free kids' tickets and do not always maintain a fixed program of artists for a single season.[7]

How we wish that the Casual Cal we saw a few months earlier in his own new circus had been there with UniverSoul. How we wish there could have been the live band that once played for Mr. Walker's show.

When DuPre broke from UniverSoul in 2005 to start up his Bumpin' Big Top, the parting left both him and his former employer worse off. The makeshift circus program that DuPre put together, built on a wide-ranging spectrum of talent from top-drawer (the Canestrelli trampoline act) to bargain basement (Genie with the animals) did not harbor well for Casual Cal's inaugural season out on his own bank account. Still, Bumpin' Big Top came with a saner sound system and, best of all, with Cal himself. It was a much easier show to sit through.

Cal tells me that he quit UniverSoul because he felt they put too much emphasis on their logo. "Cal is a product. UniverSoul is a product. What we should have done was marry them both to be powerful powerful. Okay, that they didn't do. They wanted to separate. ... We're personality. People want to see personality, especially if you've got one. If you don't have one, you go with the logo. No problem. But UniverSoul can be no bigger than the pastor of the church, so if you're the church, you got to bring the pastor right behind."

Sounds to me like the church wanted to change pastors.

That wasn't the only reason. Cal was growing antsy about Walker's obsession with black markets. "I quit because, number one, the black community is not the only community that wants to see the show.... If you ever sat in that tent when I do a show, it doesn't matter what color you are, you feel the goodness, and that's what I'm selling.... It's very important for the world to know that soul is not a color, cause we spend so much time identifying with black. Soul is an experience."

As disjointed if not more so than UniverSoul's program (well, it's new), the Bumpin' Big Top also brings its show to a close, welcome or not, with a sermon for the younger set. Guys are exhorted to "keep your pants up." Girls are urged, "Don't show it all in public. Whatever you show, be prepared to share." Then the tent is turned into a church, with a token pitch for Jesus, complete with four midgets dressed as altar boys. A long drawn-out spiritual proclaims, "I need you! You need me!" A woman ascends a heavy web and proceeds to make little use of it. We are no longer being entertained. We are being force fed a preachy black sermon. Casual Cal is walking around the central aisle with quiet reverence, shaking hands with some of us in the small crowd who turned out to patronize his very first date. We are at Jack London Square in Oakland. Really, he is the most interesting act in his own show.

The DJ turned ringmaster wears a pink and white costume patterned after the zoot suit. It adds a subtle flair to his highly personable style. He claims to have no idols for inspiration. When he saw one performance of the Ringling show in the early seventies, he walked away without long-lasting memories. What gave him the most joy were the boys he took with him to see the circus. On his own, DuPre seems to have achieved what few big top announcers are able to bring off — the image of quiet authority and a personal connection to every act on the program. He is one commanding presence in a soulful way. And yet he never puts himself in the way of the show. So, Casual Cal, would you please share with us some of your ideas about the role of the ringmaster?

"He brings that thing right into the hearts of the people.... What you're saying, they have to feel, what you know, they have to feel. 'I know why he's excited. I didn't know that act was that hot, but when he introduced them, I was wondering why he was so excited, but after seeing the act, he put it right on the money. I love it!'"

"I define circus as one step below church. It is the only family event where you captivate ages one through ninety nine.... What you're saying, they have to feel. What you know, they have to feel."

He has a unique voice, like John Strong had a voice ("Hi, ya, folks!"). Like Harold Ronk, Ringling's majestic ringmaster supreme, had a voice. Like Paul Binder, the sawdust scholar who shares bits of circus history with the audience, has a voice. They all convey a compelling respect for the artist, and we feel a deeper sincerity — beyond the bombast, beyond the rhetoric. Just good actors? Maybe. Most circus announcers fill the shoes with routine competence, if that. Few rise to the passionate level of a Strong or a Ronk or a Binder. Or now, a DuPre. And if their work is an illusion, it is not easily learned.

Another young African American who got close to the mark of conversion was Johnathan Lee Iverson. He donned Ringling red to whistle the show on. So very close. He came and went like clowns did under the Felds. In one season, out two or three later. They never stay around long enough anymore to age into vintage anythings.

Iverson's coming was hyped to the heavens by the Big Show. "The first black ringmaster, and also the youngest, in Ringling history," they claimed. From choir boy to apprentice comedy actor he advanced, courtesy of a Ringling director, Phil McKinley, who spotted Iverson's potential during his work on a diner theatre production of *The Fireside Christmas Show*. McKinley encouraged Iverson to try out for the circus gig. Thirty other souls who wanted to blow the Ringling whistle also auditioned. The job went to Mr. Iverson, not because of his ethnicity, insisted Kenneth Feld. "It was his presence and his phenomenal voice."[8]

We take everything from the media-savvy Mr. Feld as a probable act of spinmanship. And considering Mr. Feld's flair for shoplifting at other circuses in order to keep his own show stylistically up to date and competitive, we can imagine him being apprised of another circus out there specializing in hip-hop and jealously wanting to include a sampling of such soul in his own copycat smorgasbord.

The 22-year-old Iverson was said to have received a few friendly words of advice from the long-retired Harold Ronk. It showed up in subtle ways during Iverson's first season. He revealed a natural flair for the sort of understated hyperbole that suited the imperial authority of the Greatest Show on Earth. Had we another Ringmaster Ronk in the making? Many of young Jonathan's hand gestures and intonations of voice matched our higher hopes and expectations. So far, on with the show.

So far didn't last so very long. At first, Iverson blended his soulful personality with classical restraint. Gradually, though, either through direction or Iversons's own self-liberating ethnicity, he sank into gospel hall and jive. A promising new presence at the mike morphed into an act unto itself. Too much. The great ones walk a fine wire separating who they are from what we are supposed to be looking at — not them. It is no small feat, injecting a degree of excitement and anticipation without becoming the show itself. The Feld organization has never settled with any one man in red for any length of time. Tim Holst played the role superbly in the older tradition, and he lasted only a few seasons. Thereafter, he joined the corporate ranks, serving as vice president in the talent-scouting division. Most of the men who followed Holst were virtual fly-by-nighters, including the expediently short-lived Kristopher Antekeier, who spent but a single year and then turned out a helpfully informative tell-all-tome, *Ringmaster.*

None stay around long enough to develop a lasting persona cut from time, knowledge and passion. Casual Cal takes pride in what Iverson did accomplish: "He had to step in there and he handled it.... He got out there and looked good in his suit, did his job, sung his songs, and I think that's just great."

It's a pity that the multi-gifted Iverson did not last. What is more disappointing is that he did not get better direction. To require a ringmaster, as the Felds do, to also be a pitch-man during the pre-show activities destroys the necessary mystique they should bring to the program itself. Harold Ronk stressed the importance of an image carefully guarded and sustained throughout the performance. This means, for example, speaking in less dramatic tones when called upon to ask for a doctor in the audience during emergencies. It means never acting the part before or after the show or during intermission. "I don't want to spoil what's coming," Ronk declared. "Some announcers, they're always on. This is what I try not to do, because this is acting that I put into my role. Before or after the show, I don't even use my ringmaster style, because that would take the surprise out of it."

During his six-year tenure with Ringling, Iverson gradually drew more from the gospel side of his personality, sacrificing the initial restraint that had made him a much more engaging presence. He ended up as in-your-face as is the typical Feld-produced program, itself a noisy two-hour commercial for itself. Al Ringling once remarked that the profession called for someone who could be "vital yet elusive." The words still seem appropriate, at least for a three-ring extravaganza.

Casual Cal notes that his voice will change in response to the action. "It's the energy of the act maybe. If it's an aerial act that's nice and pretty and chiffon, I might come off just a little softer in the presentation, but the excitement is still in my voice."

To demonstrate, he lowers his voice and almost whispers, "What you're about to see..."

Argued Ronk, the rise and fall of intonations should be the building blocks of the ringmaster's craft. "You don't want to hear everything the same. The most beautiful voice in the world could eventually become boring because it doesn't go anywhere. It doesn't do anything."

Which reminds us of UniverSoul's new announcer, Mabeline. She comes on loud and grizzly, and she stays loud and grizzly. And she gets on our nerves. Only at the end of the program does she reveal herself to be a very petite lady with a very refined natural voice. Too late, Mabeline.

Putting more soul into his circus was no doubt what Kenneth Feld was up to when, to replace the departing Iverson, he recruited not one but two African-American announcers — "ringmaster" Tyron McFarlan and "all access pre-show host and roving reporter" Andre

McClain. They were a couple of cool dudes, either of whom would have sufficed. In prior seasons, the demographics-driven Mr. Feld included a Spanish-speaking announcer along-side Iverson in some of the larger cities with big Hispanic populations. The *Los Angeles Times*, in 2001, dubbed this one "the greatest bilingual show on earth." Just another way of bumpin' out to reach a certain segment of the public on its own cultural terms.[9]

Aside from rock concert sound systems and screeching dames on loan from the 'hood, this bumpin' out stuff may actually bring a little relief to our Cirque-decimated midway. Heck, a few of the more risqué shows out there which call themselves "circus" could be the work of Cirque-suffocated runaways screaming out for freedom from ballet. Going down and dirty may be the only politically acceptable way to reclaim the roots of a more real experience — to bring back the disgraced sideshows and barkers, the shoot-'em-up wild animal acts, the real daredevils without mechanics and the slightly loony clowns.

Maybe they're screaming out, "Let the circus be the circus again!" Consider the kinky example of Cirque Berserk, a Reno-based company of sideshow actors at Harrah's who glee-fully boast of having gone "stark raving mad." They promised to transform reality itself into a "journey of lunacy and hysteria."[10] Each of their characters bore a split-personality costume, the front side being a traditional circus figure, the back, more strange and suspect. Do you spot here an adolescent yearning for something pre–Le Cirque? For something you'd find on a weedy lot under mud-stained canvas?

Even the Big Show in Montreal — yes, that Cirque — seems to be gasping for an escape route from its own cosmic paralysis. In its high-tech hootchy-kootchy Vegas revue at the New York–New York Hotel and Casino called *Zumanity*, Cirque du Soleil peddles flesh with a certain style. Here, the ticketed voyeur will be teased by a trendy excuse for simulated sex positions and titillating maneuvers. Introducing Quebec's leather-clad drag queen, zoo keeper Joey Arias, who will sing "Sex is Beautiful," and welcome you to his Hedonistic Paradise. You'll marvel at bondage artist Laurence Jardin, working with four black ropes while doing a little ballet above the stage. You'll behold the "Gentle Orgy of Breathing Giants," consisting of fifty cast members coupling and tripling up for rhythmic breathing exercises before the mistress of ceremonies.

It's all on the inside! Come in and gawk at the kinkiest attire imaginable! Come in and have at it! Watch the rubber man twist himself into a pretzel! See Cuba's Alex Castro strip down to a sparkling silver cup! See two topless women going to work on each other in a three-high fish bowl. They splash in wild abandon! Now, you men out there who are still "men" — you'll see our stripteaser taking it all off from the top of a television set while seven guys (are they really guys?) sit around it, each staring indifferently at a football game in progress.

Come on in and test your manhood. Come on in and see if you can go "the other way." Try it for a couple of highly instructive hours. See how the other half lives. See what you've been missing. "We're adults, too," claims *Zumanity*'s producing pimp, Mr. Guy Laliberte.[11]

Casual Cal may not be taking it all off anytime soon, but he is retiring the animals from his new show for the time being. He sees himself heading into a more Cirque-like future and into more white neighborhoods. "Just as you got a lot of animal lovers, you have an equal amount of people who don't like animals. Don't like seeing 'em chained up, don't like seeing an animal trainer with them. ... To me, you have to grow and you have to change, and as long as you're substituting the same interest and energy for something for the kids and the family, you don't lose anything."

Chris Lashua identifies with youthful performers from days gone by who each sought to bring novelties to the public. "Now, I wouldn't define circus as either traditional with animals or without. Circus is ... It's so many things, that's the funny thing about what Cirque did. It is essentially what P.T. Barnum did and what the Ringlings did. They were looking for ... they had Jumbo touring, and they'd bring in the body piercing act from Africa, or the giant. They were looking for things that were just strange out there. Cirque has done the same thing. Cirque goes to Japan to bring back Tiko drumming and they built an act with drummers.... They've really gone to every corner of the earth.... They've built on what traditional circuses have done, which is go find oddities, find things that are strange."

Like fish bowl ladies and living pretzels? No, Norma, maybe the old hootchy-kootchy grind never completely went away. It's just waiting to be rediscovered, like candy apples and gaudy themeless parades. Like gruff-sounding barkers and oddball clowns. Like the fearless wire walker who truly took your breath away.

So here's the state of the circus on our midway in transition: A bumpin' big top offering a church service, Cirque du Soleil, a bathhouse. We will harbor one simple wish, neither religious nor carnal, for a season yet to come: Anything, please — other than another cerebral ballet about misplaced identity or planetary dysfunction.

19

Big Apple Delicious

Take a look over there — see — across the street in the park? The cream-colored tent, its tapering peaks as soft as whipped cream? See the red sidewalls and the white picket fence in front of it? I'd say it looks like something out of old Europe. And you? Yeah, a rather quaint, cozy setup compared to the upscale world of Cirque du Soleil and its envious copycats.

That picturesque little old-world setting represents something special to a man whose passion for tradition looms over the entire enterprise. It stands for the simpler one-ring exhibition created by Philip Astley that thrived in Europe while at the same time west of the Atlantic, P.T. Barnum and partners were saying "So what?" to the status quo, were adding rings and rails and pushing the public to expect bigger and better things. You are looking at the Big Apple Circus.

Inside the tent in the park, the old roots of the continental form are preserved year after year by two fellows who started up the whole thing thirty seasons ago. You are gazing upon the sainted expression of the show's passionate founder, Paul Binder, and his long-time co-founder, one Michael Christensen. These two guys have held firm to their oft-restated vision of a circus unencumbered and thoroughly uncompromised by pretense or technology. Under their big top, the cheapest chair is still agreeably close to the action. And the vision that guides their operation, officially stated, is "to invigorate the community we serve with the joy and wonder of classic circus."

"We believe in virtuosity," states Binder. "The artist turns the trick with grace and beauty. So, whether it's a single somersault or a double somersault or a triple, it's done with grace and beauty. They accomplish the classical form and they do it in a way that is very automatically satisfying."

Binder's boyhood memory of watching the spotlighted Unus in solo glory at Madison Square Garden seems to have guided his entire life through and around a single ring. "It's about the heart and the soul and the nerves. It's about the identification with the extraordinary nature of the human being, and that's why it's a universal language."

Says Christensen, "Paul and I had a vision of what the Big Apple Circus was — informed by our work together in European circuses and on the streets. It had a single theme that was the joyous contact between artists and audience. And that's the single greatest challenge, is protecting and maintaining that quality of the Big Apple Circus."

They started out with their hearts in academic clouds. They were determined to find and develop their own New York artists from hard-scrabble streets. Their first programs were "presented" by the New York School for Circus Arts, which they believed would one day rival those in Soviet-dominated eastern Europe. Two embittered ex-Soviet artists, Nina Krasavina and Gregory Fedin, taught many of the classes as well as performed with Big Apple.

The school enrolled 200 students the first year. Twenty-five of them were turned into apprentice performers: a six-member acrobatic and hand-vaulting group came from "the heart of the inner city" via the fledgling academy. And, like other grads decked out in sequins, the troupe supplied gusto a tad short of the "virtuosity" that Paul Binder preaches. But raise the pulse of a supportive crowd they did. Others from the school walked wires, donned clown face, foot juggled and tumbled.

The downside? Very few of these early recruits went beyond a season or two. Not a surprise. After all, New York is in the United States, and the United States does not turn out the kinds of circus acts that can compete against the superior talents from foreign lands. The first Big Apple programs were high on homegrown good will and youthful energy, and soon that was not enough. Gradually, a notable quest for local participation gave way to a largely professional roster of proven performers who had not trained in American classrooms.

What has Mr. Binder to say about this? "I know how hard it is to do. We believed we could create a professional training school and attract inner-city kids."

And they didn't.

Today, Binder confesses that the resources needed to bring off such a venture — funds and world-class instructors (not to mention the students) — were pitifully outside their reach. In his opinion, the late Irvin Feld's Clown College (since disbanded) was the best U.S.-based school. "The great clowns are born. They're not made. But the college brought them together in places with very good trainers.... Irvin Feld and Kenneth Feld were on the right track when it came to training." They went for the best teachers available, he says. "I think that was a real school."

Any other praiseworthy schools from the Pacific to the Atlantic? Binder tips his hat a little to the city by the Golden Gate. "The best school so far." Yet, the San Francisco School of Circus Arts hardly turns out any new performers of note other than, now and then, training a new crop of Chinese-style pole climbers. They are taught by the school's master trainer, Lu Yi, who is also artistic director of what is now called San Francisco's Pickle Circus. Yi came to the U.S. in 1988 when his Nanjing Acrobatic Troupe was booked by Paul Binder for "The Big Apple Circus Meets the Monkey King."

Working in a country without the will or the way to match the success of Montreal or Moscow, Binder and Christensen end up doing what virtually all big-top chiefs do: they spend their money on the most affordable foreign ring artists of indisputable merit. And at the same time, they stay connected to the community they call home. Christensen formed the generously charitable Clown Care Unit. It sends joeys and performers to hospitals, and not just to those in New York City. They appear at some 17 wards spread across the country. This sets the Clown Care Unit far above the days when a circus might dispatch a funny face or two — along with, sometimes, a few performers — to hospitals on circus day. Clown Care is in operation three to five days every week, fifty weeks a year. Clowns, magicians, puppeteers and story tellers charm bedridden children.

Christensen has reason to smile aloud. "This is unique to the Big Apple Circus. To be able to find a way to take some of the joy, some of the delight, some of the wonder, some

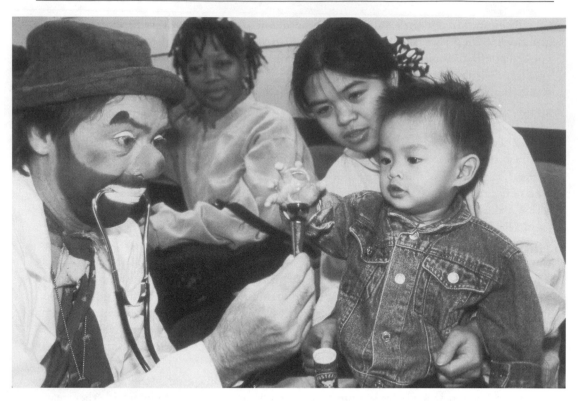

"Mr. Stubbs" (Michael Christensen) with the Clown Care Unit (courtesy of the Big Apple Circus).

of the excitement, some of the qualities that are fantastically circus, and bring them to the bedside of pediatric kids in hospitals chronically ill."

It took about ten years for Michael and Paul's Big Apple dream to blossom into a high-class, rather old-fashioned show of the kind that existed in Europe, at least until the 1970s when Ann Fratallini and others started shaking some fresh air into a very old form. Big Apple presented one act at a time, okay. Each act was formally announced by ringmaster Binder. A hard-working band provided suitable music. Programs like this rise or fall on the merits of the individual acts, for there is little extra action to spice up or gloss over lulls or ho-hum items. As already noted, in 1986 Big Apple gave the patient spectator some fairly wonderful moments. But true to the older European model, they came with little presentational pizzazz.

One thing that set the show intelligently apart were Binder's introductions, laced with neat historical bits. The two dudes who ran it, we'd say, still needed a little something more than blind duty to an aging format. Watching their show was like reviewing a dream through a musty time-warp. You got the acts, and they were good, and that was about it.

That same season of '86, Binder started doing something that would eventually help him break free of his fetish for antiquity under the tent: He started framing each program around a "theme," and from that frame forward, the show stretched its creative muscles a little more. *Bello and Friends* in 1999 highlighted the multi-talented Bello Nock. *Big Top Do Wop* came on in 2001, *Dreams of a City* in 2002. Cheers to Binder for declaring, "Themes are the only thing that make sense. Circus is not narration. It is not about the brain. It is direct and emotional."[1]

By now, Mr. Binder's valentine to the old world was having to compete with the ground-breaking sophistication of Cirque du Soleil and its imitators, most of them no respecters of hallowed traditions. The world was suddenly turning away from animal acts and from human performers appearing as themselves. What to do up against this monster with tentacles reaching far and wide, its redefining showmanship a threat to average circus companies everywhere?

Binder and Christensen faced the monster head on. And for a chapter in time — the year, 1997 — they hired its most famous director, Guy Caron himself. Yes, that Caron guy who had staged Cirque's first legendary shows. Here came Montreal, down to direct New York. A surrender to something drastically at odds with Binder's sacred vision? Michael Christensen talks of those trying times when he held a co-directing relationship with Caron. In 1997, they were planning to celebrate the twenty-year anniversary of the founding of Big Apple. And here, in essence, was Cirque du Soleil co-directing the bash.

As Christensen tells it, Mr. Caron thought up the idea of putting masks on all the performers to make them look like older people greeting Grandma in a tribute to her "birthday." A friend of Caron's up in Canada created the images. "They were wonderful masks," says Christensen. "They were characters."

And something felt strangely wrong.

From a Big Apple perspective, recalls Christensen, "It didn't feel right. It took a while to figure this out. The masks covered up our faces and personalities, and this is what I mean by balance. Theatrically, it was strong, but it wasn't right for the Big Apple Circus. We celebrate everyone's individuality and their own personality."

Off came the false fronts.

Back to earth went Big Apple. One crisis met. The next was much more daunting. And it was not something that could be redirected out, because Paul and Michael had no control over this hurdle. When Kenneth Feld booked his upstart *Kaleidoscape* into New York city the same time of the year that saw Big Apple making its annual holiday stop at Lincoln Center, now there was a box office challenge. Behind the Feld ballyhoo were the funds to launch another parting of the red sea. It caused a lot of anguish for the littler show, which nearly came unglued over the brazen Ringling invasion, afraid that its attendance would take a big hit. Then it proved to be helpful.

"In some ways," admits Christensen, "it was the best thing that could have happened to us, because it was a real threat. There was a show that was very similar to ours, and it forced us to go to the table in a hard way. To determine and be able to articulate what makes the Big Apple Circus unique among one-ring circuses."

Which is?

"New York's own circus. We grew out of New York vitality and energy and resources which is a very clear distinction. We are also a not for profit corporation, dedicated to giving back and serving the communities in which we perform."

Binder and Christensen do a lot of brain storming. With the possible exception of the Soviet big top intellectuals, we can't think of a circus director more articulate than the analytical Paul Binder. He views all events like a grad student churning out a thesis. For example, Binder took real displeasure over the *Wall Street Journal* story about power clowns, starting with the "monstrously ugly" sketch of one at the top of the article. Kelly Crow, the muckraking writer, lumped into her condemned circle of Big Egos the Big Apple's own Barry Lubin. He's the clown who invented Grandma and sometimes does the part. Now, Binder wonders just what caused Ms. Crow to crow off-key. After all, isn't she working for

The opening charivari at the Big Apple Circus's *Picturesque*, 2005 (courtesy of Bertrand Guay/Big Apple Circus).

a newspaper that, as Paul puts it, "celebrates capitalism everyday"? So why would she even question the perks and outrageously high salaries offered a handful of star funmakers at the top? Says Paul, "I think she takes the truth that these are well paid, carefully handled people and turns it into some kind of negative notion. They were well paid. What's wrong with that?"

Crow gave the impression that if Bary Lubin does not get his way, he will walk and Big Apple will fold. So far, he's been granted his wish to skip a high percentage of the dates outside of New York, to be given the title "director of clowning," to direct the 2006 show, and to receive royalties for the sale of Grandma souvenirs. Shocking? As Crow would have us believe, Lubin has a way of getting his way. According to an unidentified Big Apple "spokesman," in Crow's paraphrasing words "the circus had to accept his terms because it needed his character."[2] All of which leaves Mr. Binder fuming in disbelief and denial. "I didn't *need* Grandma's character," he insists. "I *wanted* Grandma's character."

He has no idea just who in his organization spoke with Crow or what exactly was stated that caused Crow to use the word "needed." (Crow told us that her story was fully "vetted" by a high-placed Big Apple spokesperson in public relations.)[3] Binder only knows that when the show went on without Grandma for a couple of season, business did not drop significantly. He only knows that royalties for souvenirs are fairly standard procedure, and that the title "director of clowning" was not given to Lubin under the threat of abandonment. He also knows that Lubin, like others, can make suggestions, and that he might or might not go along with them. And, lastly, he is amazed at the *Journal*'s concluding "that there is something grossly inappropriate for clowns to be paid well and celebrated."

Crow did seem conveniently oblivious to other high-paid tent stars down through the ages (like Leitzel, Codona, Gunther Gebel Williams) who made a lot more money than the average performer, and who enjoyed unusual luxuries on the train and on the lot. That's life.

Paul Binder can't say enough about his star clown. "Grandma is a symbol of the kind of gentle kindness that is the best of families, the heart of great families, so that I always adored the character."

So you've heard ringmaster Binder wax lyrical over the "virtuosity" of circus artists to the sanctity of Grandmahood. Now, let's cross the street to the park and spend an afternoon inside that cozy little tent. Let's see for ourselves what Big Apple is up to these difficult times. You might be wondering if their themes are any more obvious than window dressing, and if the format itself is still a tad staid.

In the year 2005, Binder and Christensen brought back another Cirque-related figure, Michel Barette. He appeared, you may remember, as the ringmaster in Cirque du Soleil's first show to hit the states, *We Reinvent the Circus*. Barette directs Big Apple now and then, working in close collaboration with Paul and Michael through a year-long process involving face-to-face meetings, phone calls and numerous e-mail exchanges. This year's theme, *Picturesque*, honors a number of famed painters throughout the program. The shape and colors of their pallets show up in the costumes. Museum maven John Ringling North would have loved it.

Explains Barette, "We have differences. We have agreements. But we discuss the matter. I manage to adapt to that and I have fun working with them, and I think they have fun working with me because they called me back after time. And when I go there, I try to create something new, something different, to go a little farther and to push the creative process a little further compared to the last time I was there. So sometimes it is surprising for them."

All three guys toss ideas out on the table. They argue and discuss, rethink and reargue, and manage to reach a consensus. "Each part of the threesome is fighting for their own thing," says Barette, laughing a little. Unlike Kenneth Feld's circus smorgasbord, Big Apple's big guns apparently use outside influences, such as Barette's input, in a more subtle, finely integrated manner. They do not throw a bunch of pan-global circus performance trends into the ring at one time.

"In every rehearsal process," continues Barette, "you have to find the balance back every day, in every decision you make."

Through a window in his office overlooking a rehearsal studio, Binder can keep tabs on the evolving activities. And he is usually that close at hand when his advice or approval is needed, for he has the final word. It is he who decides or passes on the acts, he who ultimately okays every element in the show.

"I don't have to be there every moment. If they need me, they'll call me. I usually am taking notes. I had nineteen years when I directed the shows, so it's come from experience."

When Barette directs, he told me, he is constantly in search of a "rhythmic potential." Usually, it will be discovered and built upon during the rehearsals. The goal is to create a kind of momentum unique to the way in which the acts begin to merge. That is something hard to foresee in advance.

Yet still, Michel Barette believes that his job is to tell a story. And don't they all? In this regard, he relates well to the preoccupation of Binder and Christensen with the emotional qualities of the performance. However, he stresses that "stories" can be told in "thousands of ways." Here is how he lays it out: "It's always referring to an intimate moment when let's say, your mother or your father is telling you a story when you're going to bed. It's exactly the same feeling. When you're in a good show, you've got this kind of mesmerizing moment when you see the story. You're in the story. You're part of that. If that happens, we have succeeded."

Story or not, in 2005 Big apple poured into the painterly mix a number of high-voltage performers from points east — Russia, Spain and China. They all grew up in circumstances that might be said to favor juggling over computer science, vase balancing over gangsta' rap. We're talking established circus family or school — the only sources that can deliver the next Francis Brunn or Miguel Vazquez.

Let's take a look at Big Apple's '05 lineup: To start with, the gifted mouth-juggler Picasso Jr. He was the only son of the great Picasso, and although Junior grew up wanting to become a tax collector for job security, fate contrived otherwise. While serving in the military, Junior chanced upon a small tent troupe, and on his own away from a famous father's heavy-handed expectations, he felt a sudden desire to change career goals. Now, the circus atmosphere grabbed him by the soul. Now, he was juggling with heart-felt enthusiasm.

Picasso Jr. competed at a circus festival in Paris. He made such an impact on the crowds that he distrusted their motives, believing that the applause was really a tribute to his father's legacy.

Whomever it was meant for, the son walked off with a bronze medal. Soon after, he joined Feld's *Kaleidoscape*. He had a great time, he says, touring the entire U.S.

In 2002, Picasso Jr. experienced the second of a pair of milestones, which he terms his two most memorable nights. At the Monte Carlo Circus Festival, he won a silver clown. That same year, another Spanish act, the high-wire Quiros, took the gold. Never before had any artist from Spain been awarded a clown of any sort at the Prince Rainier tournament, still considered the most prestigious of them all.

Next, animal trainer Svetlana Shamsheeva: She found her dealings with Big Apple to be very amicable. On the Ringling show, says she, "Office never ask you about what you think about music." Ringling's Tim Holst took it upon himself to select which of Svetlana's tricks could go into the act. In contrast, at Big Apple rehearsals, she liked the give and take. "We made good conversation. This circus is very good for that, and with costume, too.... Very nice. Very free conversation. Very glad about this. Not any kind of bad points."

Funny man Vallery started out in Russia working horses at the age of 15. He first appeared in the ring on May 9, 1985, a source of great pride to Vallery. That date marked the fortieth anniversary of the Russian defeat of the Germans in World War II. "It was a dream to become just a circus performer. It was so big. Circus performer! Proud, like you became general or something like that."

How did he switch, two years later, from running a circle of horses to running after laughs? "Third generation circus performer," he answers, pointing to childhood role models. "Grandfather was a clown, so was my father ... was all the time with them. So, I was born in circus. I saw that stuff. I saw greatest clowns. That's how I learned."

And to think of all the hours in vain that would-be artists spend at inferior schools trying to equal "that's how." Some of the luckiest don't need to attend a formal class at all, not when daddy or mommy is, by mere example, a master teacher. Some kids grow up imitating ring stars who just happen to be their own parents.

Teeterboard king Andrey Kovgar, another Russian booked for *Picturesque*, was making his American debut. He created his act six years ago at the Nikulin Circus in Moscow, and it took him a whole year to do it. He says that it was developed "from sport, nothing

Svetlana Shamsheeva and friend (courtesy of Bertrand Guay/Big Apple Circus).

GuiMing Meng (courtesy of Bertrand Guay/Big Apple Circus).

from circus." In 2004, Kovgar's troupe took a silver clown at Monte Carlo after receiving other awards at festivals in France and China. The act was choreographed by Irina Voevodina, and the troupe's costumes for the Big Apple date were inspired by the work of artist Marc Chagall.

Contortionist Mei Ling hails from a Swiss circus family. Chinese-born vase balancer GuiMing Meng, who first appeared in the states in 1985 with Ringling, followed in his father's footsteps. He learned acrobatics with the Shanghai Acrobatic Troupe, enduring 8–10 hour training sessions per day. (We won't get into the ruthless extremes that are said to exist throughout parts of Asia, forcing cruel discipline upon small helpless children against their will to learn circus skills.)

The Mongolian Angels, who work from a double trap, are from — you guessed it.

Okay, time to take our seats. *Picturesque* is now in motion. Here is a remarkable circus program that draws from three global influences to achieve something rich in rhythm, color, tone, pace and, most of all, artistry. All of the elements merge into a one-ring tent-buster. At the foundation, there is the unmistakable imprint of Paul Binder's devotion to old Europe. Above that, the delightful exploits of the foreign stars, most notably the inspired Russians. Finally, the unifying force of director Michel Barette's enchanting touches. So Big Apple is a composite of London, Moscow and Montreal, artfully transformed into almost a masterpiece.

Almost, as in not quite. Most of the best circuses are *not quite*. Why? Here are my minor qualms. There is one duplication: the aerial sculpture team of Regina Debrovitskaya and Valdis Yanovskis, a house act, do a routine in the second half too similar to, and not as good as, the one done by the Mongolian Angels in the first half. Vallery's first turn, "Paintbrush, Stick and Ball," goes on too long. So does a second half bit between Grandma and ringmaster Dinny McGuire, himself a musty, harmlessly charming old tent-show orator circling the action in a state of benign confusion and never once uttering a single "ladies and gentlemen!" Perhaps we should be wondering just what he is up to. Somehow, his being up to not much at all works.

Grandma's brief cameos are perfectly amusing and amusingly to the point; fresh comedic punctuation marks that we happily come to expect of her each time she wanders frivolously into the ring. Here, up against McGuire, she betrays the pattern established so far with an overly long run on sentence. And the pace slackens.

Other defects? Sorry to report, the liberty horses as presented by Yasmine Smart, making her first visit to the Big Apple, are too uneventful to advance the momentum.

Everything else is fine to fabulous: the young student painters who sit around the ring between acts, their creations becoming the brilliant Mirena Rada costumes worn by the performers; the musicians who make up what has got to be, hands down, the very best band with any American show at present. Credit Rob Slowik and his seven — yes, only seven — men. What a richly arranged score. What rousing sensitivity to the action. What a feast of relevant music! Any of you who think that CDs are okay for a circus program, well, go go go, no run run run to the Big Apple Circus and rediscover what a huge difference a first-rate band can make. Bravo, Slowik and Company! Bravo!

Grandma (played by clone Matthew Pauli when we took the show in on the Queens lot at Cunningham Park) is a hoot. She's a hoot whether trying to balance a vase or donning a cape. Picasso Jr., best of the class. Vallery brings down the house in his second act romp titled "Pottery Chaos." And in GuiMing Meng's Chinese Ceramics, we've not seen anything like the way he can manipulate a huge ceramic pot on his head, turning it this

Grandma takes up painting (courtesy of Bertrand Guay/Big Apple Circus).

way and that, tossing it high and gracefully bracing its fall against his amazingly solid crown. His polished routine just keeps building, as a great act will, one awesome feat followed by the next.

Svetlana's dogs, cats and birds raise the crowd to happy waves of shared delight. It's a feeling you won't find anywhere else but under a tip top big top. Don't miss the Persian fluffer who jumps aboard to ride the back of a galloping doggie around this busy ring. To quote the great Harold Ronk, "Watch him!"

They saved the greatest for last. Kovgar's springboard jumpers take the form to heights rarely witnessed. On a pair of stilts, one acrobat is thrust into the air and turns three revolutions before landing. From a horizontal perch resting on the shoulders of two men on the ground, a third man on stilts is balanced while holding a vertical perch, at the top of which is an arm chair. Into it, a fourth man is catapulted.

The Kovgar troupe climax will be a double somersault off the teeterboard followed by four pirouettes — yes, on stilts. And they land it!

These teeterboard heroes have lifted our spirits sky high. They are skipping around the ring, clapping along with us. We don't want it to end. And yet, we do, for it is the perfect place to end. What a triumphant Russian finale to an exhilarating circus of remarkable beauty and taste. What a tribute to the ageless lure of an art form perhaps more universally understood and embraced than any other. A form where humans and animals, performing together, show us a world wondrously alive with magical manifestations, a world pointing upward to friendlier stars out there.

"My hope," says Michael Christensen, "is that there will always be a place for the kind of show that we do ... that circus artists say, 'Hey, you know, I want to affect people, I don't want to be looking at my audience through a gauze of other worldly production values. I would like them to see me. I would like to have that direct joyful connection with my audience.'"

Paul Binder seems as high on circus art in 2005 as he was nearly three decades ago when he blew the first Big Apple whistle. "The magic of the primal ritual tradition is exactly what we're doing today. But we're artists doing what community members did then. What happens is that society became non-tribal, civilized, democratized and so on. Participants of the ritual have become specialists. We call them actors and musicians, and dancers, acrobats now. But they are the same people.

"When we see that we are them, they see the extraordinary nature of themselves. That's what makes them a wonderful audience."

These guys, Paul and Michael — you gotta give them their due for sticking to a core mission against so many conflicting forces of society and culture. At the same time, for finding ways in smart, discriminating collaboration with others to give the public a more stimulating and exciting version of the kind of circus they are determined to preserve. So you New Yorkers out there who take a hometown treasure for granted, why not take to heart Binder's admonition to people everywhere: "Support your neighborhood circus!"

Now, ladies and gentlemen, don't go away just yet. There's still one more big attraction left to take in before our midway of memories must pack up and move on. We're gonna bring out some of the greats — right here, right now — from yesterday, today and tomorrow. Let them throw the last thrills before tear down. Let them paint the final chapter in their own words, in their own ways. And let them take their well-deserved bows.

Maestro, if you please!

20

And in the Only Ring
That Matters

Being free — the catch — you fly out for that split second in the air, and to be caught by the catcher — that beautiful feeling that you lock hands is something that is very very special.

— Tito Gaona

The Cristianis. Wirth and Wallenda. Codona and Leitzel. Vazquez. Kovgar. Otto Griebling. Gunther Gebel Williams. Canestrelli or Zerbini or Chimal: They are the reason we go to the circus. The reason we buy tickets to sit around rings year after year, waiting on the edge of a cushy chair or a bare plank with rapt attention, waiting to be amazed by wizards in magical motion doing things that we've never seen before or things that we've seen many times before but long to see once again.

They are the reason — yesterday, today and, no doubt, tomorrow.

Most of them are destined by childhood to go the glorious distance. May Wirth, probably the most accomplished equestrienne who ever graced the sawdust circle, was riding at the age of five, a mature headliner all of eight seasons later. Al Ringling and his younger brothers, who had seen their own future when they took in Dan Rice's Great Paris Pavilion Circus on the banks of the Mississippi, started making believe they were showmen well before they were teenagers. And by the time he turned 20, Al was setting up horizontal bars in the backyard, a swing from a beam inside the family barn. He cut hoops out of wooden barrels, sanded them down and painted them up in bright colors, and said to the world, I'm a juggler. He found himself a rope, strung it between a pair of trees three feet off the ground and said, watch me walk it! He taught himself how to balance a long pole on the top of his head, and he had a third reason to call himself a circus man.

Their youthful ambitions find a way and a will. A few years later, Al was out on his own, living in a boardinghouse in Broadhead, Wisconsin, where a bed shared cramped quarters with homemade circus props and aerial paraphernalia. By day, the occupant of the cluttered room was employed at Williams and Ballou's Carriage Shop. By night and on the off days, he was practicing the acts he dreamed of one day getting paid to perform. Down at town square, Al tightened a rope strung from the tops of two buildings on opposite sides

They fly high: The Gaonas, winners of the Golden Clown Award at the Monte Carlo Circus Festival, 1978. Seen here in a later photo are, left to right: Armando, Tito, Chella and Richie (Circus World Museum, Baraboo, Wisconsin).

of Main Street. Upon it, he tickled the locals with free exhibitions of daring-do. Ringling's day job boss was so proud to have a virtual circus star seen in public, whose mere silent presence drew attention to its name and products, that Albert was encouraged to skip Saturdays at the shop whenever he felt like a little rope-walking. One Saturday, he took a very small stove aloft, lit a fire and cooked himself up a pretty fair breakfast — well, at least a slice of meat. Old timers talked about it for years. The birth of a great American circus legacy took place in the modest business center of Broadhead.

Such are the humble beginnings of most every young person who will one day make a mark under canvas domes.

Angling to shore up his credentials while still technically employed by Williams and Ballou's, Al Ringling taught himself to balance a plow on his chin. Yes, that's not an easy image to fathom, folks. The world would soon enough be entertained by Broadhead's up and coming showman when, more than a year later, he landed his first professional job with Fred White's company. After a tour, he returned to the carriage shop for off-season work. Now his name was Alphonzo Ringling, juggler and balancer. Now he wore a mustache. Now he had a track record and was ready to add his four brothers to a showbiz dream. They performed their semi-professional acts in winter hall shows, honed their skills, and started up their own circus in 1884.

Gradually, Al settled into the role of ringmaster, his brothers into management positions as they phased out their own acts and hired thoroughly professional performers to fill the bill. Not until 1891— their second year out on rails and ten years after Barnum & Bailey introduced the three-ring craze — did the Ringling boys gave up the single ring in which they had catapulted themselves to circus lords competing with the largest shows on the road. In fact, as already noted, the move was made against Al's artistic preference for the solo turn. But thirty years after the Ringlings opened in Baraboo, Al was still blowing the whistle. Why had he not retired from the tent and opted out for an easy chair in the backyard? newspaper columnist and ex-trouper David W. Watt asked him.

"Well, Dave," replied the one-time juggler and plow balancer, "I started at this work early in the game and I rather enjoy it. It seems to be hard for me to think that somebody else could do it just as well."[1]

Al Ringling to Alex Chimal. Over a hundred years later, nine-year-old Alex, having just watched a grainy, black and white video of some Ringling stars of the 1920s, the very next day set out to teach himself how to perform like one of them.

And who was the performer? Alex thinks for a moment. The guy's name, he says, was Con Colleano.

Why did he choose the flamboyant Australian for a role model? It was the man's style, he answers. He was wowed by the way Colleano ran and jumped and turned somersaults across the wire.

Alex's father did not know that the son, while traveling with his grandfather's circus in Mexico, was behind their backs pursuing a secret goal. Alex started practicing the next day. He grabbed a loose wire from the tent and tied it between two sections. He practiced in private.

They have visions of splendor in spotlights and spangles usually at very young ages. They see the great Con Colleano. They see Dorothy Herbert, or Codona or Unus, Alzana or Vazquez or Picasso, and they begin to take the supernatural for granted. Many of them, like Alex Chimal, are born into long-running circus families. They are the luckiest ones, for circus kids learn to jump high off trampolines, ride elephants and dangle freely from silver bars — by merely imitating their parents. Like mother. Like daughter.

Alex's first gig with his family's show in Mexico was in the teeterboard number. From there, higher into the air he flew, lending his agile body to the return trapeze. He loved every second of it, especially when he could touch the tent and feel like he had reached the limit. He liked wondering up there what might happen next, and feeling a rare adrenaline rush over the cheering crowds.

Alex was eventually allowed to do his rope-walking routine in the show, until he was about fifteen or sixteen, he says. His father never completely approved of the act because it caused Alex too many injuries. Too dangerous. And for Alex, who took his most recent wrist-breaking tumble in 2005, it still is.[2]

They take real risks to do astonishing things before our eyes. In the flesh. In the here and now. In real time. And that's another reason why we admire them so. In his youth, Tito Gaona idolized Faye Alexander, the actual flyer who doubled for Tony Curtis in the film *Trapeze*. Alexander inspired Gaona (as he would Miguel Vazquez) to become one of the all-time greats in his field. Ask anybody out there who has been around for more than a few seasons — what flyer thrilled you the most? Chances are, they'll answer, "Tito."

"He was the greatest showman the big top has ever had," said author Harry L. Graham. "His blindfold triple somersault and triple pirouette return and his rebounding dismount to the catch trap with an ankle-drop catch (not blindfolded, of course) are among the most astounding tricks I have ever seen."

During the late seventies, Gaona spent long hours in practice sessions trying to be the first flyer in the circus universe to execute the quadruple somersault. He never could bring it off before a crowd, although he claims to have delivered four miraculous revolutions into the hands of catcher Eduardo "Lalo" Murillo on one occasion, in January 1981.[3] That was only months before a rival, Miguel Vazquez, turned his own first quad in Long Beach, California. By then, Tito seems to have given up on the impossible quest. Out of fear? Of knowledge? Tito, Tito, please, in your own words:

"Then, later on I said, I don't want to do this. It's too much of an impact, and I don't want to do it in the show, and I just call it quits ... because I had a beautiful act. I had a great act. I had a triple every show and I didn't want to mess up my act. And if I did the quad, it was for my own satisfaction to show what the body can do."

End of a thrilling journey for the era's most loved flyer. Even they reach the outer edges of their own limits in time and space. Nobody seems to know just what became of the quietly heroic Miguel Vazquez, the only flyer so far to truly master the herculean feat — four spins to a pair of waiting hands — with persuasive regularity. Fellow flyer Tony Steele, the first to throw a three-and-a-half, expressed awe over Miguel's mystifying technique: "I've seen him on video tape and I cannot believe it — he seems to hover in the air like a helicopter. It seems like he goes up and he stays there and turns. I don't understand; it's incredible."[4]

None came close to equaling the success rate of the legendary Miguel Vazquez: over *two thousand* quads caught during an unprecedented career that may never be matched. Of the precious few flyers who have duplicated the trick on occasion, there are the Caballeros — Luis and Ruben, Jr., who first did it under the Carson and Barnes tent. In 1988, the Caballeros appeared alongside Vazquez on the Ringling show, offering spectators the thrilling possibility of watching two quads for the price of one. And in 1994, Ruben became the only trapeze artist ever to both fly the quad and, reversing positions in the air, catch it, too. At that milestone performance, Luis soared into Ruben's hands after turning four clean somersaults.

Alone in his greatness, though, Miguel Vazquez achieved a staggering 80.6 percent completion rate (408 catches) across 506 attempts during the 1988 season. That year, flying at a speed said to approach 70 mph, he caught 22 quads in a row beginning in San Francisco on September 1. He finished the season in Columbus, Ohio, nailing all nine quads during the date. When he left the Ringling show at the end of the 1989 tour, he had spun four perfect revolutions into the catcher's hands 1,600 times. In 1990 at the Circus Festival in Monte Carlo, he won the coveted Gold Clown award. After appearing on the Big Apple Circus in 1992, where he passed the 2,000 mark, and in European circus engagements, what has become of the most accomplished flyer of all time? Tito wonders himself about the current mystery of Miguel's whereabouts and state of mind, hinting that Miguel might have sunk into some sort of a post-quad depression. According to reliable inside sources, Vasquez, who evidently keeps a very low profile, is said to be working for the stagehands' union somewhere along the vast Vegas strip.

To excel in and over the starry rings that Philip Astley first formed in an open field near Half Penny Hatch — heck, just to survive almost — circus people must deliver the expected staples associated with their respective acts; better yet, they should bring the novel twist or two and the fresh flair that spells the difference between adequate and memorable.

Circuses that amaze and surprise stand the best chance of getting their customers back the next year. Svetlana Shamsheeva knows all about the public's appetite for the unexpected. "What is circus?" she asks. "Circus, it's an art where public go to see something unusual. You need to show something for public to wow."

She talks of old-hat routines that fall short of the mark, recycled acts done by the people who take the easy route just so long as producers will keep them on the payroll. Audiences are left unimpressed, contends Svetlana, and there are fewer bodies in the seats. Who can argue with her?

"Maybe I am stupid," she says, "but right now, I can't work just about the money. I'm interested in making something like my own tricks, my own ideas. Like I know these tricks. Nobody do it before."

They must continue practicing to sustain their skills and to stay above the pack. Picasso Jr. draws the distinction between his technique and that of most of the others. He mouth juggles balls not with the help of his hands. And that makes a huge difference, he maintains.

He manipulates up to five balls at a time, and sometimes, those five balls will make five tours — a "tour" meaning the passage of all five into the air and back into the mouth. Once, Picasso achieved a record eighty tours with four balls.

One wrong drop and your audience might stray. A second drop could shatter your spellbinding genius — like a flyer twice into the net. And you've lost the house, says Picasso. And that makes it doubly harder to regain your momentum and retake the audience. Performers need nerves of steel and boundless energy to survive the grueling spotlight.

They play to all kinds of people, so each performance presents a new challenge. How to read the crowd. How to grab it, and how to hold it. Our funny man from Russia, Vallery, who tries to improvise every day, will sometimes find himself up against a downbeat mass of humanity out there in the seats. Vallery told me that New Yorkers were not the easiest audience to play to. "You have to be very careful, see what you're doing, because you can't fool them there. There are so many stars."

When he first hit the big town, "I was kind of shocked, because I got a little lost when I came and I didn't get any response. Because they were serious people, so many. But, then, I get them anyway. It was different, to be honest."

For Vallery, the circus is like a party with friends: "I have big pleasure to make people laugh. That's my life. Do everything to make them laugh. I love it."

Still, it's a well rehearsed party at that.

In his twilight years while performing with the Big Apple Circus, juggler Francis Brunn observed another performer in practice, hand-balancer Jim Tinsman, trying vainly for weeks on end to perfect a handstand on a ball perched on the leg of a chair. Brunn watched with interest and doubt. One night, Tinsman shouted out in victory, "I did it! I did it! I did it!"

Brunn turned, walked over to the delirious equilibrist and said, "Yawk, congratulations! But, can you do it at eight twenty every night?"[5]

As it turned out, Tinsman could not. Whatever the artist sets out to do, it must be achieved with fair regularity.

The personal quest to be the first at mastering something never before seen is the mark of the great ones. Karl Wallenda introduced the thrilling seven-person pyramid across the high wire in 1947. Even then, Wallenda would insist that the seven-high was not as fraught with peril as the four-person pyramid he had been doing for years: Two men on trailing

They astonish: The Cristianis, circa 1940 (courtesy of the John and Mable Ringling Museum of Art, Tibbals Digital Collection).

bicycles bridge a bar between their shoulders, On top of the bar stands a chair, and on the chair stands a man with a woman standing erect on his shoulders, her arms outstretched. This trick made the Wallendas, in the words of Fred Bradna, "the most exciting act" he had ever witnessed in all his years with the Big Show.

Every night at 8:20 for some, life and death compete in the shivering spotlights high above the sawdust circle. And at 8:20, when public perceptions of danger ahead do not always match the truth, never was the circus quite so compelling as when the Wallendas performed their legendary seven-high. Even then, Karl Wallenda tells us that the most unforgettable circus performers must be dramatists, too. Of Alfredo Codona, for example, whom Wallenda held in the highest regard, he told me, "He was not just a performer. He was an actor. A good performer should be not just thinking about a good trick. He should be thinking how simpatico he is to the public."

And that, ladies and gentlemen, is the most authentic role a circus star can play: to be himself absolutely and to dramatize his every appearance before the public. This is the showmanship that made Tito Gaona so loved and excitingly watched. Harold Alzana certainly had it. So did Leitzel and Unus, La Norma and the Cristianis, Gunther Gebel Williams and Clyde Beatty. Dave Hoover, a cage boy who took over for Beatty after he died, despaired

They amuse: Lou Jacobs (courtesy of the John and Mable Ringling Museum of Art, Tibbals Digital Collection).

of ever being able to recreate Beatty's hold on the audience: "I do everything Beatty does. I shoot the gun at the same time. The lions snarl at the same time. I get out by the skin of my teeth. The lions charge at me up against the door. I do precisely the same thing and I just don't get the applause."[6]

Some will die for their art, using no undue caution in the pursuit of that which marks their courage and stamina in absolute terms. Indeed, the true aerialist symbolizes the dangers inherent in man's quest to travel beyond common terrain. The Arctic explorer or the astronaut at the edges of the unknown — they all project the same ethereal urges that propel circus artists. Each faces the certain knowledge that fate may one day catch them tragically off balance, a beat too short of a partner's saving grip, an inch below a swinging bar offering them safe return — and the end is there too soon. Risk is inherent in all courageous endeavors.

Karl Wallenda took his final fall in 1978 while walking the wire against windy conditions ten stories above San Juan, Puerto Rico. Most of us believe that this was the way Wallenda would have wanted to exit planet earth, so driven was he still, at the age of 73, to prove himself in the present tense. To remain vitally alive as a circus star. Maybe Wallenda could still hear the fifteen-minute standing ovation that had greeted his sensational premiere at Madison Square Garden.

"Human daring has but one limit: human imagination," wrote Barnum & Bailey's daredevil somersaulting automobile driver, Octavia La Tour, in 1905 for the *New York World*. "Human courage dares all, and there is no task, no feat, no exploit of bravado you can suggest to it that it will not venture.... Demand what feat you will that requires physical skill and physical courage, and we in the circus will attempt it. Nay, we will perform it successfully ... get your mind fermenting; give your imagination free play; and invent the real limit of human daring. Show us how to fly to the moon; direct the way to Mars; point the signboards down the roads of human daring. And I for one will go."[7]

Why, let's ask ourselves, are almost all the top flyers of Mexican descent? Name them — Codona, Vazquez, Espana, Caballero, Gaona. Why, Tito, why?

"Well, we just wanted to build the pyramids higher and higher, I guess."

Now, here's a tough question: Who will define what tomorrow's circus will look like? And will they return the circus to the circus or move it closer still to circus ballet? Which form will win out in the end, or will both flourish alongside each other? You want to know who will decide? "They," as in today's and tomorrow's circus performers. Yes, *they* will determine who influences them and whether they will say yes to reality and no to make-believe.

They will decide whether to keep the show real or choreograph it into oblivion. Whether to toss aside the safety wires and keep the animals. Whether to settle for the safe illusions of the stage over the life-affirming realism of genuine artistry. In their mindless embrace of other forms, performers risk reducing themselves to stick figures in a gutless pageant built on eye-candy, ballet, clowning and special effects.

Let me lay out a little common sense here, folks. The various moves of an acrobat do not tell a story. Never did. Never will. What story does the triple somersault tell us? If anything, it tells us of many human attributes from courage and resolve, to discipline, control and mastery — all of them coming together into a split-second of fleeting perfection. And that is a breathtaking affirmation of life, the need for which, as long as we are human, we are likely never to outgrow. The flyer does not assume the role of a character beyond whom he must be in order to complete his routine. He is who he is. Same for the others on parade. Each of their acts is a physical expression. They are not psychological soliloquies or encounters between figures posing as circus artists engaged in a conflict. Audiences know this. And before it's too late, maybe they will begin holding out for the difference. Let's take some heart and hope in the last-minute cancellation at the Zellerbach auditorium in Berkeley of the Moscow Circus. The Russian Ministry of Culture in pre-show publicity had promised to present *A Russian Winter's Tale*, told in the typical modern-day format of circus-theatre. The promised to include, best of all, "some of the greatest circus performers on earth!"

Did the box office on this one fail to fly? Perhaps the public is finally tiring of these elitist shows which operate on the ridiculous assumption that unless a circus can be counted on to tell a story, it does not merit our respect.

Tricks. We watch them turned before our eyes and we still marvel at how seemingly incredible they are. Most of all, we marvel because the performers have to prove themselves over and over again for every new audience. "In my time," remembered May Wirth when I visited her shortly before she died, "you learned to do it with a mechanic in practice. When you learned it properly and knew your capacity, you learned to do them with your own judgment. I was taught that way. Gives you confidence in yourself, what you know you can do. When to land, how to land — all the sort of stuff and be graceful with it. Well, I gave my whole life to riding."

They practice between shows: The Asia Boys, 1948 (courtesy of the John and Mable Ringling Museum of Art, Tibbals Digital Collection).

Nothing speaks louder of the importance of real circus than did the example of Cirque du Soleil, during rehearsals for *Varekai* in 2001, deciding that they needed a strong "circus act" to bolster a weak second half. In haste, they combed their audition CDs on file and they turned to the telephones. They located their act in Mexican juggler Octavio Alegria. He arrived shortly before opening night and was evidently rushed past the "initial phase of the preparation for the creation" stuff. No time for fluff. Get to the point, and Alegria did, taking the stage with force playing only himself, juggling up a storm of excitement and bringing down the house. Second half weakness remedied.

Let story telling take a break. Turn the fog machines off for a season or ten. Face it, purists and extreme innovators out there alike: Every time we leave a circus, it's the memory of specific feats performed by specific individuals that determines what we think of the show and whether or not we'll take the time to talk it up to others. When did you ever talk up a character or a plot to somebody asking you about what you thought of a circus you just saw? When?

Tricks. Tricks. Tricks. In his book *Big Top*, Fred Bradna described one of the most impressive he had ever witnessed, this one brought off by the two Millettes, Eddie and his son, Ira. Working from a double wide trapeze bar, Eddie stood on it without holding the ropes. "Ira stood on his head on Eddie's head. This stunt, called the head-to-head balance, had never been done on a trapeze by anyone else."[8]

We pay to be amazed, simple as that. At San Francisco's Cow Palace in 1996, a down-and-out troupe of ex-Soviet artists operating too painfully clearly on a shoe-string budget, put up what they called "Circus Russia." There were hardly any props or riggings around when you entered. Very few frills anywhere, and a chintzy little cd player for a token sound system. What a sadly lackluster setting for a struggling group who only a few years before were living like kings and queens in the once-thriving Soviet circus empire. Here they were, gratefully appearing in front of maybe fifteen hundred souls in a near-empty arena. Yet, what a wonderful little program they gave on the bare concrete floor: amusing clowns; inventive acrobats and aerialists; a high wire act doing the unthinkable up there: working without mechanics. No fake fog, laser optics or creepy characters slithering through the shadows. Not even a program magazine for sale. Almost a rumor of a show. The point? You never know what treasures may loom ahead when the word "circus" appears on a building marquee.

You could discover the likes of an Alex Chimal, who in recent times held court at Jim Judkins's recently shuttered Circus Chimera. Chimal is the kind of a showman we look for, no matter what he is up to. He is a clever chameleon, too, possessing a deft creative flair that promises a director in the making. One season at Chimera, Alex juggles with a captivating tent-wide smile. Showmanship he has. The next year, in a stunningly self-directed, self-choreographed surprise, that embracing smile has vanished. Now, Chimal is entering the tent wearing a mysterious white mask and moving in a cool mystical manner. But no, he turns around to reveal his real face and we are startled to realize that he had been actually wearing the mask on the back of his head so that when he entered walking backwards, he only appeared to be facing us. He turns around again, from real to fake, and yet again and again he builds on his skills to a mesmerizing finish, juggling a fountain of balls against the floor near his feet with exquisite, flawless control.

He has one-upped Cirque on his own terms, and in a very authentic fashion. A "wow," yes, Svetlana.

Before the show, when Alex was serving as house manager, I sat out in the seats with him. I asked him what he liked most about his work. In a very refined, soft-spoken voice both friendly and unassuming, he answered that he likes being in the ring. He likes relating to the audience. When they appreciate what he is doing, he says, that it makes all the long hours of practice worthwhile. And sometimes the people sit up, and sometimes they stand at the end of his act, and for him, that is the most rewarding thing. Con Colleano would probably agree.[9]

They inspire: La Norma (courtesy of the John and Mable Ringling Museum of Art, Tibbals Digital Collection).

What they may have to endure to stay in the business will tell the story to come. And, as Bob Mitchell sees it, the story to come may not be very pretty, for Mitchell wonders if the circus as we have known it is on its way out, "like vaudeville."

I'd say it depends on what "they" can do to keep the customer coming back. And the best of them know this.

They give us tomorrow: At age 14 in 2005, Christian Atayde Stoinev performed with the Big Apple Circus (courtesy of Bertrand Guay/Big Apple Circus).

A group of liberty horses sauntered into the rings on their own in a playful manner. Down the hippodrome track rode a striking woman in white on a fast-galloping steed. Racing furiously ahead, suddenly she caught hold of an aerial ring overhead and was swooped off the horse, high into the air! When she descended to the track, her horse rejoined her and together they walked over to the center ring. The others horses were now gathered round, and the woman in white paced them through some graceful maneuvers, after which she mounted a single trap rig and executed heel and toe catches. Then, returning to the ring, she danced serenely in a circle of balletic horses to the most beguiling music of the moment. We were transported completely, as rarely we are these days at the beleaguered Ringling show, by one Sylvia Zerbini, a ninth-generation star of the truest kind. Never had we seen anything quite like this. It sent chills down our jaded spine. May I repeat — *chills*.

No modern day performer has encompassed so brilliantly in a single appearance both the best of yesterday and today.

When Kenneth Feld was preparing his *Kaleidoscape*, he suggested to Sylvia that she combine her single trap work with her horses into one seamless display. Excitedly, she told Feld that she had wanted to do this very same thing for a long time. Here was her opportunity, and the sun smiled on Feld and Zerbini. Several years later, when the new act they created for Kaleidoscape made it into the 134th edition of Ringling-Barnum, it had evolved into something more novel, including the spectacular and dramatic down-the-hippodrome-track entrance. During its creation, Sylvia played a piece by Sting, "Desert Rose," for the show's bandleader, David Killinger. He, in turn, commissioned a composer to come up with an original setting which conveyed the flavor of the Sting composition.

So far, so fine. Against Sylvia's wishes, however, co-producer Nicole Feld urged her to accept a vocalist stationed by the ring. Sylvia was convinced that it would be a distraction.

What could she do against the Feld machine, obviously determined to incorporate Le Cirque scoring? She gave in. Nicole loved it. Sylvia never did.

What is circus to Sylvia Zerbini?

It is a feeling you bring to the public, she answers, which raises the question, has she too been Montreal-recycled? Or is she paying lip service to the artistic obsessions of today's fussy new-wave directors?

No, she most definitely is a circus realist, it seems, grounded in a tradition that goes back through her family's nine-generation history. And she wonders, with a withering sigh, if the Cirque style will in time wear thin with the public. Will people eventually tire of too much dance and too many pretty scenes? Will the Cirque experience flatten out?[10]

This much we can predict: If the day ever comes when those who genuinely excite us — from Ayak to Zerbini — are no longer there, neither will the crowds be.

So, out here on the midway of memories, folks, we've traveled a long winding road from Pittsburgh to Philadelphia and back. I've given you a lot to think about until next season. And let's hope there is a next season. The ever-changing, never-changing circus, as Earl Chapin May called it, may prove Mr. May right once again. All is not lost. The public has a way of making its will known at the red wagon. A way of prevailing upon beleaguered circus owners to reinstate elephants. A way of changing its mind even for the better. And all those fringe protesters out here on the anti-Jumbo picket lines who today sound so victorious could tomorrow be reversed by an outbreak of old-fashioned tent show popularity.

One thing is certain, and one thing only: Today's Svetlana Shamsheevas and Alex Chimals, along with tomorrow's Al Ringlings and Lilian Leitzels — the unborn kids yet to discover in their own backyards the challenge of walking a rope, of juggling a couple of oranges or coaxing two house cats instead of one to ride, jockey style, on the back of a fast-moving mutt (can you imagine?)—they are the ones who will decide for all the years to come what the circus will look like and how it will be presented and sold to the public.

So, please remember, ladies and gentlemen: whenever you see a banner in front of a tent or a building that spells out "circus," go ahead and give it a chance. You never know what you might find on the inside when the lights dim, a fanfare blows and a beautiful velvet curtain parts to admit a blaze of wonderment into your life.

You might find *them*.

Chapter Notes

Abbreviations for frequently cited sources:

BW *Bandwagon*
BB *Billboard*
HC George Chindahl, *A History of the Circus in America*
CR *Circus Report*
RR Earl Chapin May, *The Circus from Rome to Ringling*
RD Helen Stoddart, *Rings of Desire*
SS William Coup, *Sawdust and Spangles*

Unless otherwise noted, all quotes are from author interviews and correspondence conducted during 2005–2006, with the following:

Michel Barette	Jim Culver	James Judkins	John Pugh
Bunni Bartok	Garry Darrell	Sherwood Kaiser	Paul Pugh
Paul Binder	Raffaele DeRitis	Andrey Kovgar	Larry Pisoni
Barbara Byrd	Calvin DuPre	Chris Lashua	David Rawls
Patty Campbell	Hank Ernest	Dale Longmire	Svetlana Shamsheeva
Alex Chimal	Tito Gaona	Robert Mitchell	Bill Taggart
Michael Christensen	Tommy Hanneford	Bob Moore	Vallery
Norma Cristiani	Geoff Hoyle	Picasso Jr.	Sylvia Zerbini

Additional quotes are drawn from the author's interviews in previous years, as indicated, with the following:

Charles Boas and Bernie Collins, with Circus Kirk, Clymer, Pennsylvania, 8/7/75.
Noyelles Burkhart, Sarasota, 4/19/86.
Arthur M. Concello, Sarasota, 4/19/86.
Kenneth Dodd, Sarasota, various dates, 1975 to present.
Merle Evans, Sarasota, 8/75.
La Norma Fox, Sarasota, 1986.

John Hurdle, Sarasota, 1975.
Victor Kalesh, Moscow, USSR, 1979.
Jackie LeClaire, Sarasota, 1986.
Harold Ronk, San Francisco, 9/2/76.
John Strong, Santa Rosa, 1960.
Clifford Vargas, 1985.
Karl Wallenda, Sarasota, 1975.
May Wirth, Sarasota, 1975.

Chapter 1

1. *Billboard*, July 28, 1956. When did North really arrive on the show? A very different and historically fascinating account by *Sarasota Journal* reporter George Bayless (July 20, 1956), has North arriving a day *before*, in Canton. According to this account, North held a staff meeting, "canvassing the dire problems," that lasted until 4 a.m. on Sunday. If true, that meeting likely took place on the train, and likely in John's private car, the *Jomar*, while en route to Alliance.

2. *The Candid Circus, 1942–1952*, Video Editions TABU 001.

3. *Sarasota Journal*, July 16, 1956.

4. "Big Top Bows Out Forever," *Life* magazine, July 30, 1956.

5. *Pittsburgh Post-Gazette*, July 17, 1956.

6. "Death of the Big Top Blamed on Frills," *Pittsburgh Press*, July 17, 1956.

7. *Sarasota Herald-Tribune*, July 17, 1956.

8. *Sarasota Journal*, July 20, 1956.

9. *Sarasota Herald-Tribune*, July 20, 1956.

10. *Sarasota Journal*, July 20, 1956.

11. *Billboard*, July 28, 1956.

12. *Pittsburgh Press*, July 17, 1956.

13. *Sarasota Herald-Tribune*, September 9, 1956.

Chapter 2

1. RR, p. 18.

2. *Ibid.*

3. HC, p. 8.

4. RD, p. 66.

5. HC, p. 12.

6. BW, Jan.–Feb. 1997, p. 46.

7. SS, p. 10

8. BW, Jan.–Feb. 1997, p. 46.

9. *Ibid.*, p. 44.

10. HC, p. 111.

11. Twain, *Adventures of Huckleberry Finn*, p. 192.

12. HC, p. 63.

13. SS, p. 214.

14. HC, p. 82.

15. BW, Jan–Feb. 1997, p. 45.

16. SS, p. 219.

17. Ringling, *Life Story of the Ringling Brothers*, p. 26.

Chapter 3

1. SS, p. 38.

2. "Circus Trains," on *Trains Unlimited*, the History Channel, 1998.

3. SS, p. 63.

4. BW, Nov.–Dec. 2000, p. 20.

5. *Ibid.*

6. SS, p. 63.

7. BW, Jan.–Feb 1999, p. 35.

8. SS, p. 113.

9. Ringling, *Life Story of the Ringling Brothers*, p. 26.

10. HC, p. 108.

11. *Ibid.*, p. 111.

12. North, *Circus Kings*, p. 88

13. RD, p. 271.

14. BW, May–June 2006, pp. 41–42.

15. Ringling Bros. and Barnum & Bailey magazine and daily review, 1925 edition.

16. RD, p. 57

17. BW, May–June 2003, p. 13.

18. "Circus Trains," on *Trains Unlimited*, the History Channel, 1998.

Chapter 4

1. *Variety*, May 26, 1931.

2. BB, July 4, 1931 and July 25, 1931.

3. "Vest-Pocket Circus," *The Saturday Evening Post*, January 31, 1953. All biographical material on the lives of Stern and Polack, as well as how they formed their circus, was derived from this extensive article.

4. RR, p. 304.

5. BW, July–Aug. 2005, p. 43.

6. Alex Chimal interview.

7. *Duggan Bros.–Arnold Maley Tent No. 116 of the Circus Fans of America Presents Joseph T. Bradbury*, Historic Video, 1995.

8. Circus Historical Society message board posting by Buckles Woodcock (number 584), April 26, 2005. www.circushistory.or6/query.htm

Chapter 5

1. Undated King Brothers Circus advance courier, circa 1954. (Text alludes to 35th annual tour.)

2. Ringling Bros. and Barnum & Bailey Circus program magazine, 1953, p. 7.

3. Museum of Science and Industry, Chicago. MSI: Circus Timeline on the Internet. Accessed 2005. The 1956 entry, since corrected, read: "July 16, 1956, the Ringling Brothers and Barnum & Bailey Show came to an end. In 1957, Irvin Feld purchased the Ringling Bros. and Barnum & Bailey and began to tour again exclusively a an indoor presentation."

4. Author interview with Paul Binder.

5. Antekeier, *Ringmaster*, p. 109.

6. Joanne Joys, "Reflections on Ringling Red," November 4, 1984, unattributed to news source. Photocopy of article in author's collection.

7. Antekeier, *Ringmaster*, p. 144.

8. "Charity Scam Trial Opens," *San Jose Mercury News*, March 18, 2004.

9. Circus Vargas program magazine, 1974.

10. *Circus Vargas Twentieth Anniversary*, video, View Communications Group, 1989.

Chapter 6

1. Interviews with Circus Kirk personnel, Clymer, Pennsylvania, August 7, 1975.

2. Larry Pisoni interview.

3. Terry Lorant and Jon Carroll, *The Pickle Family Circus*.

Chapter 7

1. *DramaLogue*, November 5–11, 1987.
2. *Los Angeles Times*, September 5, 1987.
3. *Los Angeles Examiner*, September 5, 1987.
4. *Ibid.*
5. Cirque du Soleil Web site, under part 6: "Foin-Foin the Duck."
6. Cirque du Soleil ad, published in the *San Francisco Chronicle*, April 15, 1988.
7. Albrecht, *The New American Circus*, p. 164.
8. CR, September 12, 1988, p. 27.
9. "Billionaires: The Acrobat," March 5, 2004.
10. *Oakland Tribune*, August 6, 1989.
11. "Billionaires: The Acrobat," March 5, 2004.
12. *Ibid.* The oft-used 1768 date is when Astley started giving horse riding exhibitions; his circus was founded in 1760.
13. CR, August 1, 1988.
14. *Ibid.*, September 12, 1988.
15. Chris Lashua interview.
16. CR, August 1, 1988.

Chapter 8

1. Vasquez, *The Biggest Trick*, p. 131.
2. *Ibid.*, p. 132.
3. *Circus Vargas Twentieth Anniversary*, video, View Communication Group, 1989.

Chapter 9

1. *San Francisco Chronicle*, January 14, 1992.
2. *Ibid.*
3. *Ibid.*
4. CR, October 2, 1989.
5. Cliff Vargas interview.
6. CR, October 2, 1989.

Chapter 10

1. "Cirque du Soleil Fire Within," Bravo television channel, first aired 2002. All details of the preparation of *Varakei* are taken from this program.
2. James Judkins interview.
3. University of California Berkeley (UCB) Parents Recommendations, http://parents.berkeley.edu, October 1998.
4. New Pickle Circus program magazine, 2002.
5. *San Jose Mercury News*, December 17, 2003.
6. *San Francisco Examiner*, October 31, 2002.
7. BusinessWeek Online, December 13, 2004, and *60 Minutes*, February 20, 2005.
8. Circusnews.com; also, press release issued by LAMBA, dated July 15, 2003.
9. "Cirque du Soleil Fire Within," Bravo, 2002.
10. *San Francisco Chronicle*, May 22, 1997.

Chapter 11

1. *New York Times*, February 9, 1999.
2. Antekeier, *Ringmaster*, p. 166.
3. *Ibid.*, p. 13.
4. *Ibid.* p. 194.
5. *Washington Post*, November 9, 2003, p. W16.
6. Albrecht, *The New American* Circus, p. 230.
7. For another more long-lasting example of how the Feld fictions have made it into major circus history books, see John Culhane's *The American Circus: An Illustrated History* (New York: Henry Holt and Company, 1999).
8. *60 Minutes*, CBS, May 2, 2003.
9. *Wall Street Journal*, August 12, 2005.
10. *Ibid.*
11. *New York Times*, February 9, 1999.
12. *Austin Chronicle*, October 22, 1999.
13. *Chicago Sun-Times*, March 31, 2000.
14. *New York Times*, August 8, 2000.
15. *New York Times*, February 9, 1999.
16. Sylvia Zerbini interview.

Chapter 12

1. Center for Consumer Freedom, http://www.consumerfreedom.com, and also as seen on Fox news, March 2, 2006.
2. Animalrights.net (AR.net), posting by Brian Carnell, July 24, 2001.
3. *Seattle Times*, September 12, 1996.
4. "Dude Looks Like a Lady" (Peta on eBay), Hindustan Times.com, March 23, 2005.
5. www.iol.co.za-iol, March 22, 2005.
6. *San Jose Mercury News*, March 29, 2005.
7. CR, June 27, 1988.
8. *Ibid.*, July 31, 1991.
9. Foundation for Biomedical Research Web site release, June 17, 2005. www.fbresearch.org
10. Center for Consumer Freedom Web site, March 4, 2005. www.consumerfreedom.com
11. SS, pp. 184–185.
12. BW, May–June 2005, p. 31.
13. BW, Sept.–Oct. 2005, p. 26..
14. Sylvia Zerbini interview.
15. Barbara Byrd interview.
16. CR, May 9, 1994.
17. "Circus Spies," Peta Web site; see also "Circus Criminals," undated. www.circuses.com/circuscriminals.asp
18. Sylvia Zerbini interview.

Chapter 13

1. *20/20* television program, September 29, 1989.
2. *Ibid.*
3. *Ibid.*
4. *Ibid.*
5. Norma Cristiani interview.
6. *20/20*, September 29, 1989.
7. CR, January 21, 1991.

8. *San Jose Mercury News*, December 17, 2001.

9. Kenneth Feld, "Open Letter to Animal Rights Groups," January 7, 2002, www.feldentertainment. com/pr/aca/Open%20Letter.htm. Well worth reading in its entirety.

10. "The Animal Wars," *Eye on America*, CBS-TV, late December 2001.

11. Sylvia Zerbini interview.

12. Insight on the News Web site, August 19, 2002. http://findarticles.com/p/articles/mi_m1571/is_30_18 /ai_90753058

Chapter 14

1. "Circus Criminals," Circuses.com, Peta web site. www.circuses.com/circuscriminals.asp

2. *Variety*, July 16, 1986.

3. Jim Culver interview.

4. Gary Darrell interview.

Chapter 15

1. RR, p. 234.

2. BB, June 13, 1931.

3. *Ibid.*, June 20, 1942.

4. RR, p. 247.

5. Barbara Byrd interview

6. *Ibid.*

Chapter 16

1. "PeeWee, Bill Inspect Damp Dawn; Impresario Sleeps," *Santa Rosa Press Democrat*, May 27, 1952.

2. Norma Cristiani interview.

3. *Santa Rosa Press Democrat*, May 27, 1952.

4. Ken Dodd interview.

5. Tape recording of a Clyde Beatty Circus performance, 1953, author's collection.

6. Barbara Byrd interview.

Chapter 17

1. Polack Brothers Circus program magazines, author's collection. Scattered information on the fascinating Barbette may be gleaned from Web sites and from circus press kits and program magazines.

2. RD, p. 4

3. *Saltimbanco* program magazine, 1992, p. 12.

4. *Dralion* program magazine, p. 6.

5. Author interview with Victor Kalesh, Moscow, 1979.

6. RD, p. 17.

7. *Ibid.*, p. 79.

8. *Nouvelle Experience* program magazine, 1990, p. 25.

9. *Dralion* program magazine, p. 6.

10. www.guardian.co.uk/arts/reviews/story, January 1, 2003.

11. Slate.com, undated (circa July 27, 2005).

12. *Los Angeles Times Magazine*, December 1, 1996, p. 30.

13. *Ibid.*

14. Sylvia Zerbini interview.

15. Bradna, *The Big Top*, p. 194.

16. Barbara Byrd interview.

17. *San Jose Mercury News*, December 1, 2003.

Chapter 18

1. Hank Ernest interview. (Cedric Walker did not respond to interview requests.)

2. *Los Angeles Times*, "Hip Hop under the Big Top," *Los Angeles Times*, October 27, 1996.

3. Hank Ernest interview.

4. *Los Angeles Times*, October 27, 1996.

5. *San Francisco Chronicle*, October 16, 2005.

6. Hank Ernest interview.

7. Numerous attempts via letter and telephone to purchase a copy of the 2005 program magazine, said to have sold out before the show reached Oakland, all went unanswered. Likewise, efforts to purchase photocopies of select pages from the program containing information about certain acts. At what circus school in Africa was the Gabonese high wire troupe formed? Nobody would supply an answer.

8. *New York Times*, December 18, 1998.

9. *Los Angeles Times*, August 1, 2001.

10. *San Francisco Chronicle*, May 23, 1999.

11. *Oakland Tribune*, November 2, 2003.

Chapter 19

1. Albrecht, *The New American Circus*, p. 101.

2. *Wall Street Journal*, August 12, 2005.

3. E-mail from Kelly Crow to the author dated April 17, 2006.

Chapter 20

1. BW, Jan.–Feb. 2002, p. 33.

2. Alex Chimal interview.

3. The Gaona family have not served their tenuous quad claim by issuing conflicting information. Although Tito has held that he caught the quad once, Lalo Murillo claimed that they caught the quad at least two times in early 1977. (See CR, September 3, 1984, p. 24.)

4. http://sifter.org/-max/steele.html. A fascinating interview, apparently conducted by Karen Ruggles, with an accomplished flyer about the triple and the quad, as performed by various other trapeze artists.

5. Paul Binder interview.

6. John Hurdle interview.

7. Fenner, *The Circus: Lure and Legend*, p. 104.

8. Bradna, *The Big Top*, p. 312.

9. Alex Chimal interview.

10. Sylvia Zerbini interview.

Bibliography

Albrecht, Ernest. *The New American Circus.* Gainesville: University of Florida Press, 1995.

Antekeier, Kristopher, and Greg Aunapu. *Ringmaster.* New York: E.P. Dutton, 1989.

Bradna, Fred, as told to Hartzell Spence. *The Big Top: My Forty Years with the Greatest Show on Earth.* New York: Simon and Schuster, 1952.

Chindahl, George L. *A History of the Circus in America.* Caldwell, Idaho: Caxton, 1959.

Coup, William C. *Sawdust Spangles: Stories and Secrets of the Circus.* 1901. Washington, D.C.: Paul A. Ruddell, 1961.

Coxe, Antony Hippisley. *A Seat at the Circus.* Hamden, Connecticut: Archon, 1980.

Fenner, Mildred Sandison, and Wolcott. *The Circus: Lure and Legend.* Englewood Cliffs, New Jersey: Prentice-Hall, 1970.

Harlow, Alvin F. *The Ringlings: Wizards of the Circus.* New York: Julian Messner, 1951.

Lorant, Terry, and Jon Carroll. *The Pickle Family Circus.* San Francisco: Chronicle Books, 1986.

May, Earl Chapin. *The Circus: From Rome to Ringling.* New York: Dover, 1963.

North, Henry Ringling, and Alden Hatch. *The Circus Kings.* New York: Dell, 1964.

Ringling, Alfred. *Life Story of the Ringling Brothers.* Chicago: R.R. Donnelly and Sons, 1900.

Stoddart, Helen. *Rings of Desire: Circus History and Representation.* Manchester and New York: Manchester University Press, 2000.

Twain, Mark. *Adventures of Huckleberry Finn.* New York: Modern Library, 1985.

Vasquez, Juan, and Harry L. Graham. *The Biggest Trick: Miguel Vasquez' Quadruple Somersault.* Orange, California: Words and Pictures Press, 1994.

Wallace, Irving. *The Fabulous Showman: The Life and Times of P.T. Barnum.* New York: Alfred A. Knopf, 1959.

Index